HOW TO
STAND UP TO
A DICTATOR

HOW TO STAND UP TO A DICTATOR

MARIA RESSA

FOREWORD BY AMAL CLOONEY

HARPER  PERENNIAL

NEW YORK • LONDON • TORONTO • SYDNEY • NEW DELHI • AUCKLAND

HARPER ● PERENNIAL

A hardcover edition of this book was published in 2022 by HarperCollins Publishers.

HOW TO STAND UP TO A DICTATOR. Copyright © 2022 by Maria Ressa. Foreword copyright © 2022 by Amal Clooney. All rights reserved. Printed in the United States of America. No part of this book may be used or reproduced in any manner whatsoever without written permission except in the case of brief quotations embodied in critical articles and reviews. For information, address HarperCollins Publishers, 195 Broadway, New York, NY 10007.

HarperCollins books may be purchased for educational, business, or sales promotional use. For information, please email the Special Markets Department at SPsales@harpercollins.com.

All illustrations are courtesy of the author unless otherwise credited.

FIRST HARPER PERENNIAL EDITION PUBLISHED 2023.

Library of Congress Cataloging-in-Publication Data has been applied for.

ISBN 978-0-06-325752-8 (pbk.)

23 24 25 26 27 LBC 5 4 3 2 1

For journalists and citizens who
#HoldTheLine

Contents

PART II: THE RISE OF FACEBOOK, RAPPLER, AND THE INTERNET'S BLACK HOLE, 2005–2017

PART III: CRACKDOWN: ARRESTS, ELECTIONS, AND THE FIGHT FOR OUR FUTURE, 2018–PRESENT

Foreword

When you think of a superhero, you may not imagine a five-foot-two-inch woman with a pen in her hand. But today, journalists operating in authoritarian countries need superpowers.

They face daily threats to their reputation, their freedom, and—in some places—their life. And Maria Ressa is one of them.

To say that Maria fights against the odds is an understatement. In an autocracy, a journalist's opponent is the state—which makes policy, controls the police, hires the prosecutors, and readies the prisons. It has an army of bots active online to vilify and undermine anyone deemed an opponent. It has the power to take down broadcasters and online sites. Most important: it has a need to control the message in order to survive. Its existence depends on ensuring that there is only one side to every story.

As a famous philosopher once said, there is no greater tyranny than that which is perpetrated under the shield of the law and in the name of justice. Yet under President Duterte, the Philippine government did not hesitate to use legal tools to try to intimidate perceived opponents. The authorities revoked Maria's media license and filed civil suits that threaten to bankrupt her. She faces a barrage of bogus prosecutions that threaten her to life behind bars.

Not because she has committed any crime—but because the leaders in her country do not want to hear criticism. So she has a choice: toe the government line and be safe, or risk everything to do her job. She has not hesitated to choose the latter. And I know she will never give up.

Throughout history some of the most important voices in society have been persecuted. Gandhi, Nelson Mandela, and Martin Luther King, Jr., were all prosecuted because they criticized the government of the day. At his criminal sedition trial in India, Gandhi told the judge that he did not want mercy for standing up to a government that was trampling on human rights: "I am here . . . to invite and cheerfully submit to the highest penalty that can be inflicted upon me" because "non-co-operation with evil is as much a duty as is co-operation with good." He spent two years in prison as a result of his words. But he made India a more just society. Mandela was arrested when his views displeased the government: the charge was high treason, and he spent twenty-seven years in prison as a result. But he brought down the evil of apartheid.

Maria's struggle is one that defines our times. Data gathered in the last few years shows that more journalists all over the world are being imprisoned and killed than at any time since records began. And there are, today, more autocracies in the world than there are democracies.

This is why Maria refuses to leave the country, and is determined to defend the charges against her. She knows that an independent voice like hers is always valuable, but becomes essential when others are silent. She is holding up the ceiling for anyone else who dares to speak. Because if Maria, a US citizen and a Nobel Peace laureate, can be locked up for doing her work, what chance is there for others?

It is ironic that autocratic leaders are often called "strongmen" when in fact they cannot tolerate dissent or even allow a level playing field. It is those who stand up to them whose strength should be celebrated—and some of them are only five foot two.

Elie Wiesel warned us that there may be times when we are powerless to prevent injustice, but there must never be a time when we fail to protest. Maria's legacy will be felt for generations—because she never failed to protest, to try to bend the arc of history toward justice. And when young Filipino students study history, they will find that the first Filipino person ever to be awarded the Nobel Peace Prize was a courageous journalist determined to tell the truth. I hope that, for the sake of future generations, they will be inspired by her example.

—*Amal Clooney*

HOW TO
STAND UP TO
A DICTATOR

The Invisible Atom Bomb

Live in the (Present) Moment (of the Past)

Since the pandemic lockdown began in March 2020, I have been far more emotional than I had ever allowed myself to be. I feel the pent-up anger at the injustice I have no choice but to accept. That's what six years of government attacks have done.

I may go to jail. For the rest of my life—or, as my lawyer tells me, for more than a hundred years. On charges that should never even have made it to court. The breakdown of the rule of law is global, but it has become, for me, personal. In less than two years, the Philippine government issued ten arrest warrants against me.

I could also be a target of violence. Would the police, my government be stupid enough to target me? Well, yes. The Philippines' Commission on Human Rights estimated that about twenty-seven thousand people were killed in less than three years of ex-president Rodrigo Duterte's brutal drug war, from 2016 to 2018.[1] True? Who knows? That statistic is the first casualty in my country's battle for truth. In 2018, I began wearing a bulletproof vest on the road.

Online violence is real-world violence. That has been proven by so much research and so many tragic events around the world. I am targeted online every day, along with thousands of other journalists, activists, opposition leaders, and unsuspecting citizens here and around the globe.

Yet when I wake up and look out the window, I am energized. I have hope. I see the possibilities—how, despite the darkness, this is also a time when we can rebuild our societies, starting with what's right in front of us: our areas of influence.

The world we once knew is decimated. Now we have to decide what we want to create.

My name is Maria Ressa. I have been a journalist for more than thirty-six years. I was born in the Philippines, was raised and educated in New Jersey, and returned to my native country after college in the late 1980s. I made my career at CNN, creating and running two bureaus in Southeast Asia during the 1990s. It was the glory days of CNN and a heady time for international journalists. From my perch in Southeast Asia, I was an eyewitness to dramatic events that often foreshadowed what would happen around the world: emerging democratic movements in former colonial outposts, the terrifying rise of Islamic terrorism well before 9/11, a new class of democratically elected strongmen who would turn their countries into quasi dictatorships, and the stunning promise and power of social media, which would soon play a pivotal role in tearing down everything I hold dear.

In 2012, I cofounded Rappler, a digital-only news website in the Philippines. My ambition was to create a new standard of investigative journalism in my country, one that would harness the social media platforms to build communities of action for better governance and stronger democracies. At the time, I was the truest of true believers in the power of social media to do good in the world. Using Facebook and other platforms, we were able to crowdsource breaking news, find pivotal sources and tips, harness collective action for climate change and good governance, and help increase voter knowledge and participation in our elections. We were a fast success, but by Rappler's fifth year of existence, we had gone from being lauded for our ideas to being targeted by our government—all because we continued to do our jobs as journalists: to tell the truth and hold power to account.

At Rappler, we exposed corruption and manipulation not only in government but increasingly in the technology companies that were already dominating our lives. Starting in 2016, we began highlighting impunity on two fronts: President Rodrigo Duterte's drug war and Mark Zuckerberg's Facebook.

Let me tell you why the rest of the world needs to pay attention to what happens in the Philippines: 2021 was the sixth year in a row that Filipinos—out of all global citizens—spent the most time on the internet and on social media.[2] Despite slow internet speeds, Filipinos uploaded and downloaded the largest number of videos on YouTube in 2013. Four years later, 97 percent of our country's citizens were on Facebook. When I told that statistic to Mark Zuckerberg in 2017, he was quiet for a beat. "Wait, Maria," he finally responded, looking directly at me, "where are the other three percent?"

At the time, I laughed at his glib quip. I'm not laughing anymore.

As these numbers show and as Facebook admits, the Philippines is ground zero[3] for the terrible effects that social media can have on a nation's institutions, its culture, and the minds of its populace. Every development that happens in my country eventually happens in the rest of the world—if not tomorrow, then a year or two later. As early as 2015, there were reports of account farms creating social media phone-verified accounts, or PVAs, from the Philippines. That same year, a report showed that most of Donald Trump's Facebook likes came from outside the United States and that one in every twenty-seven Trump followers was from the Philippines.

Some days, I feel like Sisyphus and Cassandra combined, trying to repeatedly warn the world about how social media has destroyed our shared reality, the place where democracy happens.

This book is my attempt to show you that the absence of rule of law in the virtual world is devastating. We live in only one reality, and the breakdown of the rule of law globally was ignited by the lack of a democratic vision for the internet in the twenty-first century. Impunity online naturally led to impunity offline, destroying existing checks and balances. What I have witnessed and documented over the past decade is technology's godlike power to infect each of us with a virus of lies, pitting us against one another, igniting, even creating, our fears, anger, and hatred, and accelerating the rise of authoritarians and dictators around the world.

I began calling it "democracy's death by a thousand cuts." The very platforms that deliver the news we need are biased against facts. As early as 2018, studies show that lies laced with anger and hate spread faster and farther than facts.[4] Without facts, you can't have truth. Without truth, you can't have trust. Without all three, we have no shared reality, and democracy as we know it—and all meaningful human endeavors—are dead.

We must act quickly, before that happens. That's what I lay out in this book: an exploration into the values and principles not just of journalism and technology but of the collective action we need to take to win this battle for facts. This journey of discovery is intensely personal. That's why every chapter has a micro and a macro: a personal lesson and the larger picture. You will see the simple ideas I hold on to in order to make what have—over time—become instinctive but thoughtful decisions, layering experiences upon new experiences of the present moment of the past.

In 2021, I was one of two journalists awarded the Nobel Peace Prize. The last time a journalist received this award was in 1935. The winner, a German reporter named Carl von Ossietzky, couldn't accept because he was languishing in a Nazi concentration camp. By giving the honor to me and Dmitry Muratov of Russia, the Norwegian Nobel Committee signaled that the world was at a similar historical moment, another existential point for democracy. In my Nobel lecture,[5] I said that an invisible atom bomb exploded in our information ecosystem, that technology platforms have given geopolitical powers a way to manipulate each of us individually.

Just four months after the Nobel ceremony, Russia invaded Ukraine, using metanarratives it had seeded online[6] since 2014, when it invaded Crimea, annexed it from Ukraine, and installed a puppet state. The tactic? Suppress information, then replace it with lies. By viciously attacking facts with its cheap digital army, the Russians obliterated the truth and replaced the silenced narrative with its own—in effect, that Crimea had willfully acceded to Russian control. The Russians created fake online accounts, deployed bot armies, and exploited the vulnerabilities of the social media platforms to deceive real people. For the American-owned platforms, the world's new information gatekeepers, those activities created more engagement and brought in more money. The goals of the gatekeepers and the disinformation operatives aligned.

That was the first time we became aware of information warfare tactics that would soon be deployed around the world, from Duterte to Brexit to Catalonia to Stop the Steal. Eight years later, on February 24, 2022, using the same techniques and the same metanarratives he had seeded to annex Crimea, Vladimir Putin invaded Ukraine itself. This is how disinformation, bottom up and top down, can manufacture a whole new reality.

Less than three months later, the Philippines fell into the abyss. May 9, 2022, was election day, when my country voted for a successor to Duterte. Although there were ten candidates for president, it came down to two: opposition leader and vice president Leni Robredo and Ferdinand Marcos, Jr., the only son and namesake of the dictator Ferdinand Marcos, who declared martial law in 1972 and stayed in power for nearly twenty-one years. The first of the kleptocrats, Marcos was accused of stealing $10 billion from his people before finally being ousted in a People Power revolt in 1986.

The evening of the election, Marcos Jr. took an early, commanding lead and never dropped it.[7] At 8:37 p.m., with 46.93 percent of precincts transmitting, Marcos had 15.3 million votes compared to Robredo's 7.3 million. At 8:53 p.m., with 53.5 percent transmission, Marcos was at 17.5 million, Robredo at 8.3 million; by 9:00 p.m., with 57.76 percent, Marcos was at 18.98 million, Robredo at 8.98 million.

This is how it ends, I said to myself that evening. The election was proving a showcase for the impact of disinformation and relentless information operations on social media that from 2014 to 2022 transformed Marcos from a pariah into a hero. The disinformation networks didn't just come from the Philippines but included global networks, like one from China taken down by Facebook[8] in 2020. They helped change history in front of our eyes.

Starting with my Nobel Peace Prize lecture at the end of 2021, I had repeatedly stated that whoever won the election would determine not just our future but also our past. You can't have integrity of elections if you don't have integrity of facts.

Facts lost. History lost. Marcos won.

Compared to others in hiding, in exile, or in jail, I am lucky. The only defense a journalist has is to shine the light on the truth, to expose the lie—and I can still do that. There are so many others persecuted in the shadows who have neither exposure nor support, under governments that are doubling down with impunity. Their accomplice is technology, the silent nuclear holocaust in our information ecosystem. We must treat its aftermath the way the world did after the devastation of World War II: creating institutions and agreements like NATO, the United Nations, and the Universal Declaration of Human Rights. Today, we need new global institutions and a reiteration of the values we hold dear.

We are standing on the rubble of the world that was, and we must have the foresight and courage to imagine, and create, the world as it should be: more compassionate, more equal, more sustainable. A world that is safe from fascists and tyrants.

This is my journey to doing that, but it is also about you, dear reader.

Democracy is fragile. You have to fight for every bit, every law, every safeguard, every institution, every story. You must know how dangerous it is to suffer even the tiniest cut. This is why I say to us all: we must hold the line.

This is what many Westerners, for whom democracy seems a given, need to learn from us. This book is for anyone who might take democracy for granted, written by someone who never would.

What you do matters in this present moment of the past, when memory can be so easily altered. Please ask yourself the same question my team and I ask every day:

What are *you* willing to sacrifice for the truth?

PART I

Homecoming

Power, the Press, and the Philippines

1963–2004

. . .

Chapter 1

The Golden Rule

Make the Choice to Learn

Class photo, St. Scholastica's College,
third grade, 1973

You don't know who you are until you're forced to fight for it.

How do you decide what to fight for? Sometimes it's not your choice. You live your way into it because the sum of all your choices brings you to that point. If you're lucky, you realize early on that each decision you make answers a question that all of us muddle through: how to build meaning in our lives. Meaning is not something you stumble across or what someone gives you; you build it through every choice you make, the commitments you choose, the people you love, and the values you hold dear.

In my own life, I see ten-year chunks. When I was ten, my life changed dramatically; the following decade was all discovery and exploration. My twenties were all about choices: what to do after college, where to live, whom to work for, whom and how to love. My thirties were about developing expertise in what would be my calling—journalism—and the search for justice implicit in its mission. Hard work was a constant theme, the one thing I knew I could control.

Then came my forties, my "master of the universe" phase and my self-imposed deadline for finally choosing a home and making a commitment to the Philippines. Now my fifties have been about reinvention and activism: taking a stand on my most deeply held views. I suppose you could call my last decade a "coming out"—coming out against the killings and brazen abuses of power, coming out against technology's dark side, coming out and owning my political views and my sexuality.

I was born on October 2, 1963, in a wooden house in Pasay City, Manila, in the Philippines, a sprawling archipelago of disparate languages and cultures united by the Catholic Church. A feudal society, it was dominated by oligarchs who had been given their lands during centuries of Spanish colonial rule. After the Spanish-American War ended in 1898, Spain gave the Philippines to the United States under the Treaty of Paris. A year later, Filipinos say the Philippine-American War began, long a footnote in US history books, which referred to it as "the insurrection."[1]

It was a time of "manifest destiny" in the United States. Rudyard Kipling published his famous imperialist poem "The White Man's Burden" to encourage the Americans to govern the Philippines in 1899. They did until 1935, when the Philippines became a self-governing commonwealth. Its Constitution, which had to be approved by US president Franklin D. Roosevelt, was a virtual rewrite of the US Constitution. The joke about colonial rule is that the Philippines spent three hundred years in a convent and fifty years in Hollywood.

In 1964, my father, twenty-year-old Manuel Phil Aycardo, died in a car accident when I was a year old and my mother, Hermelina, was pregnant with my sister, Mary Jane.

My mom took us away from my father's family, and my sister and I lived in a half-built home with my mother and my great-grandmother, who reeked of alcohol but took care of us. We were so poor that we brushed our teeth with salt and constantly worried about where to get the next meal. Our treat was when Mom, wearing the yellow uniform of the Labor Department, where she worked, came home at the end of payday with a box of Kentucky Fried Chicken.

When I was five, a family feud re-erupted, and my mother moved to the United States to join her own mother, who had recently moved to New York City. My mother was twenty-five years old when she landed in San Francisco on April 28, 1969.

My sister and I moved in with my father's parents on Times Street in Quezon City in Metro Manila. It was a quiet, modest middle-class neighborhood with houses set back from the road.

My paternal grandmother, Rosario Sunico, was deeply religious and helped shape my values. She told me stories about my father: young, intelligent, a skilled pianist from a family of musicians. She taught me to work hard in school and instilled a mindset of delayed gratification: the coins I saved from my school allowance would go into a bottle we watched fill up. She attempted to shape my perceptions, too; she told me that my mother was no good and that she had gone to the United States to be a prostitute.

That was confusing stuff for a daughter to process, especially during my mother's periodic visits. At least once a year, Mom would stay with us, and it would turn our household upside down. Even that young, I could feel the strain between my mother and my grandmother, a seeming competition that often forced me to take a side, which I refused to do.

Black-and-white memories flicker in my mind of those visits: sitting on a bed with my mother and sister when I was about seven or eight years old. My mom was larger than life: petite, beautiful, always full of laughter. Once she was talking to my sister when I remembered a new word I wanted to show off. I waited until the right moment, then jumped in.

"Amazing!" I yelled. There was a moment of silence before my mother burst out laughing. Then she hugged me.

I went to school at St. Scholastica's College, a Catholic all-girls school. Founded and run by German missionary Benedictine sisters, the school placed me in an accelerated pilot class; my classmates and I tested well and were deemed "smarter" than the other kids. At least, that was what one of my classmates, Twink Macaraig, and I used to laugh about.

All that ended the day my mother kidnapped my sister and me from school.

It seemed like any other day when I entered the classroom, sharp rays of sun streaming through the windows. I put down my school bag and lifted the lid of my wooden desk. Then I heard a voice call my name. "Mary Ann!"

Only my family called me that, a contraction of my two names, Maria Angelita. I turned around in shock to see my mother with the school principal, Sister Gracia, at the front of the classroom. They approached my desk and helped me put everything back into my bag. As we walked out, I looked back at all my friends staring at me.

We proceeded to my sister's classroom. She was waiting outside with my mother's sister, Mencie Millonado, and another teacher-nun. When she saw our mom, Mary Jane ran to hug her. By that time, we were the only ones in the hallway. Mary Jane and Mom were both crying. Then I heard my mother mumble under her breath that she was going to take us to America.

I remember looking around the school at that point and instinctively knowing that nothing would ever be the same again. In moments like that, you look for anchors. Mine was the library book in my bag that would be overdue the next day.

As we were walking to the gate, I stopped in the middle of the courtyard, pointed to the library, and asked my mom if we could return my book. She said, "Let's do it another day."

A car was parked by the sidewalk, and we got in. As soon as we were settled, my mom introduced us to the man in the front passenger seat. "Mary Ann, Mary Jane," she said, "this is your new father."

Everything can change in a moment.

I never went back to my grandparents' house or to school. One day, they were my world. The next day, they weren't. The door to that world was forever shut, and a new reality opened. I was ten years old.

Within about two weeks, we were on a Northwest Airlines flight at a refueling stopover in Alaska. It was December 5, 1973. I was staring out the airplane window, and I told myself to remember the date. I didn't know what would happen next, but it was the first time Mary Jane and I had ever seen snow.

When we landed at John F. Kennedy International Airport in New York, it was dark and freezing cold—a cold I had never felt before. My stepfather took our suitcases. I was still negotiating what to call him in my mind, even though my mother said to call him Daddy, and my aunt Mencie said, "Try Daddy Peter." When we were still in Manila, someone had asked to take a picture with him. "They think he's Elvis Presley," Mom had whispered.

We piled into a dark blue Volkswagen Beetle in the airport parking lot. My sister and I felt a car heater for the first time as we drove about an hour and a half south. After a journey that had started on the other side of the world more than twenty-four hours earlier, we reached our destination, a suburban house in a newly built neighborhood in Toms River,

New Jersey. We unloaded our luggage. I made a perfect footprint in the light snow on the driveway. Then my sister and I entered our new home. My new dad and mom would later explain how he would petition to adopt us, formally changing our last name to Ressa.

I had left behind a country in turmoil. A little over a year earlier, on September 21, 1972, President Ferdinand Marcos had declared martial law, shutting down the largest television station, ABS-CBN, which had always been a locus of media power. Marcos's one-man rule would mark a new era for the Philippines, which until then had been overpoweringly shaped by the United States. "Territorial conquest began and ended in the Philippines," my friend Stanley Karnow wrote in his epic *In Our Image: America's Empire in the Philippines*. "Americans neglected to establish an effective and impartial administration . . . so Filipinos turned to politicians instead of the bureaucracy for assistance, a practice that fostered patronage and corruption."[2]

Feudal patronage and endemic corruption would never disappear from the Philippines. Marcos, first elected in 1965 in the midst of grave economic problems, became the first and only Filipino president to be reelected to two terms. He campaigned on national identity and independence from the United States.

After Marcos declared martial law, Congress ratified the 1973 Constitution, still patterned after the US Constitution but now with revisions that ensured Marcos's power. That was later approved by the Supreme Court, allowing Marcos to "legally" consolidate and hold power for the next fourteen years, years I would spend in my new reality in the United States.

Our family believed in America: you worked hard, you paid your taxes, and you got what you deserved. The world is fair; that was what the social contract implicitly offered. My parents lived through the erosion of that contract over decades. I know what it does to people, how uncertainty and fear grow, how those who work hard and follow

Peter Ressa on a date with Hermelina Delfin at the Statue of Liberty,
1971

the rules feel cheated when promises are broken. When you throw in social media and information operations, those same people are targeted
and susceptible; they believe the lies.

Peter Ames Ressa was born in New York City, a second-generation
Italian American. He dropped out of school when he was sixteen years
old to help his family make ends meet and then started a job inputting
data at the investment bank Brown Brothers Harriman & Co., where he
painstakingly worked his way up the ladder. By the time he retired, he
was the senior IT manager for mainframe computers, and then he went
to work for IBM. Hard work drove him, as well as an uncanny talent for
remembering minute details.

He and my mother had met literally bumping into each other on the
streets of New York City. After dating for about two years, they got married in 1972, and the following year, my sister Michelle was born. Just
a week after that, my parents asked my aunt Annie to take care of their

new baby and boarded a flight to Manila to get Mary Jane and me. For my mom, it was both a difficult and a victorious journey.

Peter and Hermelina were a striking couple, something all their children were aware of, like having a spotlight on your parents all the time. In those years, I saw the United States largely through the lens of those hardworking, glamorous figures: leaving the house before dawn for the two-hour commute to their jobs in New York City, returning after dark, working all the time.

At one point, to save money, my mom began sewing our clothes but then realized the time it took wasn't worth the money she saved. By the time she gave birth to my brother, Peter Ames, Jr., and her youngest, Nicole, I was leading the back-to-school shopping trips behind my mom, pushing the grocery cart in Grand Union, Sears, and other bargain stores every August. I knew how to choose the cheapest clothes and shoes.

During that time, my father's company paid for his education, enabling him to finish high school. While I was going to high school, he went to college at night. It was only later I realized how much my parents had sacrificed to give their children a fighting chance. They wanted their children to have a good life and go to good schools—and we did.

When I walked into my third-grade classroom at the sprawling redbrick Silver Bay Elementary School, I was, at four feet, two inches, the shortest kid in the classroom—and the only brown one. Though I understood and could speak English, my primary language at home was Tagalog, or Filipino. I marveled at the loud, easy confidence of my classmates and was shocked by how rude they were to our teacher.

I was happy to see that the school, like St. Scholastica's back in the Philippines, used the SRA Reading Lab, one of the earliest personalized learning programs for reading, writing, and comprehension, which allowed students to move at their own pace. I liked racing against myself and my classmates and had already moved quite far ahead at St. Scholastica's. When I went to the back of my new classroom to get my SRA reading comprehension card, which tracked our progress, one of the tallest and loudest kids announced to the rest of the class that they were opening for me the box of a whole new section, one no other student was using yet. In that moment, everyone knew I was advanced.

I am by nature shy, an introvert. The transition to American life was so jarring for me that my teachers recalled that I stopped talking for nearly a year. I remember my silence as learning, a continuation of the "speak when you're spoken to" mentality from my upbringing and schooling in the Philippines. I was soaking in my new world like a sponge.

Somehow, the educators at Silver Bay Elementary School understood the roots of my silence and helped me adjust. One teacher, Mrs. Rarick, gave me free piano lessons every week, which grounded me. My grandmother had always emphasized that my father had played the piano, that her family were patrons of the arts,[3] and that my uncle was a concert pianist.[4] Somehow you adopt the dreams that float in the air around you.

Playing the piano connected me to the past and gave me a sense of freedom: no need to speak or learn a new language. All I needed to do was to practice until I could play and create music. I grasped early on that in order to play music really well, you have to spend hours and hours practicing so you can let go of the work when you perform. When the world became overwhelming, I channeled my energies into hours of practicing the piano.

But of course, I also wanted to be like everyone else. I would stand in front of the mirror, trying to pronounce English words properly, wishing I had lighter skin and blond hair. When you don't know who you are and your world has been turned upside down, you don't want to stand out.

Three lessons have stayed with me from that year I moved to the United States. They have come up again and again in my life even as the context shifts. Each time, the lessons gain new meaning.

The first was always to make the choice to learn. That meant embracing change and mustering the courage to fail; success and failure are two sides of the same coin. You cannot succeed if at some point you haven't failed. Most people, I realized, chose comfort, remaining in what was familiar: old friends, routines, habits.

Moving to the United States tested who I was. What do I take with me? What do I leave behind? Who am I? Even my name was different: I had been Angelita Aycardo when I left my classroom in Manila, and now I was Maria Ressa. I had moved into a completely new world, with a new language, new customs, new cultural signals that everyone understood but me. It was so overwhelming that at some point that first year, I didn't want to leave the house.

So I focused on what I could measure: my progress through the SRA Reading Lab; how quickly I could go through Hanon's exercises for the piano. I learned a lot of things from books, including how to play basketball. On weekends, I would take a book outside onto the school basketball court, put it on the tarmac, and follow, step by step, the instructions for how to dribble a ball, how to shoot a foul shot. I made real everything I learned. All I had to do was practice.

A few months after I had settled in, my teacher whom I idolized, Miss Ugland,[5] asked me if I would consider moving to another classroom: the school wanted to push me a grade higher. I was just starting to feel comfortable, and the potential change scared me. That was when she told me, "Maria, don't be afraid. Always push to learn; you have nothing more to learn in my classroom."

So midyear, I was moved from grade three to grade four and started all over again. And I learned my second lesson: to embrace my fear.

The trigger? I didn't know what "pajama party" meant. We didn't have them in Manila, or at least we didn't call them that. But I got an invitation for a "pajama party" from Sharon Rokozny, the coolest kid in my third-grade class, and when I asked my mom what the party was, she replied, "It's a party you wear pajamas to!" That made sense. And I was still in disbelief that Sharon had invited me.

On the appointed day, I put on my pajamas and got into the car with my dad, my mom, and my sister. When we turned into the cul-de-sac, I saw my classmates playing kickball on the lawn of Sharon's house. No one was wearing pajamas.

I turned in panic to my mom, who sheepishly admitted she didn't really know what a "pajama party" was, either. By that time, my classmates had already seen our car; we couldn't leave. When the car stopped, I looked at my parents before I opened the door. Then I stepped out.

My classmates stopped playing and looked at me. I didn't know what to do. And then Sharon came to the car. "Oh, you're wearing your pajamas," she said.

"I thought we were supposed to," I mumbled, on the verge of tears. It had taken all the courage I had to step out of the car, and now I had none left.

Then Sharon took my hand, grabbed my bag, and led me to the house. "You can go inside and change," she said while I wiped my eyes and waved to my parents. Good thing I'd packed extra clothes.

When you take a risk, you have to trust that someone will come to your aid; and when it's your turn, you will help someone else. It's better to face your fear than to run from it because running won't make the problem go away. When you face it, you have the chance to conquer it. That was how I began to define courage.

My third lesson was about standing up to bullies, which was connected to a lot of things: fear, acceptance, joining a group, being popular. Since everything was foreign to me, I usually had no choice but to stay quiet, observe, and learn. Because I was already so different from the others, I felt the need to conform much less and had the luxury of observing and understanding the crowd without ever being part of it.

That year, I had a classmate I will call Debbie, a quiet, plain girl who was ridiculed because she wore polyester pants. Everyone made fun of her, although I didn't totally understand why. I certainly didn't want to speak up and ask—what if they started making fun of me?

Today, I have a phrase for this situation: silence is complicity.

I played the violin and Debbie played the viola, and one day after our school music rehearsal I saw Debbie crying in a corner of the orchestra room. My instinct was to walk away because if I stopped to ask her what was wrong, people might notice, making me a target, too. No one spoke to Debbie except to make fun of her. Then I remembered the Bible's Golden Rule: "Do unto others as you would have them do unto you."

I made a decision. I walked out of the rehearsal room into the bathroom across the hall, got a tissue, brought it to Debbie, and asked her what was wrong. She told me that her father had been in the hospital for months.

Talking to her gave me the courage to keep talking to her. At some point, I invited her to sleep over. She wore polyester pants, it turned out, because her family was struggling to make ends meet and the pants were cheap.

Well, after that, I started standing up for Debbie. Once, when her worst bully was picking on her in orchestra, I told him to stop. Right when I thought he would turn on me, some of my friends jumped in to help. All it takes is one person to stand up and fight because a bully doesn't like to be challenged publicly.

That was an early lesson in pushing back against the cruelty of the herd mentality. Here's what I learned about popularity: people like you if you give them what they want. The question is: Is it what *you* want?

Toms River's public school system gave me free music lessons, computer programming classes, and advanced placement classes that enabled me to compete for admission to Ivy League schools—a future that promised that you can accomplish anything if you work hard enough. By the time I graduated high school, I had been president of my class for three years and been voted "Most Likely to Succeed."

Because my parents were constantly working, I spent a lot of time with my teachers. The one who helped make me who I am was Donald Spaulding, the head of the Toms River Regional Schools Summer Strings program, a heavyset but fast-moving man with a bearded face that was always breaking into a smile. Mr. Spaulding was not only my violin teacher and orchestra conductor; he helped me learn to play up to eight different instruments. He nurtured me and others like me: kids looking for our place in the world. He would pick me up from the other side of town so that I could join actual gigs. We played at Sunday brunches, at the Ground Round with the peanut shells on the floor, at our local mall in Ocean County, and at Six Flags Great Adventure.[6]

He pushed me to be better as a person and as a musician. No idea I had was too far-fetched.

"Mr. Spaulding, how about we play 'The Devil Went Down to Georgia'?" I asked after I heard a riff I wanted to learn. He stopped to think, took out his violin, pulled out blank sheet music, and began to write down the notes so I could follow.

"Why not?" he always responded. Always make the choice to learn.

But there was another lesson you learned while in Don Spaulding's orbit: that no one can accomplish anything meaningful alone. That's what the orchestra taught me, and what I would learn again from the basketball and softball teams, the theater productions, and student government. Yet how good a team player you are depends on your skills, your drive, your endurance.

I loved being in the swirl of music, one part listening and soaring, another part counting the beats, watching the ups and downs of our bows, always part of me focused on the conductor, ready to follow, and, as concert mistress, ready to lead. The magic happened when all of the work faded into the background and we lived inside the music, interpreting the notes and creating music together. To get to that point required hours and hours of practice.

Later, I would realize that an orchestra was a perfect metaphor for a working democracy: the music gave the people our notes, our systems, but how you play, feel, and follow—and how you lead—that's all up to you.

I continued to play sports partly in an attempt to avoid being labeled a nerd. But I was a huge nerd. Above all, books were what explained everything to me that people couldn't—or answered questions I couldn't ask. I loved Harlequin romances and science fiction novels, which helped me imagine different worlds such as the ones Isaac Asimov built. But first and foremost I was one thing: a die-hard Trekkie.

I read all the *Star Trek* novelizations by James Blish and had a shelf at home where I collected them. The books helped me understand my own mind. Sometimes I was Captain Kirk, the leader who listened to his emotions and gut instincts; sometimes I was Mr. Spock, the logical Vulcan, who deconstructed problems. Only much later would I realize that they were two sides of the brain and of human nature—thinking fast and thinking slow, as Daniel Kahneman would later put it. To this day, when someone asks me who my heroes are, I point to the combination of Mr. Spock and Captain Kirk, rational logical analysis tempered by empathy, instinct, and emotions.

Something I didn't grasp until later was that I was sublimating my negative emotions, like anger. I could never shake the feeling that I was on the outside looking in, trying to understand what was happening so I could fit in. That's probably why somehow, the extracurricular activities I chose were connected to the Philippines. I played basketball, the most popular sport in the Philippines, and joined the chess team because somewhere in my memory those were important parts of a past I couldn't return to and that I was yet to fully understand.

Some of those feelings came into the open when it was time to apply to college. I wrote in my application essay about how I regretted that so many of my achievements, so much of who I had become, were a reflection of what others—teachers, my parents—wanted me to be. I had gotten straight A's when it mattered, but through it all, I had felt as though there was a devil on my shoulder driving me to keep doing better and more, to keep racking up achievements and superlatives because if I didn't, then I didn't belong there.

I applied to thirteen colleges including six-year med programs, military academies, and several Ivy League schools. My parents wanted me to be a doctor. I thought I needed discipline. In the end, I didn't really know who I was, but I felt I needed to achieve. Something. Anything.

I knew that drive came from a place of insecurity. Still, I was pragmatic. Even if I didn't understand the devil on my shoulder, I knew that learning—and learning beyond standard school books—would only help me.

I figured you can't go wrong if you make the choice to learn.

Chapter 2

· · ·

The Honor Code

Draw the Line

Last name Reyes	First name Maria	Middle initial A.

To the Honor Committee:

> I agree to abide by the rules and regulations adopted under the Constitution of the Honor System. I understand the full implications of the Honor Code and the responsibilities (responsibilities) which I must undertake as a member of the class of 1986 in maintaining the high standards of the Princeton community.

JUN 17 1982

Signature *Maria A. Reyes*   Date 6/13/82

JUN 17 1982

Part of every Princeton application is a pledge to follow the Honor Code.

College was when I began to explore and think for myself. My Manila education had emphasized rote learning and memorization: to follow the rules and speak when you're spoken to. In the United States, I did just that. Until college.

Princeton University was my choice. I loved the idea that students could attend precept classes or small discussion groups with world-renowned professors, even a Nobel laureate. It was also roughly an hour's drive away from Toms River, so I wasn't too far from home. I would spend hours walking around the gorgeous campus with its buildings that radiated history, watching the leaves change. Or sitting inside the chapel, which quieted my mind. Sometimes, if no one was around, I would stop at the imposing Blair Arch to find the point in the middle where my whisper would reverberate around the walls. Late at night, coming home from Firestone Library, I would stop at the 1879 Arch to listen to impromptu performances by our singing groups before walking back to my dorm, singing the last song.

I had been assigned an eighty-eight-square-foot room, just big enough for a bed, a dresser, and a desk. My mom brought along a huge statue of the Virgin Mary that she placed on top of my dresser, looking over the bed. I didn't even realize how strange that was—although it did make for some great conversations with my boyfriends right before we fell asleep.

Religion was a huge and thorny issue for me. My grandmother's deep religiosity had pounded organized religion into my sister and me. She made us say the rosary twice a day, in the morning and at night, and attend Mass almost every day. My freshman year, I studied all five major world religions: Christianity, Buddhism, Islam, Judaism, Hinduism. I wanted to define what I believed logically; but of course, there's nothing logical about religion. For a time, I thought about becoming a Buddhist, but then daily life took over, and my beliefs intertwined with what I studied.

I entered Princeton pre-med, and I finished all the requirements for medical school in my first two years. I saw how the rules of science, of physics, were philosophical, like the laws of thermodynamics: how everything moves to maximum entropy or chaos, and how it takes energy to maintain order. Or Newton's laws of motion; my favorite was the third: that for every action, there is an equal and opposite reaction. Or the Heisenberg uncertainty principle, which I would use as the epigraph of my first book: that the very act of observing changes what you observe and that the more you drill down, the more unknowable what you are searching for becomes. Who said religion and science don't go hand in hand?

But the thing that infused my values and shaped me the most at school was the Honor Code. On every paper and every test, students at Princeton must write the Honor Code Pledge: "I pledge my honor that I have not violated the Honor Code during this examination."

When you write that, you guarantee not only your own behavior but also that of everyone around you. Once an exam is handed out, the professor leaves the room. Implicit in that pledge is that you will report anyone else you see cheating, because if you don't, it will tear down your own honor. You are responsible not just for yourself but also for the world around you, your area of influence.

I love that idea. Though I didn't think much about the Honor Pledge while I was in college, I was already living it. Only later did I realize that I assumed everyone was doing the same: taking responsibility for the world around us. Some family and friends would later criticize that trait of mine as dogmatic and elitist, and it can be annoying, I suppose. But the strict code of honor simplified the world for me and helped me make quick decisions.

That Honor Code helped me define my values early and clearly—before any moral dilemma could tempt me to rationalize selfish, bad behavior. It helped me avoid situational ethics later in life. It was simple. Draw the line: on one side you're good; the other, you're evil.

It turned out at Princeton that my passions were in the arts, not the sciences. I took an excessive course load so I could squeeze in all my enthusiasms: comparative literature, Shakespeare, theater, acting, playwriting, psychology, history. Those subjects taught me how to cope with the stresses of daily life and how to understand my own history and identity. They made me realize how much I had compensated for being an outsider, always pursuing perfection to fill the absence of belonging. And they nurtured my tendency to inquiry, probing why we were on this planet and what I was here to do.

Of them all, I learned the most from theater, even things as simple as breathing: lying down, breathing deeply, visualizing air and energy going in and out, centering yourself in the moment. Letting your mind and body work together to be absolutely present. Another theater exercise was mirrors, in which a leader and follower find the line between leading, following, and creating. These may seem like simple exercises, but they have proved incredibly useful in some of the worst moments of my life.

It was in one of those theater classes, too, that I called out what I considered unfair behavior and ended up solidifying one of the most important relationships of my life.

Leslie Tucker, a light-skinned black American, was among the first people I met at Princeton. Tall, pretty, and charming, she seemed to be my opposite. She was funny, a born storyteller, someone who naturally captured the spotlight. She was also brutally honest, at times even mean, which somehow, instead of offending people, would make them laugh with her.

Every week in playwriting class, we would submit scenes that would be critiqued by the class. Leslie always had insightful comments, and her best friend was the handsome Andrew Jarecki. The two were constantly laughing with each other and, I imagined, poking fun at others. At some point, there came a period when Leslie wasn't doing the assignments and turning in her own scenes but was still participating in the critiques. One day, I'd had enough.

Our chairs were in a circle, and Leslie was offering her usual criticism that was blunt but nevertheless always charmed our professors.

"I'm sorry," I interrupted. "We haven't read a scene from you yet, Leslie."

There was stunned silence, including mine. I had actually said it aloud.

I went on, addressing the class: "Don't you think that Leslie should hand in her scene?"

Leslie looked at me quizzically and tried to respond. "I'm not sure what Maria is getting at here."

I interrupted again, my heart in my throat. "It's been a few weeks that this is happening. Is this actually fair?" Our professor was forced to address the problem, and I felt a small sense of justice.

After class, Leslie asked me why I had called her out, which set off a series of conversations between us. Leslie's easy laughter, her casual deployment of tough criticism, scared me. But her sharpness and brutal honesty taught me something else: that in order to have a clear view of the world, you have to ask yourself the toughest questions. Leslie always went for the jugular, but her insights inspired my own introspection.

That day in class, I not only did the same for her; I learned that drawing the line, calling out unfairness and being honest, though uncomfortable, often means moving life forward, bringing something new to fruition.

Challenging Leslie, and understanding her own code of honesty, not only sparked one of my most important friendships but transformed my way of being in the world. Staying silent or compliant changed nothing. Speaking up was an act of creation.

In playwriting class, I also learned to be more consciously creative, to gain comfort with uncertainty and continue to explore. I had always tended to avoid negative emotions like anger, but my acting teacher pushed me to immerse myself in the emotion. One day, in the middle of a scene in class, I finally felt an explosive release, and all the anger I had sublimated came rushing out. For the next two weeks of my junior year, I couldn't control my anger, which kept erupting in strange flashes.

Trying to understand why led me back to the past. My boyfriend urged me to read Alice Miller's *The Drama of the Gifted Child: The Search for the True Self*, from which I gained a key insight: that there are successful people who, because of their childhood experiences, learn to suppress their emotions as long as their life is peppered with achievements. "They do well, even excellently, in everything they undertake; they are admired and envied; they are successful whenever they care to be," Miller wrote, ". . . but behind all this lurks depression, a feeling of emptiness and self-alienation, and a sense that their life has no meaning."[1]

And I remembered the devil on my shoulder, always driving me to do better, when I read this: "Their access to the emotional world of their own childhood, however, is impaired—characterized by a lack of respect, a compulsion to control and manipulate, and a demand for achievement."[2]

I would come to see that I might have suppressed many of my childhood experiences—the abrupt departure from my homeland, the terror of being an outsider in New Jersey—as a way to survive and become a successful, even powerful person. And it would be critical for me never to be manipulative or abuse that power. I wanted to balance my ambitions with the Golden Rule: do unto others as you would have them do unto you.

Another key text for me during that time was T. S. Eliot's essay "Tradition and the Individual Talent." He argued that the way you read William Shakespeare is affected by the last novel you read, and the last novel you read is affected by the fact that you read Shakespeare. This notion collapses time, space, and tradition because both past and present coexist, changing each other and creating the future. "The emotion of art is impersonal," he wrote. "And the poet cannot reach this impersonality without surrendering himself wholly to the work to be done. And he is not likely to know what is to be done unless he lives in what is not merely the present, but the present moment of the past, unless he is conscious, not of what is dead, but of what is already living."

The present moment of the past.

I began to realize that the work of art you're creating is your life; that the person you are today has been created by all your past selves (for example, the person you were at ten years old), but that your actions today actually change those earlier versions of yourself. I didn't have to remain that achievement-oriented child, the one alienated from myself, my past, and my emotions. The person I am is an act of creation; I can seize the past and transform all I have learned and turn it into something new. I control who I am and who I want to be.

Ever pragmatic, I was now aware of a problem. So I set out to solve it in as constructive a way as possible: Captain Kirk and Mr. Spock combined.

I set myself a twofold challenge: how to understand the world and my place in it, and how to build my confidence while controlling my ego. I wanted to achieve an "empty mirror,"[3] a concept I took from a book about a Buddhist monastery: to stand in front of a mirror and see the world without my image obstructing the view. I wanted to know myself to such a degree that I could take myself out of the equation when approaching the world around me and responding to it. That is clarity—the ability to remove your self and your ego.

At that point, I had no interest in politics or world events. When I passed a group of students on campus demonstrating against apartheid in South Africa, I didn't stop to sign their petition.[4] I didn't know what it was about, and I was rushing to class. The Philippines for me existed as a vague, intriguing memory.

But for my senior thesis, I began research for a play called *Sagittarius* that would be my attempt to work out my own personal demons—a political allegory that would reflect on the situation in the Philippines as well as my family history.

Ferdinand Marcos had remained president of the Philippines well into my college years. By then, he was also a dictator who manipulated elections, used the military to impose his power, and built a kleptocracy that allowed him to steal up to $10 billion from his country. His wife, Imelda, with her infamous shoe collection, bought expensive perfume not by the ounce but by the gallon. Their ostentatiousness was so lurid that it humiliated their people.

On August 21, 1983, the exiled opposition leader and longtime Marcos opponent Benigno "Ninoy" Aquino, Jr., returned to the Philippines. He was aware of the risks in returning to Manila; he even told the media that he would wear a bulletproof vest. As he descended from the plane, he was shot in the head on the airport tarmac by security forces thought to be working for Marcos.[5] It was one of the most shocking moments in the history of the Philippines.

Aquino's widow, Corazon, more familiarly known as Cory, became the opposition leader. Against all odds, the widow stood up against the dictator in 1986. The year I would graduate from Princeton, President Marcos, now in power for more than two decades, declared a snap election. Cory ran to challenge him. It was David against Goliath, good versus evil.

Marcos declared victory, but Aquino and her supporters refused to accept it. Hundreds of thousands, later millions, of people poured onto one of the largest highways in Manila, EDSA, a bustling, multilane avenue flanked by lush acacia trees and high-rises, which separated the headquarters of the police and the military. The protestors also swarmed Malacañang Palace, Marcos's home, the Philippines' equivalent of the White House. Many expected that the military would open fire on the crowd. Instead, the soldiers defied Marcos's order to shoot their own people.

The protests were called People Power and would remain in the collective memory of Filipinos as one of the most heroic, democratic moments in our history, proof of what the Filipino people could do in the face of the worst repression.

The peaceful uprising ousted a dictator who had been in power for nearly twenty-one years[6] and would spark pro-democracy uprisings around the world—in South Korea in 1987, Myanmar in 1988, and China and Eastern Europe in 1989, when former dissident and Czech president Václav Havel thanked Filipinos for inspiring his country's democratic revolution.[7]

In my play, I imagined a grandmother, a Marcos figure, fighting a mother, a Cory Aquino figure, for the custody and love of a child: the Filipino people. By writing the play and framing my own personal quest for the truth in my own family in a Brechtian framework, I found my way to what I think of as the micro and the macro of life. What was revealed in my writing—even though my conscious mind may not have recognized it—was a deeper sense that what's personal is political. Conflicted about loyalty to the different characters in my play, I also discovered a greater sense of empathy within the political and for political actors. It was my own private exorcism, a way for me to ask questions my family had done its best to avoid.

My family came to the opening night of my play at Theatre Intime, the campus student theater. When the lights came up and they called us onstage, I saw my parents crying in their seats. I was crying, too. A few months later, we opened my play at the Edinburgh Festival Fringe in Scotland.

That "present moment of the past" was a time of great intellectual exploration, but even then I knew that intellect without emotion is flawed—and that some of the greatest insights can come only from letting go, something I still was reluctant to do. My Mr. Spock side ruled a lot of what I did in those early years. I was learning how to make decisions, but, afraid to make mistakes, I sometimes took too long to make them. It felt as though there was so much at stake before graduation.

Still, whenever I was lost or needed to make a quick decision, I began to develop a formula: I look at what I'm afraid of, downplay my ego, then follow the Golden Rule and the Honor Code.

It always works.

We all want to belong somewhere.

I had never felt completely American. I knew something was missing, so I decided to look for it. If I wasn't American, I thought, then I must be Filipino. (I miss the simplicity of those days.) The year I graduated, after doing everything I was supposed to do, I set aside the corporate job offers, medical school, law school, and applied for a Fulbright fellowship. Continuing the journey that my playwriting had unlocked, I would return to the Philippines—in search of my grandmother, in search of my roots, in search of home.

Home. A safe place. A sanctuary. The word taps into something visceral. It means safety; no matter what we do, at home we're accepted for who we are. When I was ten, inside that car leaving St. Scholastica's with my mother and my new father, I remember wondering whether I should run away. Should I find my way back to my grandmother's house? When a teacher asked where my home was, I avoided the existential question and answered with the left side of my brain: I gave my address.

Home is about emotional roots: culture, food, implicit values, the warmth of familiarity. You belong there. It has its rituals that mark the passage of time and give it meaning.

I finally felt comfortable being an outsider looking in, wanting to belong but comfortable with observing. I learned to listen and learn, to achieve and excel, but it wasn't until after college that I found the courage to really explore the world.

Chapter 3

...

The Speed of Trust

Be Vulnerable

Jungle training exercises, late 1980s

Sliding doors. I had always wondered how different I would be, what life I would be living if my parents had left me in the Philippines. What hit me when I walked out of the Manila airport was a blast of humidity, heat, and noise. It was my first time back in thirteen years.

I went to Quezon City to visit my paternal grandmother, so large and imposing in my child's mind. Past and present collided when I realized that we lived only houses away from Cory Aquino's home on Times Street, newly surrounded by security after she had become president. As I waited in the living room, I looked at the marble floor, which in my mind had stretched endlessly, and outside at the unkempt yard. Now everything looked small.

My grandmother came out of her room and walked in front of the altar in the hallway, where we had all once prayed together. I stayed rooted in my seat as she sat down before me. She was much smaller than I remembered, a little bent, not quite as imposing. She started speaking, and her accent was strong. That was jarring. Somehow in my mind, she spoke American English. I looked at the overgrown grass in the backyard and remembered the walk to the maid's quarters in the back. Or did I make that up? There was an air of decay, and it all reminded me of Miss Havisham in Charles Dickens's novel *Great Expectations*.

Everything adjusted in the present moment of the past.

I was there in part to thank my grandmother for giving me the values that had helped make me who I was, but real life is far more awkward. Memories are deceptive. She proceeded to launch into a sidewise critique of my upbringing, still trying to turn me against my mother. As I was listening to her, I began a running commentary in my head, all the time nodding in agreement. I felt lost, partly because I was so American and my grandmother was so Filipino. I think I disappointed her as much as she disappointed me. Somehow I'd thought that coming back would give me instant answers to my own identity.

I focused instead on my Fulbright. Before I returned to Manila, I had finished the production of my thesis play, *Sagittarius*, at the Edinburgh Festival Fringe in Scotland. For the play's poster, I had used the last cover of the *Philippines Free Press*, a Filipino English-language newsmagazine. The front-page editorial cartoon a day before Ferdinand Marcos had declared martial law had asked, "Do You Want to Live Under a Dictator?" My Fulbright proposal was to explore the role of political theater in driving political change.

So I joined the nineteen-year-old Philippine Educational Theater Association, or PETA, a home of agit prop theater, which had played an important role in the development of People Power, getting people out into the streets to bring down Marcos. For a time, the atmosphere in the country had been jubilant, Filipinos proud of themselves for their courage and hopeful about what the future might bring.

My mom told me that when she had taken us from school in November 1973 to head to the United States, one question I had asked her was "What about Twink?"

Muriel "Twink" Macaraig and I had known each other since we were four and five years old, respectively. (Strange diminutives are normal in the Philippines—grown men named "Boy" and government officials called "Joker.") I remembered Twink as one of the tallest in my third-grade class, raucous, always running around, a thin sliver of sweat on her upper lip. But we hadn't seen each other since I had left that classroom thirteen years earlier. Through my cousin, she'd heard that I was returning to the Philippines. She would later tell me what a ruckus our "kidnapping" had created in 1973, which was why she was so curious to find out what had happened to me.

Twink had grown into a petite, beautiful, self-assured woman who, along with many, had decided after People Power to audition for anchor positions with the government station, People's Television 4, or PTV4. She came from a family of lawyers and journalists and loved to tell stories: funny, engaging anecdotes that taught me a lot about her Philippines.

She pursued and restarted our friendship, bringing me into her world. One evening, she took me to the station for her early-evening newscast. When we got to the newsroom, I saw the manual typewriters ringing the desk area in front of a bank of televisions set to different stations, all of them blaring. At the right of the room, the teletype was literally spewing out stories. There was a faint smell of cigarette smoke in the air.

I followed Twink to the studio through hallways that were completely dark. After the buildings had been overrun after People Power, little money had been spent to fix broken tiles or busted lightbulbs. The stench of urine permeated dark corridors where stray cats lurked.

But there was nothing like the excitement of a live television newscast! I loved how all the disparate parts—from the writers in the newsroom to the script runners to the technicians and cameramen—came together to bring a live program to people's homes. The scripts were sometimes written only minutes before and even during airtime. I was fascinated by scripts being torn and handed to the anchors seconds before they had to read them on air, as runners with VTRs—three-quarter-inch tapes—arrived just in time to slot them into the U-matic players seconds before the director yelled, "Roll!"

Like the student orchestra of my youth, it was a group of people making music together, except this time it was the first page of history being created with tremendous impact. The systems, which needed to adapt to broadcasting breaking news, were only as powerful as the strengths and weaknesses of the people on the team.

Twink introduced me to her coanchor, Betsy Enriquez, the most experienced of the station's anchors. The third anchor was Judith Torres, a former singer whose unaccented English, I would later learn, translated into crisp, clear writing. Little did I know then how our lives and careers would intertwine.

Since Twink also anchored the late-evening newscast, it became a near-daily ritual to get dinner in between the newscasts. The director of the 10:00 p.m. newscast was a gray-haired veteran everyone liked, but he kept falling asleep in the control room. I marveled that the studio team kept going. Even though I had never directed a newscast, I figured I could do better than someone who was sleeping. Within weeks,

I had convinced the managers at PTV4 to let me direct the late-evening newscast.

The problems of the Philippines media industry mirrored those in the country's political and corporate culture. This is true of any democracy, which is defined by its institutions, but especially true of a democracy emerging from a dictatorship, one whose people are struggling to create a democratic culture. Because the strength, transparency, and trustworthiness of the media was linked to the survival of the Philippines as a democracy, I quickly saw how high the stakes would be— that in journalism, I might contribute more to the evolution and health of the country than in anything else. We have lost sight of this now— and the social media platforms have done their best to destroy these once-universal values—but in the 1980s, another agreed-upon fact, a foundation of our shared reality, was that without good journalism, without the sound production of facts and information, there would be no democracy. Journalism was a calling.

Corruption was one of the Philippines' most corrosive problems. It existed in government, in the media business, and in everyday lives. Politicians and the police abused their power with impunity, TV channels censored themselves for greater access, officials demanded petty bribes from ordinary folks. What had happened in media was happening in every industry in the Philippines as well; people preserved relationships over facts. Even President Cory Aquino stated as part of her philosophy that Filipinos should privilege reconciliation with one another rather than retribution for the Marcos years. At the time, that attitude made some sense: the country needed to heal after emerging from a dictatorship.

Not only did the media have a long history of state control under Marcos, but it had its own tradition of corruption, or what we then called "envelopmental journalism," referring to the envelope of money that organizers of press conferences often handed out to the journalists attending. Good journalists refused the envelope but stayed quiet about those who accepted it. The attitude of most working journalists then was to privately acknowledge that corruption existed within our ranks but to look away. After all, the thinking went, that person has a family to feed. The journalists who exposed corruption were often the first attacked. That hasn't changed.

Even PTV4's studios and broadcasting facilities in Quezon City were a focal point of contemporary Philippine history, and a symbol of democratic transition. Originally built by the news station ABS-CBN in 1968, the brand-new studios were shut down and seized by the government after Ferdinand Marcos declared martial law in 1972. Marcos cronies took over the facilities from its owners, the Lopez family, and turned them into Maharlika Broadcasting System, or MBS. When People Power kicked out Marcos, MBS became PTV4.

There was a disconnect between the newbies like Twink, Judith, and me and the old guard, who had been there when the station was still MBS under Marcos. The old guard had learned to do the bare minimum because doing more didn't bring more rewards but often brought punishment instead.

Those prominent anchors during the Marcos days had no place in the new world. Everyone who had appeared on camera before, the established broadcast anchors of the Marcos government, were tainted and thrown out. Twink and Judith were women who, along with many others, had auditioned for anchor positions at PTV4 after People Power. Over several days, the audience voted for their favorites, and then the channel's management chose the new anchors to represent the new country. That new group who had auditioned publicly became as much a symbol of the new Philippines as the protestors storming Malacañang Palace. Twink and Judith bucked the stereotype of Filipino women. Empowered and smart, they drew bold lines; they called out hypocrisy and highlighted the difference between black and white, especially after Marcos.

PTV4 agreed to hire me for several reasons: I didn't ask to be paid because I was on a Fulbright, and with Twink and Judith, I had a ready-made team. Within a few months, we had approval to write, edit, supervise, direct, and produce a daily live newscast—just us.

That was what I used my Fulbright for: real-life theater. I chose journalism.

I was spending 7:00 a.m. until midnight in the newsroom and studios. What I learned early was the connection between good broadcasts and the sustenance of a free media organization. In addition to the basics of producing, I pushed to create better standards and programming. The news head would just shake his head and dismiss me as foreign, but Twink and Judith were Filipinos who wanted better. The more we did, the more we wanted to do.

I began to understand the concept of a "workflow": a standardized, step-by-step process for executing excellent stories. Every step required strict quality control. In the Philippines, there was a personal cost to calling out an error or demanding better in a work culture; SIR, or "smooth interpersonal relations," had long been prioritized. So we created our own team and energized them with a vision of what we wanted our newscast to be.

We wanted video with the tightest editing, sequenced properly to tell a story, instead of a B-roll that unfurled lazily and meaninglessly. We wrote our text in the present tense: short, tight, declarative, active sentences instead of the run-on, complex sentences that had become customary. I demanded tighter camera shots, which meant that our studio cameramen—yes, they were all men—couldn't sit on their chairs during a live show.

I also began to understand self-censorship in a new way. Old habits formed under a dictatorship are hard to shed. It was always easy to spot self-censorship in an anchor read because the phrasing was angled to please the boss, at best, or avoid angering power, at worst. The first time I pointed out an instance of self-censorship, I truly hadn't understood why the script had been written in such a circuitous manner. It seemed ingrained in the government newsroom to deflect responsibility for the government. Twink immediately took out her pen and rewrote the line I had questioned, and for that she was called into the news head's office to defend her decision.

Within four months, I had created and was leading the network's first newsmagazine program, *Foursight*,[1] with a team of young, energetic creatives that I still think of as a template for all my future endeavors. There was an incredible sense of mission; we felt that we were writing the present and rewriting history, righting the wrongs of the past. It was a time when journalists, the gatekeepers of the public sphere, took our responsibility seriously. We all went through our programs line by line—first the reporter, then the producer, the executive producer, and the legal department. We held ourselves accountable for every word in every sentence.

I renewed calls for more funding for PTV. I asked if we could clean the hallways, change the busted lights, get rid of the stray cats and the stench. I received long lectures about government funding and budgets and how much work and money it takes just to keep things going. In my mind, that was the mindset of mediocrity, when you settle for what you can get instead of pushing for more.

The transition from a dictatorship to a democracy proved to be a turbulent one. The year I returned, President Aquino faced six coup attempts. That's what happens when the military kicks out a long-standing ruler like Marcos and realizes it has the power to do so again. Unhappy with what they perceived as a weak woman leader, the soldiers who had successfully ousted Marcos—soldiers who called themselves the Reform the Armed Forces Movement (RAM)—kept trying to oust

Aquino, too. The first five attempts were discovered and quashed relatively quickly, with little violence.

We were inevitably caught in the middle of some of the coup attempts because, as I soon learned, during a military takeover one of the first things rebellious soldiers do is seize the government radio or television station to control information. Media has always been crucial to the maintenance of political power; the airwaves are the first thing any dictator must control. Indeed, the spark of the People Power revolution had been the radio, when Jaime Cardinal Sin, the archbishop of Manila, encouraged people to take to the streets. That is why I grasped how important the news media were, how existential their survival and integrity were for a democracy.

The sixth and most violent coup against Aquino began during the early-morning hours of August 28, 1987. Rebel soldiers seized our broadcast compound along with Malacañang Palace, Villamor Air Base, and other strategic sites. I had spent the previous night editing in the basement of our office. Once I realized what was going on, I sneaked out to the nearby Camelot Hotel, where my visiting college boyfriend was staying. There we watched on television while a brief firefight between the rebel soldiers and the police returned the facilities to government control. More than fifty people were killed in the attempt. The relationship between media and politics was seared into me early, especially because, in the Philippines, it always seemed that our political past kept returning to haunt us.

Around that time, I got a call from Cheche Lazaro, who was then the head of public affairs at the newly re-opened ABS-CBN and the anchor of its well-respected news documentary program, *Probe*. The Aquino administration had given the Quezon City broadcast compound, once the mouthpiece of Ferdinand Marcos, back to ABS-CBN, which had agreed to share it for a limited time with PTV4. Unlike the existing newscasts, which aired in English, ABS-CBN's prime-time newscast used Filipino, and it dominated the ratings. When Cheche asked me to join her, I said yes. So in addition to directing newscasts at PTV4, I directed, produced, and edited *Probe*'s documentary programs with Cheche.

I had my hands full, and I was exercising power that someone my age should never have had and gobbling up the experience. But I was nearing the end of my Fulbright fellowship. My college boyfriend had come to visit in part to make sure that I would come back to the United States.

Then Cheche decided to start her own company and asked me to come with her. She had a vision for a real investigative newsmagazine program, and she infected me with her zeal. We wanted to prove that Filipinos deserved better programming, and there was no better time to try to do that than after People Power, when the people's demand for better leadership needed to be met with good governance.

We had one problem: I had expensive student loans to pay off, and *Probe* couldn't afford to pay me a salary that would allow me even to rent an apartment. Cheche offered a solution: in addition to working for her, she wanted me to live with her family. I didn't hesitate.

My parents thought I had gone crazy; they said I was throwing my Princeton education away. Instead of returning to my life in the United States after the Fulbright, I went home to say good-bye to my family and friends and returned to Manila on the round-trip ticket Cheche had bought me. It was a life-changing decision—one of the best I ever made.

I made the choice to learn, but it was more than that—I learned to trust: to drop my shields and be vulnerable. I have rarely been disappointed when I do. That, to me, is strength and why I believe in the goodness of human nature. When you're vulnerable, you create the strongest bonds and the most inspiring possibilities.

Much of what I am today as a journalist and leader was formed at *Probe*, where I set up systems and developed our program templates by doing each job myself: writer, director, producer, video editor, and executive producer. In my early twenties, I learned how to create and build a team that was more powerful than the sum of its parts. *Probe* gave me the most rigorous training in the broadcasting industry—probably better than I would've gotten if I worked for a television network in the United States. I wasn't just learning by doing; I was learning how to lead. We tackled projects and timelines that someone older would have turned down, setting a frenetic pace for work. That's what happens when you let crazy young dreamers set up a system.

I lived with Cheche and her family in the lush, stately neighborhood of Dasmariñas Village for more than two years. At the time, Cheche was a famous journalist and a household name, and her husband, Delfin Lazaro,[2] was the Philippines' secretary of energy; in other words, two journalists shared meals every day with a public official. We drew journalistic lines, creating rules for ourselves, such as "No questions at the dinner table." Hard as I looked, I saw no corruption, greed, or selfishness in Cheche and Del. Although they were public figures, they lived private lives, shunning ostentatious behavior.

Del and Cheche were so unlike the Marcoses of the world. They gave new meaning to often abused Filipino terms like *delicadeza*, doing the right thing when you wield power, and *utang na loob*, literally "the debt from within." Del and Cheche modeled those values in their purest forms: *delicadeza* that showed professionalism and pride and *utang na loob* that never degenerated into patronage and corruption.

Their values came in part from Cheche's family lineage. Cheche's grandfather, General Vicente Lim, was the first Filipino graduate from West Point. She told me about how he led an underground resistance against the Japanese in World War II until he was captured and later beheaded. It was a story of conviction, courage, and passionate belief in a people fighting for its freedom.

That time in my life showed me it was possible to live my ideals—to successfully bridge the gaps between the way you choose to live and the realities of a stratified, class-conscious, feudalistic Filipino society. Cheche and Del taught me that you can succeed without compromising your ideals. It was a choice; so choose to be better.

Cheche's energy drove all of us: she was always fair, always transparent, and willing to do anything that needed to be done to meet our insane deadlines. She also taught me to embrace and love the Philippines, despite its imperfections. Like most Filipinos, Cheche's life revolved around her family, but her heritage turned that love for family into love for her nation. That love of country was a core value of *Probe*, and because we were young, we gave it everything we had.

As I learned to make judgments on complex and thorny issues after all the rational debate, I always went back to the Golden Rule and my values: Where to draw the line between good and evil?

In 1988, the Philippine Tropical Fish Exporters Association filed a case against a story *Probe* had done on cyanide fishing, claiming that it was libelous. I had written, directed, and produced the twenty-minute piece. Our lawyers immediately put my name onto the defense witness list. It was the first time I had ever dealt with anything like that, and I was scared.

Cheche stepped in and said she would testify instead. She went to battle for me, and the judge ruled in favor of *Probe*, upholding the Philippine Bill of Rights, which had been patterned after that of the United States.

What she said then has stayed with me until today and still influences the way I defend our journalism. "Our integrity and our credibility are on the line here," she said. "So if anybody comes and says that we cannot air a piece or wants to preview a piece, that to us is tantamount to muzzling our freedom of the press. . . . And we will never, never, never agree to be intimidated by anyone, no matter who he is."

Cheche's words that year aged well for me, gaining more meaning in the present moment of the past. Never, never, never agree to be intimidated by anyone, no matter who he is.

For all the agonizing I did about East and West, we harnessed the power of both worlds to help get *Probe* off the ground. In 1988, *Probe* got a big boost: a commercial deal with CNN.

Gary Strieker, CNN's Nairobi bureau chief, was looking for a reporter in Manila and invited Cheche for a camera test and interview. At the time, CNN was seven years old, not one of the big three US networks but starting to make a name for itself. Cheche asked me to come with her, and after I did, Gary asked me to apply, too. I demurred, explaining that I had no on-camera experience, but Cheche convinced me to do the camera test. Then she sat me down and coached me. I got the job.

Going on camera is the most unnatural way of being natural. When I deconstructed it, it seemed that it required putting on a facade of arrogance; the cadence newscasting required was so different from what I used as a person. Without it, though, my pieces were perceived to lack energy and authority. The first time I did a stand-up report, my boss called me up from Atlanta and told me that I looked too young and my voice was too high. His solution: wear a suit, put on makeup, and drink brandy to lower my voice. The first few times I think I got drunk before I even finished my on-camera report.

I was horrible in the beginning, convinced that the only reason CNN had hired me was because I had an American accent and I was cheap. I started as its freelance reporter while still doing *Probe*, a win-win for both and certainly a windfall of experience for me.

But it was more than that. What you choose to do shapes the person you become. Nothing shaped my personality—or my ability to withstand threats—more than becoming a breaking-news television journalist, learning to maintain my composure while live and even under literal gunfire. That became my superpower. In breaking-news TV, if you panic, you can't get the video, and when you're live, a second is a lifetime. Later in life, I would often fall back on those skills: pushing my emotions down, staying calm, and summarizing a story in three bullet points. Like muscle memory, that skill set kicks in to help me survive crisis after crisis.

At CNN, I also learned that ideals are harder to live by when you actually have to get things done. Early on, I got a delivery of six months' worth of big, bulky U-matic videotapes for shooting. When I went to pick up the shipment, one of the customs officers asked for a bribe. I refused. But as the weeks dragged into months, the burden of actually getting the tapes began to weigh heavily on my own performance. CNN wanted me to do whatever I needed to do to get the tapes, but it would never give me official permission to pay a bribe—the Foreign Corrupt Practices Act, or FCPA, makes it illegal for a US business to pay bribes to foreign officials. Usually, I later learned, American businesses hire an agent to deal with such issues instead.

I still refused to pay. I'm stubborn that way. I didn't want to turn a blind eye; it came down to principle, didn't it?

So the tapes stayed in customs. It took nearly a year and a half and Cheche stepping in before we finally got those tapes out without paying a bribe. That was the first time that I thought: Why bother having a law if you're not going to stick to it? If a democracy is to survive—if a media organization is to survive—the insidiousness of corruption, does that mean that lines have to be drawn every time, that every cut against the truth must be resisted?

In December 1989, the military attempted its seventh coup against President Aquino. The previous ones had already exposed an unholy alliance between soldiers loyal to Marcos and those who had once helped end his rule. Now, just a few years later, the soldiers who had once been on opposite sides joined forces and recruited thousands more fighters, including elite scout rangers and marines. They accused Aquino of incompetence and corruption—mostly unfounded claims.

I was twenty-six years old. By that time, I had about two years of reporting under my belt. Doing double duty for *Probe* and CNN meant that I was now a good producer but still a horrible television reporter. Yet doing both jobs had doubled my sources, the number of which is the real measure of a reporter's skill. The foundation of getting the facts is trust. Before social media, that depended on your track record and the integrity of your news organization. Cheche and *Probe*, with its deep roots in our society, expanded my area of trust; CNN's global reach helped me amplify the stories that mattered. Early on I had a unique view, both local and global.

When the coup started, I went out to cover it for CNN. I felt the adrenaline of breaking news and conflict reporting. If you're a war zone reporter for any period of time, it becomes addictive, but you don't know that in the beginning. The flurry of activity requires a journalist's real-time clarity: simultaneously listening to the radio, contacting (or back then visiting) sources to know what they are experiencing, and then quickly relaying all of it to CNN Atlanta so it could get the news out. All that while I was running around trying to anticipate events so that I could miraculously be there when they happened and catch them on video. That was the part of the job I loved: I had to be there to capture the video.

The tall, taciturn Rene Santiago, my cameraman, was my teacher in breaking news. He was a man of few words, but he taught by repetition and example. I learned to hang on to his belt as he pushed his way to the front of the crowd. He didn't care if he pissed people off; he got the video.

We soon learned that the rebels had taken over the InterContinental Hotel, among other high-rise buildings in the financial center. Shortly before dawn, we drove carefully toward no-man's-land. A day earlier, gunfire and mortar shells had crisscrossed the area; no one knew where the sniper fire was coming from, so most journalists stayed away. But I wanted to get to the rebel soldiers who were making the decisions. We took a white bedsheet along in the car and attached it to a mic boom pole. As Rene drove in, we turned off the air conditioner and opened our windows.

It was so quiet you could hear the birds chirping. I caught myself holding my breath. We entered the wide, deserted Ayala Avenue, the main six-lane thoroughfare of the financial district. Flanked by high-rise buildings on both sides, it was where, in 1983, the body of Ninoy Aquino was paraded amid the people's fury. It was also where, three years later, confetti-strewn parades heralded the end of the Marcos regime.

"Can I sit on the window ledge, Rene?" I asked. I thought that if I waved the boom with the white sheet tied to it, the sharpshooters would see that I wasn't a soldier.

He started pointing out where he thought the snipers were in surrounding buildings.

I got up to sit on the ledge so I could wave the white flag. We drove in slowly. It took several excruciating minutes.

I was never happier to jump out of a car. I untied the white flag from the mic boom pole, and Rene and I walked quickly into the lobby of the InterContinental Hotel. Colonel Rafael Galvez, the rebel commander, granted us an interview, his first for international viewers. He then assigned a rebel escort for us to drive to the Peninsula Hotel and other surrounding buildings in Makati and talk to rebel soldiers and the few citizens who had ventured into the deserted streets. We got our story.

Rene and I built a lot of trust during that 1989 coup attempt. We built trust as a team, which was the first step in creating good journalism. Our partnership would continue for nearly twenty years.

The coup lasted nine days. It was the bloodiest coup attempt of all: 99 people died, including 50 civilian bystanders, and 570 were wounded. Cory Aquino's presidency survived, but her administration never recovered. She had attempted to forge a democratic leadership after a dictatorship, but she had never managed to quell the habit of military dissent that had been forged during People Power.

By 1992, the Philippines would have a new leader, President Fidel Ramos. Anointed by Cory Aquino, he had led the military under her after he helped oust his cousin Ferdinand Marcos. Under his leadership, the Philippines was poised to flourish, to become what was then the ideal for the region, an "Asian tiger." For all of her disputes with the military, Aquino had set up the Philippines for a shot at stability and prosperity.

Those were years of work and self-discovery. I was burning the candle at both ends, directing and producing *Probe*, as well as serving as a reporter and bureau chief for CNN Manila. I would direct Cheche's shoots, do my own stand-up after her, write and edit her twenty-minute piece, then write, track, and edit my CNN report. Work would begin at 8:00 a.m., and by 9:00 p.m. most nights, I would go out to dinner and hit the clubs until at least 2:00 a.m. Who needed sleep? I stretched the twenty-four hours each day held. Those were the glorious twenties—I didn't want to waste a moment.

I missed theater and music, so, on top of everything else, I began to direct musical concerts. One of the biggest I directed was at Manila's Music Museum with some of the top singers at the time: Janet Basco, Jose Mari Chan, and Ariel Rivera. That was around the time when I began to explore my sexuality. Even that I had to somehow fit into my schedule.

As I approached thirty, marriage became an issue; in the Philippines, you are an old maid if you're not married by then. With CNN, I had the best of both worlds, allowing me home leave so I could go back every year to spend a week in Atlanta headquarters and a month in the United States. During one of those trips, my high school boyfriend and I reconnected and started dating again. He came to Manila and lived with me for a few months. But when he asked me to marry him, I hit a wall.

I knew something didn't feel right, but that marriage proposal, my age, and the expectations society has of women all weighed on me. The easiest thing would have been to say yes; my boyfriend was ready to move to Manila, and we had a good relationship. But I realized that I had compartmentalized sex and love. I wasn't in love. I didn't know what the word meant.

Perhaps that was because until that point, I had spent my energy avoiding the craziness of love. Too much had been written about its power and irrational impact. I had watched friends lose themselves in it, and it seemed too dangerous and volatile. I avoided touching it. So I chose relationships I could control, which goes against the loss of control that love seems to demand. At the very least, I knew I needed to experience love, and I also knew that if I got married, I would no longer be able to explore the unanswered questions I had kept in a locked room.

Twink and I had always helped each other through our careers and our relationships, and she helped me at that crossroad.

"Do you love him?" she asked.

"I don't know."

"That should be an easy answer," she replied. "If it isn't, then you don't. Don't let anyone pressure you into doing anything you don't want to do."

The most important choice you make is the person you will spend your life with. That person's values and choices will sway you as you create yourself, as you make the most important decisions about who you are.

So I said no to marriage, and it was painful. I lost a friend for many years. If he hadn't asked me to marry him, we might have lasted longer, but the proposal was a trigger. At that point, I had dated several men, but I had never fallen in love. That didn't happen until my first girlfriend, when I was thirty years old. Maybe it was because I had refused to be vulnerable until then. Or maybe it was because I am gay.

When I finally began to date a woman, it shook my world. She was a sexy, beautiful singer with a shy dimple who had majored in computer science. Neither of us had ever been with a woman before, but with each other, we jumped in.

First, there were basic questions I had to ask: How do you dress for a date? A suit or a dress and stockings? Or jeans and a shirt? Lipstick or not? What do you do with gender roles? It was like being a teenager again. The Manila community for gay women was like in the 1950s in the United States, largely organized around notions of butch and femme. Since I identified with neither and both, it raised a lot more questions for me. Butch-femme seemed to just adopt the gender and identity stereotypes of heterosexual relationships.

It's confusing when you throw away gender signals ingrained since birth. They are far more basic than cultural standards; they are embedded into your identity, affecting the way you present yourself to the world—the way you dress, the way you speak, the way you act. Did I need to fundamentally change?

I didn't get the answers when I asked the questions, so I learned to be patient. I did get resistance both from people I trusted and from people I didn't know; I felt the censure in their eyes. As an overachiever used to people's praise, that was new.

But I fell in love. We were together for five years, even shifting to a long-distance relationship when we both moved away from the Philippines and had to fly at least seventeen hours to see each other.

In the end, I think neither of us could break entirely from society's standards. We still cared about convention on some level. A phrase she used a lot in the last few months foreshadowed the end: "If only you were a man." I'm not, and I didn't want her to be anything other than who she was. My friends called her a femme fatale and thought she was playing me. My parents prayed that I would just move on.

Society's tendrils are invisible but can be like steel cables holding us in place.

I also learned a lot about beauty during that time: my relationship to it, my fascination with it. I grew up in a family where beauty was important. For my mom and my sisters Mary Jane and Michelle, beauty and femininity were built into their identities, how they viewed and moved through the world. Beautiful people, women and men, have an advantage in the world we live in. They get a lot more for a lot less effort, especially if they are charming. Some of us are born with advantages, which might be part of the reason I work so hard. I didn't want to live in a world where the only currency is physical beauty.

One's attractiveness was inevitably linked to fairer skin (I'm dark), to how well you cook (I can't), to how well you obey (huh?). I rebelled against all that. We are all on a sexual spectrum. I was attracted to passion and intellect, energy and empathy; whether in a man or a woman, I loved connecting with people at a deeper level to share that inspirational spark. At some point, I stopped looking through the binary lenses of straight or gay and just accepted what is.

After my relationship ended, I dated an older man for a short while. My next relationship was with a powerful woman, an investment banker at the time. We had a lot in common, including having grown up in two cultures, and had similar values and ambitions. She was unashamedly gay and helped me come to terms with what that meant.

Love is powerful and irrational. And that's okay. Maybe I approached it like playing an instrument: be strong in the technical exercises so you can let go and actually let the music flow. I hadn't trusted myself to let go until I knew I was strong enough. As with most of the way I build my world, it begins in my mind, and I make a choice.

Two things happened when I chose a woman as my partner: my parents refused to let her come home with me, and I felt Cheche—my mentor, my friend, the person who to a large degree had made me a journalist—pull away.

There are always repercussions to our choices. My ex-boyfriend who had proposed marriage got so angry after I told him that I was attracted to women that he made me wonder whether I should have been that honest. But I was learning that honesty was essential to a good life.

So how can you be honest without tearing everything apart? How honest will you be when you break up? Or when you deal with a cheating partner? Or when you cheat yourself? How honest will you be when you're firing someone? Or admitting that what is happening around you in your country or company threatens our collective future—when you yourself may be complicit in its deterioration? Before you can even get to those, you have to conquer the toughest question: How honest will you be with yourself?

We often let ourselves off the hook, refusing to look at our own difficult or ugly truths. We rationalize our behavior, but the world will not cushion us against those lies. So: embrace your fear. Learning to be honest begins with your own truths: self-assessment, self-awareness, your empathy for others. The only thing you can control in the world is you.

After a year, my parents asked us—both of us—to come home. I talked to Cheche, who denied that we made her uncomfortable and welcomed us.

I knew I didn't want my sexuality to define me; it's only one part of everything I am. Plus, for CNN I was working in several countries where it was illegal to be gay. Or uncomfortable at best.

In September 1998, I was at a press conference in Malaysia. Prime Minister Mahathir Mohamad had thrown his deputy prime minister, Anwar Ibrahim, out of his post, though previously he had treated Anwar like his son and was even grooming him as his successor. The reason? Anwar had allegedly had sex with a man, his family driver. There was a video of Malaysia's intelligence chief taking a stained mattress out of his house, which supposedly showed semen stains from that homosexual act.

In a press conference, Mahathir said that Anwar was "not suitable" to be a leader and looked as if about to cry. There were only a few of us invited; I was there because I had earned the trust of Mahathir: I was from CNN, and I was Asian American (yes, it definitely mattered). I was also—privately—in a relationship with a woman. My heart was pounding when I raised my hand.

"Prime Minister Mahathir, are you saying that you can't be gay in Malaysia?" I asked.

He looked at me and explained that unlike in the West, Malaysians had "traditional values." He was uncomfortable. I was uncomfortable. I followed up by asking about the Malaysian gay and lesbian communities, but he skirted the question, at one point looking directly into the CNN camera behind me to address our global audience. Mahathir, prime minister since 1981, was a skilled, aggressive communicator, often attacking Western "superiority." Anwar would be jailed for up to nine years for sodomy and corruption, on charges that he maintains were part of a conspiracy from the top.

I did not say in that moment that I was gay. I drew a line between the personal and the professional. At the beginning, it wasn't hard because I lived on the other side of the world from CNN's corporate headquarters, but as the years passed, it became an open secret. I didn't hide it, but I didn't trumpet it, either.

It's not in my nature to rail against the world; I accepted it, didn't let it stop me, and kept doing what I needed to do. I was more focused on telling other people's stories, fine-tuning the craft of journalism.

...

Chapter 4

The Mission of Journalism

Be Honest

In a remote area en route to a clandestine interview with Falintil guerrillas in East Timor, early 1999. That's a satellite dish pointing up from the phone box, and I was using the compass to find a line of sight to transmit and let Atlanta know our vehicle had broken down while crossing a river.

After a few years of this hectic life, on one of my home leave trips to Atlanta, my boss at CNN, Eason Jordan, asked me to come to his office. Eason knew and understood Asia; it was under his watch that Asian American women were hired as bureau chiefs, starting with me. He said he wanted to make sure that the faces reporting overseas reflected the countries we were reporting from. I owe a lot of the way I am today, the journalist I've become, to the opportunities he gave me.

But that day, he had something else to say—he gave me an ultimatum: "Maria, I'm told that it's taking you a long time to turn around stories," he said. "I'm going to give you six months, and if it doesn't improve, we'll have to revisit your contract."

I was shocked. When I got back to Manila, I revamped my life, shifting my focus away from *Probe* and to CNN. Due in part to that conversation with Eason, the Manila bureau would become the most prolific of CNN's bureaus our size within a year.

Part of the reason I was patient with Facebook's early mistakes at first was that I was with CNN when we were "Chicken Noodle News," a channel the veterans laughed at. We were still a few years away from becoming the world's leader in trusted and breaking international news. So I know what scaling up quickly does to an organization; everyone has hit-and-miss calls. If you have a good team and a good process, you hit more than you miss. But a shared mission stated by a strong leader is paramount.

Eason credited our success to our leader, Ted Turner.[1] "Ted's position was never 'We need to make as much money as possible,'" Eason said. "He really cared about the world and saw the news as the stand-up thing to do for the planet." Ted decided that no place in the world should be "foreign," so he fined anyone who used that word a dollar.

Plus, in those early days, a strong standard of fact-based, reportage-focused news ruled contemporary life. From 1980, when CNN launched, until 1996, when the more opinion-fueled Fox News and MSNBC launched in the United States, CNN had no competition from other twenty-four-hour news channels, especially ones with totally different reporting standards. CNN was serious; it covered the whole world.

About three weeks after my meeting with Eason, CNN offered me my first story outside the Philippines—in Singapore. The trip proved to be an eye-opening experience. I loved the questions that begged for answers, the people I was meeting, the cultures and systems I was learning. Once our bureau began traveling, my beat grew to include Malaysia, Brunei, and Indonesia as well. I never refused an assignment. I would get 2:00 a.m. phone calls directing me to go to New Delhi, and we would not only have the visas in our passports, we would be ready to get on a flight at the crack of dawn. When a story broke in Asia, it was standard operating procedure to apply for visas for my team to Pakistan, China, South Korea, Japan, and many more.

At some point in 1994, Eason told me to research what it would take to open a Jakarta bureau. By the numbers, the world's most populous nations in 1994 were China, India, the United States, and Indonesia. "Why in the world do we not have a bureau in the most populous Muslim nation in the world?" he asked.

Two things had become important to me by then: bridging worlds and highlighting cultures outside the West. I saw myself as a conduit and as someone reporting for the West from countries in the Global South. I wanted the stories to be recognizable to both cultures: the subjects of my pieces and my audience (the gap is often huge). It wasn't my job to judge people, events, or customs; that would be arrogant. Only by learning the context and observing a society's or people's actions over time can you assess what is happening.

International media had been dominated by a decidedly Western perspective. After all, the Western countries were the ones with the resources and with the networks that made global news gathering a high priority, at least back then. That meant that companies like CNN and the BBC got to determine what was newsworthy, filtered through their cultural lenses.

Up to that point, Asian and many non-Western countries did not have similar financial resources, nor had we had the chance to hone the skills to highlight our ideas. We hadn't had reason to seek a global stage. But now we must. To do that, I believed, we would need to dial up the sophistication of our message and expand our worldview.

By the time we opened CNN's Jakarta bureau, Indonesia had five television stations, most tied to its longtime dictator, Suharto. Its relatively underdeveloped—meaning low-skilled—commercial television industry was part of the argument I used when I advocated for moving the Manila team to Indonesia, which we did in 1995.

We celebrated our launch at the Shangri-la Jakarta, and in attendance was one of CNN's biggest stars, Peter Arnett, who had become one of television's most recognizable faces during the 1991 Gulf War. In 1966, he had been awarded the Pulitzer Prize in International Reporting for his work with the Associated Press during the Vietnam War from 1962 to 1965. Before he had been assigned to Vietnam, he had reported from—and been thrown out of—Jakarta.

I took Peter to lunch at my favorite Indonesian restaurant and peppered him with questions. At sixty-one years old, he was nearly double my age. I described the role I saw journalism playing in the Philippines and the countries I reported from.

"You need to know and understand journalism's role in our democracy," he said, "that the work is so important that you will risk it all to get the story."

During the Gulf War, CNN was the only network that had a four-wire—two direct pairs of telephone lines (one pair in each direction)—that ran across the Iraqi desert floor and connected to a microwave transmission dish in Amman, Jordan. The dish relayed the phone signals by satellite directly to CNN headquarters in Atlanta and simultaneously allowed producers to speak with those in Baghdad who were live on air. The world was glued to CNN and especially to Peter.

That also meant he bore the brunt of the US government and military's attacks. Those began when Peter reported about civilian casualties in what the Iraqis told him was a baby milk factory. At the time,

CNN also explicitly stated that Peter had done his reporting during "guided tours" with the Iraqi government and that his reporting had been "cleared by Iraqi censors," to make sure that audiences understood the newscasts' limitations.

That didn't stop the then chairman of the Joint Chiefs of Staff, General Colin Powell, from declaring that the "baby milk plant" was a front for a secret laboratory producing biological agents such as toxins, bacteria, and viruses to use as weapons of mass destruction. White House press secretary Marlin Fitzwater began calling Peter "a conduit for Iraqi disinformation."

Those in power have always attempted to control the narrative, especially during wartime. That was true even before social media. Peter would make mistakes later on (including "throwing his team under the bus," according to an insider), but the lesson he gave me that day was always to hold power to account, even if it nearly wrecks your career. Hold the line; that is the journalist's duty.

At the same time, something was changing the way journalists gathered and reported the news: technology. When I set up the bureau in Manila in 1988, it took two weeks to ship a tape to Atlanta. By the time we opened a Hong Kong bureau in 1989, there was overnight delivery. Then I received a big, bulky cell phone that was as heavy as a suitcase. I had to sling it over my shoulder, and it often hit the ground when I ran.

When we moved to Jakarta in the mid-90s, we became one of CNN's testing centers for new technology: first-generation satellite phones that allowed us to connect to Atlanta for on-air voice reports. We also received a huge white Toko box, which compressed video and transmitted it over an ISDN (terrestrial data) telephone line to another Toko box in the studio. On a story, I would spend hours transmitting low-quality video, then waiting longer to finish the transmission of the audio.

Those were the early years of "live via videophone." It was fun, relatively easy, and cheap. Now we could set up a live shot anywhere, even in the remotest parts of the world. It created what was then widely referred to as "the CNN effect"[2]—although it included all global twenty-four-hour television news outlets and was directly attributable to the rapid growth and effect of satellite news gathering.

All those technological advances had a profound impact, especially on the often contentious debate about how much mass media shapes political policy. The new technology allowed us to deliver information to the public faster than any government's ability to get information on its own. It meant that government officials had less time to think before declaring their positions and less time to deliberate before acting on them. And governments would soon learn to shape public opinion by using those technological developments.

It also meant that a reporter like me had less time to learn, and it minimized our time to explore and discover stories. Whatever was thrilling, faster, easier also seemed to diminish the depth of our coverage; somehow technology both saved us time and stole it from us.

The demands of a twenty-four-hour news network required me to do all the prework before even getting on the ground. My competition might still have attempted to read everything written about a country before reporting on it, however, so I ended up with an advantage: I had been covering the same nations for decades. Often when I landed, within an hour of leaving the airport, I was live.

It was an incredible, magical time for news for our Jakarta team, right at the time when dramatic change came to Indonesia. Since 1965, the country had been ruled by Suharto, who would become the longest-serving president of the country. Transparency International called him the most corrupt leader in modern history, just ahead of Ferdinand Marcos. Working at CNN helped me not just to study leadership, both of countries and of media companies, but to understand the ebbs and flows of the people leaders lead. Finding the balance between stability and change—created by the expectations seeded by leaders—sometimes took generations to bear fruit.

After we opened the bureau in 1995, each year brought something new: 1996, the Jakarta Megawati riots, triggered by a woman's political challenge to Suharto; 1997, the Asian financial crisis and the forest fires in Indonesia, leading to the recurring Southeast Asian haze, a massive environmental and political story. And then in 1998, after nearly thirty-two years in power, Suharto fell, which triggered massive social change and unleashed a kind of violence I had never seen.

Interviewing leaders showed me how their weaknesses were embedded in the cultures of the people they led. At CNN, we chronicled several societies in transition as they emerged from strongman rule to clamor for and develop their own democracies—from Marcos's Philippines to Lee Kuan Yew's Singapore to Suharto's Indonesia and Mahathir's Malaysia.

Marcos and Suharto left behind similar problems that lay just beneath the surface. In the Philippines, it was cronyism and patronage politics. In Indonesia, it was called KKN (pronounced "ka-ka-en"): corruption, collusion, and nepotism. That top-down oppressive, controlling political system took its toll on the people. Their leaders' biggest sin was that they failed to educate their people.

I became frustrated by the lack of initiative and creativity among both countries' workforces, but why should the people have those values? Under Marcos and Suharto, if you stood out, you took a risk. Better to sit back and conform. It didn't help that the countries' cultural values reinforced that view.

When I taught at the University of the Philippines in the years I was with *Probe*, I wanted to understand what—and how—students were learning. What were their values? What I saw being rewarded was respect for authority: knowing your place, rote learning, the ability to memorize and mimic answers back; neatness and punctuality; and above all, submission to their teachers and their views. They rarely articulated what they really thought.

In Indonesia, the lack of creativity and independent thought was even more pronounced. To set up the CNN bureau, I spent seven trips looking for Indonesians I could hire. No one I interviewed had the skills, experience, and work ethic that I needed.

In the streets, the lack of education would take a violent turn in a country where the word *amok* had originated. Still, I struggled to understand the disconnect between the violence I was reporting on and the kind and respectful people I was meeting on the streets. That was when I began to realize that understanding the way a large group behaves is very different from dealing with and understanding individuals.

What I was learning in Indonesia was emergent behavior: that the way a system behaves can't be predicted from what you know about the individual parts. In fact, the system as a whole exerts pressure on the individuals, a kind of peer pressure exerted by group dynamics, which often makes people do things they wouldn't do if they were alone.

When it leads to a group becoming a mob—whether online or in the real world—emergent behavior is unpredictable and dangerous. Up until then in the countries I had reported from, including South Korea and China, I had never seen such fickle violence. I began to categorize what I was living through; there was not only political violence but also economic violence, religious violence, separatist violence, and ethnic violence.

Every week in the late 1990s, I traveled to another of Indonesia's twenty-seven provinces and reported on the phenomenon of mob violence. It started in 1996 in the largest riots in Jakarta in more than two decades. The riots began innocently enough; one of my sources warned me in a phone call before dawn that action would be taken against the supporters of opposition leader Megawati Sukarnoputri, the daughter of Indonesia's first president, Sukarno. She led the smallest of three rec-ognized political parties, the Indonesian Democratic Party, or PDI. The government had just engineered a takeover of the party by a former mil-itary general named Suryadi. Megawati and her supporters refused to accept his leadership and challenged it legally.

That was the first time I saw how Suharto consolidated and main-tained control. It was also a tactic I would see play out over and over in other countries—when military and paramilitary forces infiltrate and taint a movement for democracy and foment violence.

I called Rene and woke up my sisters Michelle and Nicole, who were visiting me for the first time in Jakarta. I had promised to take them sightseeing that weekend, so I told them to join our coverage. They could help with equipment and learn how a news-gathering team worked.

We were among the first to get to the PDI headquarters, where Mega-wati's supporters were camping out. I saw trucks pulling up and a group of bulky men changing into red PDI T-shirts on a side street. When I asked them who they were, they said they were Suryadi supporters, allegedly members of the PDI. Yet they wore military-issue boots. I re-ported that on air but didn't go further.

We saw Suryadi's supporters throwing stones at the PDI sign. Mean-while, truckloads of police set up barricades to prevent more Megawati supporters from entering the conflict area. Around 8:00 a.m., the po-lice stormed the building and led Suryadi's supporters inside, arresting Megawati's supporters. By 11:00 a.m., Megawati's supporters breached the military blockades, and sporadic battles began with the security forces. The burning of buildings began a little after 3:00 p.m. on Jalan Kramat Raya, a main road in the city.

By sunset, about ten thousand people were rampaging the streets and torching nearby buildings. As we ran in front of the mob, my sisters and I became separated from Rene and Ikbal, our sound-tech driver. I pulled my sisters into a backyard to hide and made them promise not to tell our parents they were with me. I don't think it had dawned on them how dangerous it had become. They were stunned by events but excited by what their big sister did for a living.

Analysts at the time would attribute the violence to political oppression, the people's suppressed anger. That Saturday, 5 people died, 149 were injured, and 136 people were arrested. It was my first lesson in why Suharto was called the "puppet master," a *dalang*, who, in an Indonesian *wayang* performance, manipulates from the shadows the puppets projected onto a screen. The projected shadows are all the public sees. When there was a challenge to power, the leader tried to shape the narrative by controlling the press.

Live shot for CNN on the rooftop of the Sari Pan Pacific Hotel in Jakarta in May 1998. Around-the-clock coverage with at most three to four hours' sleep a night.

By the time Suharto stepped down in May 1998, 1,400 people had been killed in riots in Jakarta. After he resigned, the violence only escalated, seemingly beyond the military's control. The target, as in the 1960s, was the ethnic Chinese, because the Asian financial crisis had sparked a scramble for survival, and institutionalized racism spread. In Jakarta and other parts of the country, mob violence became the norm. Neighborhood rivalries turned into urban warfare: men with machetes slicing each other in Jakarta's streets. The scenes I witnessed of senseless killings and beheadings made me realize how Suharto's oppression had acted like a pressure cooker, how covering up violence only led to more violence.

In West Kalimantan, ethnic violence between the Madurese and Dayak tribesmen killed hundreds of people. The Dayaks had once been known as the headhunters of Borneo. They believed that if you chopped off the head of your enemy and ate his liver, you received his strength. That old, traditional, animistic belief still flourished—never addressed because under Suharto, discussing issues of race, religion, or ethnicity was banned. It was too "emotional," too contentious, and in a society where order was largely imposed by the military, it was "unnecessary" to discuss and debate contentious issues because it only made things worse.

In one weekend, I saw eight people beheaded by rowdy, partying groups of men wearing colored headbands designating their ethnic group. At some point, I walked out onto a field where there was a group of boys playing soccer. They seemed to be having a lot of fun. Then I realized that the ball they were kicking around was the head of an old man.

In Muslim-Christian Ambon, religious violence killed more than four thousand people in a little over a year. By 2002, the number killed hit more than ten thousand. I remember at one point asking the people exhausted from the fighting, living in enclaves divided by Muslim or Christian checkpoints, how the violence had started, hoping that going to the root cause would help stop the communal violence. The answer I always got was that it was "the people from outside; it wasn't us."

That was always the answer when violence broke out. The force of the mob destroyed individual control, giving people the freedom to be their worst selves. What I was seeing in Indonesia was something I had seen in the Philippines and someday would see in countries around the world as the power of disinformation began to devastate the minds, and transform the behavior, of often less educated people or those less familiar with the internet. Education determines the quality of governance. An investment in education takes a generation to bear fruit. Likewise, countries feel the impact of this disregard for education a generation later. That determines their productivity, the quality of their workforce, their investments, and ultimately their gross domestic product (GDP). A nation's budget line item for education is an investment in its people.

The ability to discern and question, which is crucial to both journalism and democracy, is also determined by education. Journalists and news organizations are a reflection of the people's power to hold its leaders accountable. That means that ultimately the quality of a democracy can also be seen in the quality of its journalists.

My experience in journalism was the norm among the journalists of my generation because I had come up during our profession's golden age, when news organizations gave their staff enough resources and protection to do our jobs.

I loved reporting. Being a reporter gave my twenties and thirties a tremendous adrenaline rush for meaning; it was a deadline-driven school about the world. I was privileged to experience and tape some of the most sensitive moments of many people's lives: tragedy and joy unmasked. Living through those moments together created true connections if I treated it as the privilege it was. I walked into every situation ready to listen and learn; to be open; to be vulnerable—because good journalism starts with trust. Your subjects must trust you, and your stories over time must build trust with your audience.

I felt tested at every level: physically, intellectually, socially, and spiritually. Intellectually, I developed expertise by following stories over time and jumping from politics to economics, governance, security, climate, sustainable development, and so many more.

Socially, I formed a network of sources until I could gather inside information on how and why decisions were made. A reporter is only as good as his or her sources; that's the difference between press conferences and independent investigation. Honesty, delineating lines clearly and asking for permission for what you want to reveal publicly are essential to cultivating sources. I never broadcast a sensitive story until I let all sources know so they could protect themselves from vengeful or autocratic leaders. As you build your sources and the sophistication of your reporting, you build public trust. Over time, you and your sources learn each other's values, and you may even fight the battles of integrity and justice together.

Circumstances and deadlines stretched me physically, too. War zone and disaster coverage required meticulous planning and resilience. It meant eating instant noodles and canned goods for weeks at a time (if I could pack a spare vehicle with food) and weeks of short naps, with maybe at most two or three hours of sleep during breaking-news cycles. It meant enduring extremes of heat, cold, hunger, thirst. And it meant facing fear, including staying still in a darkened home, hiding under a bed, while an armed militia hunted my team.

In 1991, I drove endless hours after a flash flood in Ormoc, Leyte, Philippines, swept parts of the city out to sea in the middle of the night. It would be a story about the denudation of the forests, climate change, local government's ability to handle disasters, and the consequences of wrecking our environment. Anywhere from four thousand to ten thousand people died. (The gap in the death toll estimates was in the vested interest of those who wanted to keep the casualty count low.) As we entered the city, the stench of death was overpowering. We crossed the bridge into town and stopped the car to shoot video of the damaged skyline. I was half asleep when I stepped out of the car onto something squishy. I looked down and nearly gagged when I saw that it was a human hand.

When you bear witness to senseless deaths, violence, and cruelty, you're forced to confront the existence of God. I watched more than six hundred corpses being buried in a mass grave in Ormoc, heard the wailing of their families, was surrounded by the stink of rotting flesh.

That was when I chose to believe in God. Part of me was raging that a flash flood tidal wave could kill so many in their sleep—would a God have allowed that? Another part of me thought of the God of Noah's ark, teaching a deadly lesson to mankind. We couldn't be only tissue, so easily discarded. Despite myself, I prayed for their souls. I needed there to be something more. Moments like that taught me that faith—regardless of whether God is Buddha, Allah, Yahweh, Jehovah, or El Shaddai—is about more than just religion.

Being a journalist taught me to have faith in myself and our shared humanity.

By 2000, I was a recognizable CNN face in Southeast Asia. I came home to the Philippines that July to give a speech at the Rotary Club of Manila about education, journalism, and democracy. The speech was one of the first times I articulated my vision for our journalistic future.

I didn't tell war stories but instead spoke about something more conceptual: the myth of the "objective journalist." I distinguished that idea from the principles of journalism, which, through an organizational system of checks and balances, have built a goal of objectivity into the process of reporting. But there is no such thing as an objective journalist; anyone who says otherwise is lying.

It was important to define what people meant by "objectivity" because it is the word used to attack journalists for somehow being dishonest or biased. That's why I react to it as strongly as I do. I always replace "objective" with "good" to describe a journalist.

A good journalist doesn't look for balance—as when, say, a world leader commits a war crime or outright lies to his or her citizenry—because that would create a false equivalence. When a journalist confronts the powerful, it is easier and safer to write it in a "balanced" way. But that's a coward's way out. A good journalist, for example, would not give equal time and space to known climate deniers and climate change scientists.

Good journalists lean on the side of evidence, on incontrovertible facts.

Good journalism is a professional discipline and judgment exercised by the entire newsroom operating under a strong standards and ethics manual. It means having the courage to report the evidence even if it gets you in trouble with the powers that be. The words *impartiality* and *balance* are dangerous when used outside this context, often hijacked by those with vested interests.

Now I look back longingly at that era. Even in the early 2000s, the news media were still the gatekeepers, when their audiences counted on the skills of the reporters and the track record of the news organization, when professionals on an entire editorial team made judgment calls according to the same manual. The mission was to protect the public sphere; our values and principles had been hammered out in countless meetings and set down on paper. According to one of those principles, journalists listened to different sides of an issue and consolidated what they learned to help the public make their own informed decisions. The pact felt sacred.

There was also a balance between market forces and accountability. Journalists and news organizations were legally accountable for everything we published and broadcast—both the creation of the news and, crucially, how it was distributed: how many times an audience saw a news story, what headline appeared on top of it, how sensationalistic the font or imagery looked, how fair and free of bias the language we used. A wall existed between business managers and journalists to prevent those in the organization with vested financial interests from influencing the news.

What you saw was what we all saw. Everyone read the same articles, watched the same news reports. We agreed on the facts. Though the visual medium was more emotional than print, there were limits to what you could ethically do, unlike the design and algorithms of social media today.

The goal was not to win an argument or win a popularity contest; it was to create the more informed citizenry necessary for a democracy to work. Journalists were part of a shared culture of democracy: to listen, debate, and compromise. Aside from legal accountability, there was a sense of moral responsibility—to help create a better future.

The understanding of how power works also felt more concrete. We knew that all governments would attempt to co-opt truth tellers and control narratives. In most democracies, journalists were the Fourth Estate, deriving power from the people's will, their desire for knowledge to form opinions about their lives, their country, their leaders. In exchange for this access to the people's hearts and minds, the state gave access to journalists. At its best, the relationship is a checks-and-balances system. At its worst, the access becomes contingent on whether a journalist told the stories the state wanted.

In most news groups, there was an internal battle between those in charge of the business, which needed to be on the right side of power, and the independent editorial hierarchy, which needed to be responsible to the people. That was another check and balance.

Now remove all that and replace news organizations with technology companies, which have largely abdicated the gatekeeping role of protecting facts, truth, and trust. These companies welcome an alliance with power, which guarantees market access and growth because their incentive system is built around power and money. In the past, the information we all got was protected from vested interests. In the cases of some corporate media firms, that information was only slightly affected by vested interests. Now, under the technology companies, the information you get is directly determined by the corporations' drive for profit.

This is the transition we are living through.

On January 20, 2001, Gloria Macapagal Arroyo, a US-educated economist, was sworn in as the Philippines' fourteenth president.

Every president had been a reaction to the one before: dictator Ferdinand Marcos replaced by Cory Aquino, the simple housewife and widow of a hero. She was followed by Fidel Ramos, the former general who ousted Marcos and then helped Aquino weather coup attempts as her military chief and then defense minister. Ramos was followed by Joseph Estrada, a movie star.

When Estrada faced allegations of corruption, the Filipino people took to the streets to oust him, in what some called a second People Power. But Estrada wasn't a dictator like Marcos; he had been democratically elected and had survived an impeachment process. Did the protests violate the rule of law? Where was the line between the wisdom of the crowd and mob rule?

The military, by now a politicized kingmaking force, abandoned Estrada and backed his vice president, Gloria Arroyo, as president. The protests catapulted Arroyo into what would be a troubled presidency, but those events began to change the legacy of People Power. In one live shot, I described it as "a bastardization of People Power." Arroyo served the rest of Estrada's term and then won her own, giving her nearly a decade in office, but she would leave a country shaken by persistent charges of corruption against her. The people knew that the old problems hadn't been fixed at all.

Eight months later, 9/11 shocked the world. That day exposed the vulnerabilities of a global security paradigm anchored in Cold War principles, which were no longer relevant in a time of global terrorist groups' asymmetrical warfare. The powers of the nation-state were being replaced by a different kind of powerful movement, fueled by passion and a sense of mission. Discovering al-Qaeda's links became my obsession. And it alerted me to a new phenomenon: how a virulent ideology can radicalize networks and shape something I by then knew well: emergent behavior.

September 11, 2001, ripped off a veneer, the collective lie we had built about post–Cold War peace.[3]

What many did not realize at the time—and what I was intent on reporting more fully—was how Southeast Asia had served as an early breeding ground for al-Qaeda.[4] By September 11, it had been operating for a long time in the region. Mohammed Jamal Khalifa, Osama bin Laden's brother-in-law, had come to the Philippines as early as 1988 to set up Islamic charities that spread Wahhabism and radical ideas. From 1991 to 1994, the number of terrorist acts in the Philippines increased by nearly 150 percent.[5]

On 9/11, I rushed home from my gym in Jakarta to dig out my files and intelligence documents (the only way a reporter kept track of events and relationships then) and pulled out the Philippine intelligence service's 1995 interrogation report on Abdul Hakim Murad, a licensed commercial pilot who trained in flight schools in the United States. He may have been the first pilot recruited by al-Qaeda. He was arrested in 1995 in Manila, turned over to the United States, and at the time of the 9/11 attacks was sitting in the supermax prison in Florence, Colorado.[6]

Once I reread Murad's interrogation report, I asked Atlanta to send me to the Philippines so I could interview the Manila police chief from 1995 about the al-Qaeda plot. The names I first reported from the Philippines are now familiar.[7] Ramzi Yousef and Khalid Sheikh Mohammed had both been in the Philippines in 1995, plotting to assassinate Pope John Paul II and US president Bill Clinton.[8] The plot we all reported was called Oplan Bojinka, a scheme to bomb US airplanes flying from

Asia. What we ignored then—because it seemed too fantastic—was another plot to hijack commercial planes and crash them into buildings: the World Trade Center in New York City, the Pentagon, the Sears Building in Chicago, and the TransAmerica Pyramid in San Francisco.[9] The more I reported, the more I could see how every major al-Qaeda plot from 1993 to 2003 had some link to the Philippines, the United States' former colony,[10] from the attack on the World Trade Center in 1993 to the 1998 bombings of US embassies in East Africa to the JW Marriott Hotel attack in Jakarta in 2003.

That means that the two biggest stories of my career had to do with the Philippines as the testing ground of two menaces threatening the United States and the world in the twenty-first century: Islamic terrorism and information warfare on social media.

After 9/11, I became obsessed with tracking down that global terrorist network, to identify which members were linked to each other and perhaps discover similar plots.[11] I looked up longtime contacts—investigators who had risen up the ranks in the Philippines, Indonesia, Singapore, and Malaysia and were all scampering to harness their resources and gather intelligence. They were more than willing to share past intelligence reports on al-Qaeda figures in exchange for analysis of what they could mean. At that point, I had more information than they did because there was no centralized database or formal intelligence sharing program in Southeast Asia. I began to keep my own database of the classified intelligence reports they shared with me.[12] Often, to bypass unwieldy bureaucracies, investigators picked up the phone and called me to find out whether a newly discovered name was familiar or to brainstorm about what some new information could mean. That was how I broke exclusive story after exclusive story for CNN in the decade after 9/11.

Studying terrorists and the spread of the virulent ideology that espoused violence led me to examine how people change when they join groups—a concept I had already witnessed in Indonesia. To study radicalization, I started with groupthink and the experiments of the psychologist Solomon Asch in the 1950s, in which, when confronted with simple questions in twelve critical trials, 75 percent caved in to the pressure of the group rather than sticking to their own conclusions.[13] His experiments showed the power of peer pressure and how being part of any group changes each of us. To understand terrorists' reaction to authority, I turned to the famous experiments of Stanley Milgram (remember "six degrees of separation"?) and Philip Zimbardo's prison experiment. Milgram found that most people follow instructions, even when told to administer potentially lethal shocks to other people.[14] Zimbardo's study has been challenged, but he stands by his findings: that people lose their individuality and take on the characteristics of the roles they're given.[15] In other words, authority can give us the freedom to be our worst selves. Those experiments would come to my mind again later in the context of social media: how easy it is to rile up a mob against a target.

Later, I would learn how extremism and radicalization could spread through social networks like a virus. Social network theory offered the Three Degrees of Influence Rule, a theory first posited by Nicholas Christakis and James Fowler in 2007.[16] Their work showed that everything we say or do ripples through our social network, creating an impact on our friends (one degree), our friends' friends (two degrees), and even our friends' friends' friends (three degrees).[17] For example, if you're feeling lonely (which you might assume spreads the least), there's a 54 percent chance that your friend will feel lonely, a 25 percent chance that your friend's friend will feel lonely, and a 15 percent chance that your friend's friend's friend will feel lonely.[18] Emotions such as happiness and hope, as well as smoking, sexual diseases, and even obesity, can be traced and spread through social networks.[19]

I first learned[20] the mapping of social networks using techniques we fine-tuned working at the CORE Lab at the Naval Postgraduate School in Monterey, California.[21] In tracking terrorists, we saw that al-Qaeda and Jemaah Islamiyah (JI) in Southeast Asia and Australia operated the same way as disinformation networks someday would: they hijacked disparate groups, trained and funded them, and infected them with the jihadi ideology that targeted both the "near enemy," their own governments, and the "far enemy," the United States.

Both JI and al-Qaeda saw their centralized command structures collapse in the years after 9/11. But the old networks continued to spread the jihadi virus. The cells carried out attacks without central leadership. The training camps were smaller and operated in a more ad hoc manner. The threat became more dispersed and harder to track down.

I have since repeated that sentence in many different ways when talking and writing about the impact of counterterrorism operations on terrorist networks.[22]

Transpose that to online political radicalization twenty years later: Facebook's cybersecurity and intelligence experts, including former employees of the US National Security Council, would come to the same conclusion about how online disinformation networks that spread through Facebook regenerated after years of takedowns: "The threat became more dispersed and harder to track down."[23]

By 2003, I had been a journalist for seventeen years, and my learning curve had hit a plateau. I could now do breaking news with my eyes closed, and I was starting to see the same themes emerging in every story I was doing. My Jakarta team's workflows were the best they could be; we outproduced every other bureau our size. But I had stopped learning. I wanted something more.

I was turning forty, but I was still living like a student with no concept of work-life balance. My work was my life, and my life was my work. I was aware of the sacrifices: inevitably a really big story might mean the end of a romantic relationship; I missed my brother's wedding because I couldn't leave breaking news in a conflict zone; and, after months of consideration, I decided to choose journalism over having a child. I tried to stay conscious of those decisions because I wanted to live a life of no regret, and despite what I'm living through now, I'm happy I chose the life I did.

Around that time, the owner and chairman of ABS-CBN, who had once been imprisoned by Marcos, Eugenio Lopez III—known as "Gabby"—again offered me the job of heading the largest news company in the Philippines. I knew that someday I wanted to retire in the Philippines. Somehow, viscerally, this country, imperfect and flawed as it was, had become home. So it was only one step to the next conclusion: If I was going to retire in Manila, why don't I contribute to making it a better place to live in? I was old enough to have real experience but still young enough to want to work hard for an ideal and to have the energy to do it. Besides, I had spent my career writing about what everyone else was doing, what kinds of institutions governments and companies were building. I wanted the experience of putting the lessons I had learned from them into practice.

The kicker was Gabby's challenge to me: "Can you turn ABS-CBN into a world-class news organization?" I also saw a survey done after the May 2004 elections suggesting that nearly 90 percent of Filipinos got their information from television, not newspapers, like before. TV was now the Philippines' most powerful medium, which meant that it would be an incredible tool for nation building.

I couldn't say no.

I packed up my Jakarta apartment, went to Atlanta to say good-bye to the people who had mentored me, and returned to Manila in early December 2004—my second and final homecoming. I was slated to go on board with ABS-CBN on January 1, 2005.

Manila by then had become a sprawling, wealthier city. I settled in Taguig, in Bonifacio Global City, a new neighborhood being built on an old military base—shiny new apartment buildings and clean, relatively quiet streets—and set up my new life. ABS-CBN was housed in the same media compound in Quezon City, a half hour away, though in Manila, traffic always made a difference.

I felt uncertain: so much of who I had become was tied to my CNN identity. If I left CNN, who would I be? Would I be anyone without CNN? And now I was going to become part of a media system whose faults I knew all too well. Could I survive the internal politics of ABS-CBN, an organization still struggling with corruption, self-censorship, a culture of patronage, and all the flaws of corporate, political, and social life in the postdictatorship years, and help build a stronger institution? I asked to start as a training consultant for the first six months to give me and the people I managed the chance to get to know each other outside any power structure.

By now I knew that crucial to whatever I would do next was a challenge I kept growing into: Learning how to tell even the harshest truths. To avoid white lies and rationalizations. To be transparent and honest.

Breaking news had defined me; it had created in me a bias for action. But I had other goals. Part of the reason I chose to leave CNN in 2005 was that as a reporter, I had little role in shaping policy or organizational goals. Especially in a nation still transforming from a dictatorship to a democracy, the actions of every organization, group, and individual mattered. I was ready to experiment with the ideas I believed in.

I wanted to build my vision for journalism, a news organization in the Philippines so strong and committed to the truth that no government could dream of touching it.

PART II

The Rise of Facebook, Rappler, and the Internet's Black Hole

2005–2017

Chapter 5

The Network Effect

Hitting the Tipping Point

At ABS-CBN, May 2010

When I took over ABS-CBN News, I was given the freedom and resources to create something new, a vision of how a country's largest network could help in nation-building. I believe now that the steps we took to change ABS-CBN's values, culture, and content in the early twenty-first century offer clues for how the media can help rebuild democracy around the world. The news shapes the public as much as the public shapes the news. That's something that news organizations like ABS-CBN, ones that had formerly experienced state control, knew well.

In 2005, ABS-CBN was the largest news group in the Philippines, with about a thousand people working for the news division alone. Our main base was in the capital, Manila, but we ran nineteen provincial stations and six overseas hubs: two in North America, one in the Middle East, and one each in Europe, Australia, and Japan. We distributed content on radio, TV, and the internet. I also managed the Philippines' only twenty-four-hour local English cable news network, ANC, the ABS-CBN News Channel, which was also distributed globally.

My first challenge at ABS-CBN was changing the work culture. The media was a microcosm of what our nation's leaders had to deal with: when situational ethics and patronage politics determine whether you, your family, and friends are rewarded or not. I was used to a certain standard of performance at CNN, where loyalty didn't trump merit and the group had to deliver or face the consequences.

The most immediate task at ABS-CBN was upgrading the skills of our journalists. I believed that their mastering the craft would lead to higher ratings. So I began training programs with employees in January 2005 with the help of my second CNN team in Manila,[1] whom I recruited to join me in this experiment of culture change.

Early on, we institutionalized three words, which I felt were necessary not just to ABS-CBN but to our country. I promised our team transparency, accountability, and consistency because I wanted to create systems that would function regardless of personalities. Like the government, we needed to institutionalize systems that would work regardless of—and in spite of—personal connections. That is why those three words were so important to me then and remain so today. They are key to building a functional democracy and resisting the cultlike power of a dictator.

As in all things, our greatest strengths are our greatest weaknesses. Filipinos are known to be kind, caring, and loyal. Personal loyalty is a key value we enshrined in the phrase *utang na loob*, literally meaning "the debt from within." But that quality also has sustained our feudalistic society. Whether in government, at work, or at home, there still exists a system of patronage dating back to our feudal past. Creating an environment of excellence and professionalism required confronting that tendency head-on. If we could succeed in doing that in our company, then perhaps we could spread it to the circle beyond it.

That was when I began to use the phrase "Be cruel to be kind." Managers weren't assessing the work of their subordinates honestly because they wanted to be nice, to avoid conflict. We needed to be cruel to be kind for three reasons: because we wanted to be the best; because we wanted to be world class; and because as a media organization responsible for reporting the truth about a country's state of affairs, we had an outsized role to play in our society.

That involved some harsh measures. Six months in, we downsized what had become a bloated news organization, firing a third of the news group, softening the blow by offering three months' severance pay for every year of service. It was a painful process, and I was personally present for many of the firings. In every move I made as a leader, empathy was essential. It was hard to see the surprise, the anger, the anxiety on our employees' faces, and then the understanding and acceptance as I explained why we were letting them go. That process strengthened my conviction that the hardest decisions are the ones that you must communicate yourself. If you don't have the courage to deliver the news to the people affected by your decision, think twice.

Bit by bit, we began to change a culture that emphasized loyalty above performance, demanded blind obedience, suffocated initiative, and emphasized group loyalty instead of the greater good. All of these are the common features of a political party grabbing power or of a resiliently authoritarian country. All of these go against the core values of any news organization, which relies on collective intelligence, personal initiative, and coordinated immediate action.

A question I asked every one of our people to ask themselves was: *Why* do I do what I do? The answer led us to core values; we urged our people to define their personal values and, if possible, mesh them into our organization's values. We eventually narrowed our philosophy down to one phrase that we lived by: "Excellent journalism to make the world a better place." Then we wrote a 116-page Standards & Ethics Manual, which included a strong anti-corruption theme. We lived by it, and we suspended and terminated people based on it.

By mid-2007, ABS-CBN was competing with the best news organizations in the world. Some of the moves came at great cost, not just to the company but to me personally. Some of the attacks, in fact, were very personal, and often they were legal.

In my nearly two decades with CNN, doing hundreds of investigative stories, no one had ever slapped me with a lawsuit. In my first year leading ABS-CBN News, I was served with one lawsuit from within the company every month. One of the people we fired for corrupt practices filed a case to have me deported—not realizing that I was a Filipino citizen. And every few weeks, I would face some sort of ugly, retaliatory smear campaign from those within the company who didn't like the way I was changing things.

If you try to change a culture, it will fight back. You have to have the stomach for it. Not only that, these were signs of the angry, resentful mood that would multiply and spread along with the internet in my country and beyond. It was a culture I was determined to take on, and, in my area of influence, to change.

During that period, the government was increasingly under siege. Not long after I arrived at ABS-CBN, we received information that Gloria Arroyo might have rigged the 2004 presidential election. The allegation was substantiated by the release of cell phone conversations that sounded as if Arroyo had asked for a million more votes from an election commissioner.[2] Those revelations would spark three failed impeachment processes and massive protests.[3]

Arroyo went on the offensive. She signed Proclamation 1017[4] on February 24, 2006, the twentieth anniversary of the 1986 People Power revolt, declaring a "state of national emergency."[5] She claimed that opposition politicians, elements of the extreme Right and the extreme Left, and "certain segments of the national media" were working together to mount a coup against her government. About the coup, she was actually correct, and ABS-CBN knew about it, too.

Arroyo's declaration severely curtailed press freedom. The government raided a newspaper office, carried out warrantless arrests, threatened to close down news organizations, and stationed an armored personnel carrier outside ABS-CBN. During that period, they tried to control journalists through intimidation tactics and libel suits. Some people believed that members of the security forces were involved in the extrajudicial killings of journalists and leftist leaders. The government feared the media's power, not least because the country had peacefully ousted two presidents by using the media to call for protests in the streets.

Arroyo was right to be afraid. ABS-CBN, in fact, could have been the spark that unseated her government. Soldiers were actually waiting for the media—for ABS-CBN, specifically—to trigger their actions. We had a reporter with the elite Scout Rangers, and they told us they would march out into the streets the minute we showed them live on television. Through our reporter, I told them that we wouldn't show them live until *after* they marched out. The line was clear in my mind: they must act first.

In the end, we never put them on air live because they never marched out. But if we had agreed to the soldiers' demands, we would have set off the coup. That was the power of ABS-CBN.

Arroyo's presidency survived that miserable episode, but it wasn't the last time she attacked press freedom. The most serious challenge to the media was on November 29, 2007, when fifty-one journalists, including twelve from our network, were arrested while reporting a one-day takeover of the Peninsula Manila hotel in the financial district by—again—rebels within the military. The government warned all news organizations to pull their people out of the hotel before they sent in troops. We chose to keep our people in the hotel, because if we complied with the government's demand, the only account of what happened would be the government's. Why should we voluntarily retreat from reporting a coup attempt?

By turning conflict coverage into a "crime scene"—at which anyone could be arrested—the government had repurposed existing laws to clamp down on the free press, which was a clear constitutional violation in the Philippines. It was also the first time the Philippine government tried another tactic: using the national police as the lead agency in a political conflict situation. Every other coup attempt or "passive withdrawal of support" in the past twenty-one years had been handled by the Department of National Defense and the military.

That was the beginning of what we're living through today. The attacks of the future Duterte administration were based on those tried and tested by Arroyo. Indeed, many of her loyal supporters and cabinet members became part of the Duterte administration, including his national security adviser, Hermogenes Esperon.[6] The seeds of Duterte's subversion of the Constitution were planted during Arroyo's tenure. The cuts were so small and insidious at the beginning that the public barely noticed them. We should have raised the alarm earlier. That's another reason why we #HoldTheLine today.

There was something else I learned in those Arroyo and ABS-CBN years that prepared me for a present in which dictators attack media companies and journalists face jail time: how to manage a crisis.

There is a "golden hour" in every crisis during which you can proactively shape and tell a story before someone claims it for their own and it becomes a crisis. You need to know clearly what message you want to send over which distribution networks (phone calls, emails, and so on)—and all this was before the age of social media. The goal is to tell your story first, especially if it's about you, not only to gain control of the narrative but to protect the people at risk. If you handle that well, almost everything else follows. This is how an organization survives threats to its integrity and its people.

At ABS-CBN, our toughest crisis was when I received an early-morning phone call from ABS-CBN anchor and friend Ces Drilon to let me know that she and her two cameramen had been kidnapped for ransom. The kidnappers were the Abu Sayyaf Group, a homegrown terror group linked to al-Qaeda, that had been wreaking havoc in the Philippines for decades.

Ces's terrifying phone call kicked off ten days of negotiations, improvisations, and high-stakes maneuvers that I hope never to have to live through again. It's far more complicated to make decisions that could mean life and death for the people you manage.

I asked for—and received—full responsibility for handling the crisis. I asked Libby Pascual, our head of human resources, to gather the immediate families of our kidnapped employees, and we all took over two floors of a nearby hotel, stationed security around us, and spent ten sleepless days and nights negotiating our team's release. Early on, I wanted to assure them that we would do everything we could to get them out safely. We were with them, and they were with us. We started with trust. When you don't know what's going to happen next, being vulnerable and open is the first step to bring everyone together.

Our little team made decisions in minutes, often with the buy-in of the families. I explained every decision I made. It was also clear that if I made the wrong call, it would be my fault, which would provide an out for my network and allowed me to do everything I thought was right to bring our people home. This was a matter of life or death. The

kidnapping of laborers a month earlier had shown us what happened
to those who refused to negotiate: the laborers had been beheaded and
their heads delivered to their company.

Having journalists manage the crisis was the best thing ABS-CBN
could have done. I had deep sources inside the police and counterterrorism forces; Glenda Gloria, whom I had just brought in to head our
twenty-four-hour English cable news channel, had deep sources inside
the military.

We got Ces and her team out in ten days.

Managing that crisis forged a deep tie among Glenda, Libby, and me
that laid the bedrock for Rappler's ability to handle the crises we would
face in the Duterte years.

Despite all the turmoil, it was an amazing time to be leading the
country's largest news organization, using its resources and vast
audience to strengthen civic engagement. That period was the beginning of my embrace of technology and social networks. The challenge
was how to combine our power of traditional broadcasting with the new
media and mobile phone technology, not just for coverage but for social
change. We wanted to encourage people to use their cell phones to work
with us in reporting the news. What I saw in those years was the power
of journalism to transform a society and strengthen a democracy.

In those six years, we created award-winning programs that spurred
concrete, quantifiable results in our society—and even led to a democratic tipping point. We used mass media as the megaphone to broadcast
a call to action and the internet and mobile phones to create a participatory culture to energize our citizens and our youth.

The changes were incremental, building one on top of the other. We
changed the workflows of news gathering and production, shifting our
emphasis to quality and standards and ethics. We moved the editorial
agenda away from sensationalism and crime, which, like in many coun-

tries around the world, drove the ratings (which drove revenues), and added "the vegetables to the sugar," as I called it. We rebranded our late-night newscast *Bandila*, which means "flag," because we decided to make it cool to love our country.[7] We gave the newscast a bold look and appealed to youths. The leading force in all those moves was Beth Frondoso, who would later become one of Rappler's founders. All the changes until then had been internal and organizational. *Bandila* was the tip of the iceberg.

One area in which we wanted to have real impact was the Philippines' record on elections and encourage more of our citizens to vote. We wisely aimed all of our news network initiatives toward the May 2010 presidential elections, for which I co-opted two ideas popularized by American writers: the tipping point and crowdsourcing.[8]

The idea of the tipping point has its roots in epidemiology: when a virus multiplies below the radar screen and then hits the point when it changes the entire system. Crowdsourcing suggests that if a group's members have diversity of ideas, independence of one another, a decentralized structure, and a mechanism for turning judgments into a collective decision, they can make smarter decisions than any lone genius can. Those four elements create the "wisdom of the crowds," not mob rule.

For our get-out-the-vote election campaigns, we used a gradual, studied tipping point approach. To try to build a community, we held eleven all-day, on-air multiplatform voter registration drives in more than twenty-one provinces. We registered Filipinos not only for the vote but also to become citizen journalists, or "boto patrollers," for ABS-CBN.

To draw them in, we held more than fifty lectures and talks nationwide, which included youth activist speeches, concerts, and workshops, many of which I led. After just four months, the Commission on Elections asked us to slow down our efforts because its systems couldn't keep up with the number of voter registration applications pouring in.

I focused our resources on two big goals: spreading empowerment and hope; and fostering debate and engagement.

My ideas for the first goal built on what I had learned while studying terrorism and mob violence in Indonesia. I relied on ideas from social network theory, the experiments of the psychologists Solomon Asch, Stanley Milgram, and Philip Zimbardo, and the Three Degrees of Influence idea, that everything we say or do impacts our friends, our friends' friends, and even our friends' friends' friends. Our network's focus group discussions showed us that Filipino youths were dissatisfied and disillusioned with our country's political processes. We decided to use the power of group dynamics and social networks to do something positive: spread hope.

We used a simple tagline or slogan: "*Ako ang Simula*," which means "I am the beginning."[9] In spirit, it means "Change begins with me." We drew from universal messages. This one was inspired by an idea often credited to Mahatma Gandhi—"Be the change you want to see"—but it went all the way back to the ancient Greeks: Plutarch's "What we achieve inwardly will change outward reality."[10]

We decided to spread hope through empowerment. It was a call to action.[11]

The sustaining vehicle was a crowdsourced citizen journalism program on politics and social concerns. It first aired stories three times a week in our newscasts through our different multimedia platforms, then shifted to nightly stories in our prime-time newscast in the month leading up to the elections. We used a tipping point approach, banking on the cumulative effect of each action we took and using repetition to help our citizens understand that if they saw something bad or good happen, they could take out their phones and record it. Three months before the elections, we held a concert with fifteen bands that was attended by about twenty thousand of our citizen journalists.[12]

We then hit a tipping point in our citizen journalism program with the Maguindanao massacre.

———

On November 23, 2009, fifty-eight people, including thirty-two journalists, were killed in broad daylight in Maguindanao Province. The murders had been a premeditated act orchestrated by a rival politician and were the Philippines' worst election-related violence in its history. The Committee to Protect Journalists called it "the deadliest single attack on journalists anywhere around the world" and "the deadliest attack on the press ever recorded in CPJ history."[13] And one citizen journalist revealed the truth of what happened.

At 3:47 p.m., nearly forty-five minutes before the military verified that people had been killed on a remote mountaintop in the province of Maguindanao, ABS-CBN received a message saying that the relatives and associates of the gubernatorial aspirant, Esmael "Toto" Mangudadatu, as well as journalists covering them that day, had been kidnapped. The message also said that the national police had failed to act because they were under the control of the incumbent Maguindanao governor, Andal Ampatuan, Jr. According to our citizen journalist, the military, too, had "played dumb and blind despite heightened reports that there is a plot against Toto Mangudadatu."

That message told us what happened, who was responsible, and why law enforcement officials hadn't acted.

Our source's second message arrived just eleven minutes later:

> We plead that this incident be given attention and that in-depth investigation be given as well as impartial report. The atrocities of Ampatuan family in Maguindanao is a secret public knowledge. All are immobile for their fear of life. These people are playing gods here.[14]

In those two messages, the source told us what happened, where it happened, who was involved—and gave us the mood. At that point, everyone was afraid of the Ampatuans; the person who sent us those messages did so at tremendous risk. We guessed that it was most likely a soldier.

A half hour later, the spokesman of the Philippine military confirmed the kidnapping and killings. The death toll rose in the following hours.

The third and last message from our citizen journalist came later that evening. It was the first picture of the grisly massacre site—three bodies spread-eagled on the grass as if dumped there—but when we received it, we had no way of proving its authenticity. All the journalists who had flocked to report the event, including ours, were being held by authorities in a hotel in the city center.

Once we confirmed that a white Toyota HiAce van in the picture was part of the Mangudadatu convoy, that the bodies must have been among the kidnapped, we released the picture publicly. We were right: a soldier who had visited the site and been horrified by what he saw had emailed us the photo. Only the military had access to the scene at the time. I believe that soldier became a citizen journalist because he wanted to prevent any possible whitewash of those crimes.

The Maguindanao massacre was a milestone for our citizen journalism program and proved the tremendous potential of embedding citizen journalists in communities and institutions. And it made me realize that the core of a citizen journalism program in a country such as the Philippines is rooted in an individual battle for integrity: How far will you go to correct what you perceive to be wrong? Or evil?

By election day, May 10, 2010, we had nearly ninety thousand registered citizen journalists. Our Facebook page was 400 percent more engaged than a regular news site.[15] That was how we hit the targets of our first goal for social change for elections: we seeded empowerment and hope and got out of the way when our citizen journalists answered our call for action.

There were many times leading up to and after the Maguindanao massacre when citizen journalists blew the whistle on bribery, corruption, election violence, intimidation, and much more. Their actions helped shape the days after, making it more difficult for candidates and their supporters to openly violate the rules of the election code. Anyone with a cell phone could capture their act, report it, and get the full broadcasting power of ABS-CBN behind them.

What I saw then was how powerful participatory media can be: how citizens using their cell phones are enfranchised to demand justice and accountability. It showed me how technology could be used for good: for citizen empowerment, voting and democratic engagement, and integrity and truth. It is why I still believe that the Philippines was not destined to become the country it did under Duterte and that ultimately, average citizens won't stand for a dictator's repression if there was a free press they could run to for help.

Another goal I set for social change was to foster debate and engagement. I wanted to see honest-to-goodness, no-holds-barred debate on issues that mattered, something most Filipino politicians still avoided doing publicly. In fact, at the beginning of 2009, the election candidates wouldn't even face each other on the same stage. They would answer questions from journalists, but they didn't want to be challenged by a competing candidate. We wanted to change that.

So every month for twelve months, we hosted different politicians for debate. Each month, we also added another layer of engagement. One year before the elections, we gathered the presidential candidates in front of a live audience of students. We layered in internet engagement, particularly with the relatively new platform of Facebook, and then we added Twitter and Multiply, a platform popular in the Philippines that was actually the precursor of Facebook, and instituted live bloggers for each candidate and live chat sessions on our own news website. By the fourth month, citizens could engage with the election campaigns on four devices: they could watch on their television screen, vote on their cell phone, and write comments on Facebook and Twitter. No other television network in the Philippines had developed such a multifaceted approach.

In March 2010, we hosted a vice presidential debate in which all six candidates faced off, rotating two at a time at two podiums that faced each other. One candidate would ask a question of the other candidate, who then had a certain amount of time to respond. We asked the candidates each to bring a live blogger to answer viewers' and readers' questions live online.

We posed a simple question to our audiences on Twitter, Facebook, and other online platforms: "Do you believe what he/she said?"

The audiences had a spectrum to choose from, between, in Tagalog, *naniniwala* (believe) and *hindi naniniwala* (don't believe).

We put the results onscreen instantaneously. We found that people responded not only to what was said but to how others reacted to it, which then fostered greater dialogue and engagement online on Facebook, on Twitter, and in the chat box on our website. The candidates were able to ask each other more knowledgeable and pointed questions than ordinary journalists could because they simultaneously had to gauge and navigate the public's responses they were seeing in real time.

That night, I felt the physiological impact of technology, adding to my normal breaking-news adrenaline. I knew that I must have also had elevated levels of both dopamine, which causes addiction, and oxytocin, which increases the feeling of being "connected" (it's also known as the "love hormone").[16] I was engaging with what was happening on my television screen through three other screens: Twitter, Facebook, and online chats. That was reflected back to me through periodic announcements of audience feedback, which then fueled more feedback—a network effect for good, I liked to think.

The debate initiatives were as close as we came to being able to measure honesty, quantifying the often hard-to-measure instincts that make you decide whether you trust someone or not. We saw what political tactics worked and what didn't, and we did it all together.

Innovation and engagement, sharing your power with your community, makes for good business. After we had introduced "Boto Mo, iPatrol Mo" citizen journalism in 2007, we had seen nearly a 400 percent increase in our gross profit rate compared to the last presidential elections. That trend continued until I left the network at the end of 2010. After a decade of operations, ANC, the English-language station, made money for the first time.

In the next years, we monitored the impact of our experiments. In July 2010, a survey by the trusted polling institution Pulse Asia showed the full impact of our *"Ako ang Simula,"* or "I am the beginning," campaign: Filipinos had reached the highest level of optimism nationwide since the Pulse Asia surveys had begun in 1999, with 53 percent of people feeling optimistic and only 11 percent pessimistic, the lowest the group had recorded. The survey also confirmed a boost in our network's credibility ratings, putting ABS-CBN first in all of the Philippines.

Our plan had worked.

It worked, that is, until the old-style network effect—the power of the country's largest media organization—was turned upside down by technology's own, far more powerful network effects.

ABS-CBN taught me the best and the worst of Filipino culture—the kindness and loyalty, the tendency toward patronage—and helped lay the groundwork for how I handle Rappler today. For six years at ABS-CBN News and Current Affairs, we turned things around. Three years in, we had achieved stability and created a new Standards & Ethics Manual that we entwined with the labor code. As I had expected, once the system and its leaders were transparent, the group felt a sense of justice, which led to accountability and consistency. We rewarded people based on their merit and performance.

One of the people I had brought to ANC in 2005 was Twink. A little more than a year later, she was diagnosed with breast cancer. She told a few of us and then dealt with it: she had a partial mastectomy and thirty sessions of radiation therapy. She worked the entire time she was receiving treatment, coming in, editing, and anchoring her programs. She boasted that she "carried around that little pouch of pink serum attached to [her] armpit with such aplomb that strangers assumed it was a new kind of power drink." And she beat the cancer.

I saw her much less in those days, but her anchor desk was steps away from my office, and every now and then, she would stop by. She often told me I was too black and white, made too many enemies, tried to tackle too many problems at one time. Twink told me to choose my battles; Cheche told me to hold the line.

Those who want power will do all they can to get it. In the end, it wasn't among the reporters and producers and editors in the news group that I encountered the strongest resistance to all of the dramatic changes I demanded. The real resistance came from a small power center at the corporate core of ABS-CBN and their efforts to weaken the unity and purpose of our News division. After all, if News takes a zero-tolerance approach to corruption—for example, that all parts of ABS-CBN should not give money to entertainment reporters to cover their network stars—what happens to those people who may have been dependent on corrupt practices for their success?

One by one, that small group of people splintered my deputies and allies away through gossip and petty disputes that tore apart decades of friendship and trust. There was even a point when my boss, Gabby, assigned me personal security because of internal threats.

Most of what I'm experiencing in 2022—the legal cases, the smear campaigns, the homophobic slurs, the vicious personal attacks—I have lived through before, on a far smaller scale. Though painful, it was good training. I smile as I write this because it did make me stronger and helped prepare me for today's battles.

When you try to change the system, it fights back.

One day in October 2010, Gabby called me into his office. It was a gorgeous time of day in Manila, right before sunset, when the Pacific light turns pink and purple and the air is at its most sultry. It's my favorite time of day. I smiled when Gabby asked an aide to get us martinis.

He wanted to talk about Noli de Castro, a former prime-time anchor, whose return to the network I had been blocking for nearly a year. De Castro was one of the most popular anchors in the Philippines, and most recently he had served as Gloria Arroyo's vice president—which tells you something about the intimacy of media and politics in the Philippines! De Castro wanted to return as our prime-time newscast's main anchor, and Gabby was afraid to lose him to a new rival network. I felt that we had to transition him back properly and be transparent: after all, as our nation's vice president, he had also faced charges of corruption.

I wasn't sure what I would do in that meeting, but if your lines are clear, so are your points of action. When the owner of the company wants to do something you don't, either you accept it or you leave. By the time the meeting ended, I had handed in my resignation, helped choose my successor,[17] and worked out a timeline of transition.

Later, in a written note, I thanked my team for six amazing years.[18] We took risks together to help define the future of journalism and our nation; we took a stand and said no to corruption; we embraced the growth of social media; and we joined hands with citizen journalists to patrol our elections and the integrity of our nation. I told them to value and protect their editorial independence. I wished them clarity of thought, stamina, and the courage to fight for what is right. I reminded them to avoid the compromise of mediocrity.

Key to my time at ABS-CBN were three women whose expertise and values had turned us into lifelong friends and allies. Together, we had fine-tuned our vision of journalism and its role in a democracy.

We began to dream of how we could make that happen. At a dinner with Chay Hofileña, Glenda Gloria, and Beth Frondoso, I raised my glass. "Okay, enough of the problems," I said. "We survived!"

We all laughed. In succeeding years, our enemies would call us witches.

That was the foundation of a company we would later call Rappler.

Chapter 6

Creating Ripples of Change

Build a Team

The founders of Rappler (*from left to right*): me, Chay Hofileña, Beth Frondoso, Glenda Gloria. Selfie photo outside Estancia Mall, Capitol Commons, Manila, March 7, 2017.

Rappler called its four cofounders *manang*s, which loosely translates to "older sisters." That was how we behaved toward our team. We were a strange mix of personalities and work habits. We even had different political views, but that was not something that concerned us much; we always put our commitment to good journalism, truth, and justice above politics.

I had spent nearly two years at ABS-CBN recruiting Glenda Gloria to head ANC. From Marcos country, she knew firsthand exactly how feudalism and patronage-driven politics could capture a province and a nation. She was also perhaps the best newsroom manager I had ever worked with and would be my partner in building Rappler, the bad cop to my good cop, the disciplinarian who laid out our expectations, and woe to whoever disappointed her.

Chay Hofileña had worked with Glenda at what had become the largest newspaper in the Philippines, the fledgling *Philippine Daily Inquirer*, where the two had led the labor union—every policy they crafted was a reflection of their long-held labor principles. An author of several books on politics and media, she had written the bible on media ethics and corruption for our country and helped prepare our staff for the comprehensive Standards & Ethics Manual we wrote for ABS-CBN. Chay was the teacher, part of the reason each member of our Rappler team grew so quickly. She helped instill a culture that didn't exist at many cutthroat and secretive news organizations.

The last Rappler creator, Beth Frondoso, was an eleven-year ABS-CBN veteran whose formal and informal leadership of the network helped me navigate its stormy political waters. She had worked her way up the ranks, which meant that she understood how politics and infighting bred inefficiencies. She handled the largest budget in the news group and was often the final word on the daily deployment of news gathering, determining the form and substance of what aired every day. She was the one who found the right balance—the magic point where we had enough serious news but still grew our ratings. Beth believed in spending money on ambitious reporting because it was part of our news agenda.

And me? Well, I know that after a few cups of coffee, I can bounce off the walls with energy, and that's both good and bad. Other Rapplers said I was driven, always coming up with ideas, but often setting impossible goals. One of our first twelve employees, Natashya Gutierrez, said I looked innocent, but I was a weapon: "Her wheels in her brain are always turning, always churning, never stopping. Depending on the situation, she is often democratic but sometimes makes a call on her own despite consensus."

In 2011, the *manang*s had five things in common. One was that money wasn't what drove us. We had resigned from ABS-CBN knowing that we were giving up anywhere from 30 to 90 percent of our monthly pay. We all had extensive experience managing news groups and had worked in at least one independent organization that had challenged the ethos of the mainstream media. We all believed in the power of journalism—its mission and its standards and ethics. We all worked hard, fourteen- to sixteen-hour days, and were used to being in the daily trenches of the creation of news. And we all wanted to create something better than what we had lived through before.[1]

Our complementary personalities enabled us to make quick, instinctive decisions under pressure. I would often be the most aggressive and Glenda the most deliberate, while Chay would always find the middle and Beth would weigh in tactically and philosophically. Together we would find the perfect action point. We were two Libras and two Leos, and we made a team far better than simply the sum of all of us, with the expertise and courage to bring the mission of journalism into the twenty-first century. We were creating something entirely new, not only in the Philippines but in the world.

We are all women, and our decisions were based not only on facts but also on emotions and values. Still, each of us could be personal and sensitive. Sometimes we didn't take criticism kindly. Our deep loyalty to one another sometimes affected our decision making, a weakness we tried to guard against. But we all knew that ultimately our work was about our friendships, the trust that was forged in the trenches—because even before Duterte, we were fearless together.

We incorporated our company in July 2011. Our plan was to launch the news website in January 2012 and to break even in five years, half the time it took traditional news groups.

The *manang*s met in my apartment in Taguig, light streaming through the glass windows on both sides. We had decided on our name for our new company: "Rappler," a portmanteau of *rap*—to talk, a throwback to the 1980s of our generation—and *ripple*, to make waves.

It was a grand experiment: we wanted to put television news in our viewers' pockets on their mobile phones; in 2010, that was still a dream. But our success at ABS-CBN showed me that we could, through crowd-sourcing, create participatory journalism and help build our country's institutions from the bottom up. That gave me more hope than the top-down governance we had been covering for decades. Government always does better when the people are involved.

We all wanted to do more than just tell stories. We believed that excellent journalism could change the world; we had a theory of change. We imagined three interlocking circles—investigative journalism, technology, and community—on a Venn diagram, with Rappler at the center where they converged. My elevator pitch was "Rappler builds communities of action, and the food we feed them is journalism."

Fundamental to our discussions was that the journalists at Rappler would have editorial independence and commercial power, meaning that the buck would stop with the journalists. We would consult our board and our shareholders, but the final decisions would rest with us.[2] We had learned at ABS-CBN and other corporate media that editorial independence wasn't as valuable without the commercial decision-making power. We also knew that we would have to make enough money to pay our people decently so we could stay independent. Our primary goal was to create a sustainable business model.

What also made us different was our approach to the internet. Traditional media looked at the internet as an add-on. We set up our sales team around a native advertising model we called "BrandRap," for which an entirely separate team produced sponsored articles, which were clearly labeled on our site, the first in the Philippines. From the board to the journalists, we fused experience with innovation. The four *manang*s, the heads of Rappler's business, had deep journalistic field experience. Our founding board members had a deeper sense of the mission, too. We weren't just millennials playing with new technology; we had run old-world organizations and then jumped in to understand this new one.

One of our first initiatives was experimenting with Facebook, which we had recognized at ABS-CBN in 2008 as an undeniable force for mobilization. We started posting our experiments on our Facebook page, Move.PH.[3] If the search function on Facebook had worked better, perhaps we would never have launched our own website. In the beginning, we felt so much excitement, so much optimism, about what Facebook and its founder, Mark Zuckerberg, might do for a country like the Philippines and our democratic future.

We launched our first public event on social media: a four-hour workshop for five hundred students at the University of the Philippines in the cool northern city of Baguio, about a four-hour drive from Manila. The idea was to train those students in how to use social media for good; we focused on local environmental concerns and ways to use social media to address them. The title of my keynote address was "Social Media for Social Change."

We set up a stage and a livestream for the event.[4] In 2011, before any of the livestreaming platforms, we wanted to take what we knew from television and apply it to our brave new internet world. Already at that time, the Philippines was leading the world in social media use. Mobile penetration was at 94 percent; the average web user was below twenty-three years of age. The internet had just overtaken television in terms of the number of hours consumed each week.[5] TV still earned the most revenue, but we were convinced that the future was the internet.

In the workshop, I spoke about the possibilities I saw in the internet: the cataclysmic way it was changing the way we thought and acted.[6] At that point, I saw only the positives for democracy.

With my keynote presentation, I took the students to the Middle East and North Africa—Egypt, Tunisia, Bahrain, and Libya—which had just experienced the Arab Spring that year. In the West, those revolutions had triggered a debate about whether Facebook and Twitter had spawned them.[7] But regardless of where the academics came down on the question, clearly the internet, and social media specifically, had been a critical factor in igniting long-standing grievances, breaking down people's fears, enhancing their courage, and fast-tracking protests that might otherwise have taken months and years to organize. The result had been the downfall of dictatorships.

The medium that carries the message shapes and defines the message itself, I told the students, invoking the media theorist Marshall McLuhan's seminal work, "The Medium Is the Message."[8] Social media's instantaneous nature had accelerated the speed at which the revolutions had taken place. Authoritarian governments couldn't keep up or control the messaging because those protest movements were modeled on the networks of the web: loose, nonhierarchical, leaderless. Dictators didn't know whom to arrest; there were no political parties to tear apart, no underground revolt to dismantle. This was the people, and any government that fought its people would ultimately fail.

I cringe now when I remember that presentation. Those very same developments I welcomed in 2011 would soon be fine-tuned by the platforms' business models, co-opted by state power, and turned against the people, fueling the rise of digital authoritarians, the death of facts, and the insidious mass manipulation we live with today.

It's not that we did not also see the downsides of the internet back then; I highlighted its impact on our biology. The five hundred young people in that audience were undergoing major physiological changes. More than 75 percent of those in the room had Facebook accounts. A smaller number were on Twitter. Participation in the platforms had the effect of tweaking our emotions by increasing the dopamine levels in our brains.[9] Because our emotions were heightened, our expectations, and the way we reacted to them, were shifting. And it was not just social media but all the technological interruptions in the modern world that were conditioning us to prefer sensationalism over objectivity.[10] When I looked out at that audience that day, I warned them not to become the generation that couldn't focus.[11]

But even I quickly looked past the downsides of social media because I thought the upside was so exciting. "We're more engaged," I told the students that day. "We're more social. We can decide—with minimal costs—to act together." The purpose of the workshop that day was ultimately to show them that they could use social media for social good.

What emerged from those weeks was MovePH, the civic engagement arm of Rappler. We would keep the journalism core small, giving facts and policy questions to our civic engagement team and partners, who would take the stories we did and change our world for the better.

Of course, nothing is perfect because among the people we trained in the thousands of workshops we conducted were some who later became key propaganda voices of the Duterte and Marcos armies.

We also started playing with form, using multimedia and video on the internet. Because of our television background, we embraced live transmission via cell phones several years before social media platforms made it easy to do that. We built metal casings for our iPhones, which our reporters used as their primary cameras (and could be anchored on a tripod). By the time we launched in January 2012,

In 2013, Rappler's multimedia reporter Natashya Gutierrez holds up the equipment they brought: a metal case we built, tripod, and lights.

each Rappler reporter carried that equipment and worked alone. Unlike typical television production crews, they did all the reporting, live social media, and livestreaming or recording themselves.

In the field, some of the men from other networks would laugh at our reporters who were doing their stand-ups in front of their cell phones. But once Rappler began publishing video in or near real time—which eliminated the ride back to the office and the editing of video—we were breaking news hours ahead of the television stations. Our competitors soon adopted our methods, eliminating our advantage after about a year.

We adapted our knowledge of broadcast television to the internet for live transmission. An outdoor broadcasting (OB) van used television transmission, with a total cost of about $1 million. Rappler created an IP satellite van, one that used the internet for transmission, which we built on an Isuzu chassis; that van cost us $100,000. Now we could drive anywhere in the Philippines and do a live broadcast. Especially during natural disasters, the van allowed our reporters to file stories and do crowdsourcing, uploading posts asking whether the area we were driving through still

had a cell phone signal and creating a real-time map of electricity and cell phone service. The key moment for our DIY van was when supertyphoon Haiyan, known as Yolanda in the Philippines, hit in November 2013. Rappler, along with the government and other NGOs, was able to transmit information outside the disaster area. But like our metal phone casings, which were no longer necessary after lighter plastic models came out, our IP van would be made obsolete by Facebook Live in 2016.[12]

Rappler's first few years were backbreaking in terms of the pace of change, but we were experimenting with what a whole-of-society approach to solving governance problems would look like and changing our company workflows accordingly—all while our investigative journalists worked to hold power to account.

Within our first year and a half, Rappler became the Philippines' third top news site.[13] In our first three years, our reach and revenue grew from 100 percent to 300 percent. There were some key factors that led to that success. One was that our investigative journalism had a video-first focus long before other media organizations did and long before Facebook and YouTube made video ubiquitous. Another was that we used social network analysis to understand how information flowed from Rappler's site to the public and vice versa. Finally, we harnessed engagement through moods, enabling us to see how a story rippled emotionally through our society. In fact, we rolled out our mood meter and mood navigator nearly four years before Facebook introduced emojis.[14]

Using social cartography, the analysis of social networks' impact on human behavior, we began to use social media to anticipate emergent behavior in a rapidly changing information ecosystem. I was certain that we could use their data for everything: to jump-start the site's development, to help fight political corruption, and to build more civic institutions from the bottom up.

New technology was giving journalists new power. Instead of fearing the dramatic shifts in our industry, we were using it to try to help solve age-old problems that would allow us to go beyond storytelling and into crowdsourcing and community building. Media was powerful, but could we use the new technology to determine exactly how powerful? In a country like the Philippines, where institutions are weak and corruption is endemic, we used the mood meter to capture the zeitgeist of a frustrated society. Could we somehow employ the right stories, the right information to inspire real-world action, whether that was to vote, help a village during a flood, or call out corruption? Studies[15] had shown that 80 to 95 percent of how we make decisions is based not on what we think but on how we feel.[16]

I thought of it like an iceberg: the tip was the story you could read and see (with performance metrics we could measure), but each story carried an emotion, which traveled over social networks—now social media, four times more powerful than physical networks. Over time, our theory went, that mix could change behavior. If we could map those networks, we would have an idea of how and why the emotions associated with stories traveled through society and changed human behavior.

The tool we used to measure how stories provoked our readers' emotions and how they traveled through society was the mood meter. The

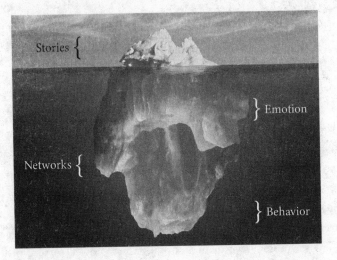

most immediate, easiest action for people was to click how they felt about a given story. If we embedded in each story a mood meter that a reader could click, every mood vote would be aggregated into a mood navigator that would display the top ten stories on the site, as well as the overall mood of the day. Over time, trends would become apparent, giving us more insight into the public we served, not only how they were feeling but what issues they cared about most.

We measured three metrics at the tip of the iceberg—unique users, page views, and time spent on site—but I was careful about how we handled the information. I chose not to let our reporters see all of the metrics, for example. If they did, would they stop doing stories that mattered and pursue only those rewarded by traffic? That could change the incentive away from quality journalism to clickbait. We also wanted to foster a culture of collaboration and thought that reporters chasing online traffic could lead to corrosive competition.

But we did report those mood metrics annually in "The Year in Moods."[17] That was how we knew that before the great propaganda wars began in 2016, "happy" was overwhelmingly the most prevalent emotion in five years among our users.[18] Over time, disinformation networks would exploit the greed of Facebook and YouTube and we would see in real time how behavior changed, with information operations artificially inflating the votes for "anger" and creating a new normal.

The daily mood navigator also gave us an idea of how the day's stories were filtering through society. It revealed vested interests in our country, like when politicians or companies repeatedly voted on a mood. We kept track of attempts to manipulate public opinion, in some cases reporting them publicly. We began tracking trends over months.

Rappler's first election coverage was of the midterm election on May 13, 2013. If you look at the moods that month, you can chart when "happy" became "angry" and "annoyed"—in this case, after a minor glitch in reporting election results after the polls closed. The spike of anger at the end of the month was due to a rape joke and the fat shaming

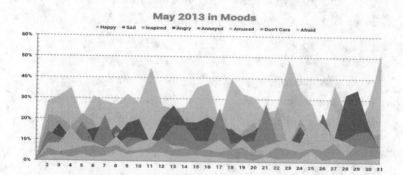

of a journalist by a rival network's entertainment figure.[19] Interestingly, engagement increased for both "happy" and "angry" responses.

We unveiled the ecosystem not just for our journalists but for our government and civil society partners, as well as our advertisers. The same growth and distribution model worked for both. We all had to understand what the people wanted, what they cared about. Rappler remained transparent and open about all of it.

By 2014, we were beginning to see concrete results for our most ambitious goals. Four of Rappler's campaigns spurred by issue-focused stories were turning social media crowdsourcing into civic engagement.

The first was #BudgetWatch,[20] our first anti-corruption campaign. We knew that the only way to stop government corruption was to show taxpayers where their money went. So we presented budget data in easily digestible and visually engaging ways—like a game of Slides and Ladders,[21] to illustrate the budget approval process, or another interactive game[22] that allowed the public to submit their own proposals to see how they would affect different government sectors.

Our second campaign, #ProjectAgos,[23] was our climate change and disaster risk reduction campaign—our most successful initiative in our first five years of operation. That made sense because the Philippines has an average of twenty typhoons every year and in 2012 was the third most disaster-prone country globally. Disasters meant calling all hands on deck.

In collaboration with nearly forty groups, including the Philippine Climate Change Commission, the Office of Civil Defense, private-sector partners, the Australian Agency for International Development (AusAID), and later the United Nations Development Programme (UNDP), Rappler piloted and built a one-stop online platform[24] for enduring climate-related disasters. It included a risk knowledge database[25] and interactive tools like hazard maps and compliance trackers that aided officials as they prepared for a storm to hit and included a wide range of information necessary before, during, and after any major weather disturbance. During a typhoon, for example, a crowdsourced map of calls for help enabled first responders to see them and reply, while also giving others who wanted to help a broader view. From 2013 to 2016, that initiative helped reduce the death toll from weather-related disturbances from triple digits to low double digits. The hashtag was #ZeroCasualty.[26] That successful initiative would eventually be abandoned by the Duterte administration, and death tolls would soon rise to triple digits again.

Our third campaign was #HungerProject,[27] which we created in collaboration with the UN World Food Programme and the Philippine Department of Social Welfare and Development. We did this because our country's incidence of hunger, among the highest in Asia, continued to increase despite our growing GDP. Stunting, or low height for age, the result of chronic malnutrition, was a particular problem in the Philippines. By creating a repository of information on Rappler, we were able to reach some of the most vulnerable sectors of society; instead of an extra cup of rice, poorer communities began to look for the right kinds of food.[28]

Our fourth campaign, #WhipIt,[29] was a commercial partnership with Pantene focused on gender bias and women's rights. Rappler commissioned a survey[30] looking at how society perceived women[31] in the Philippines and organized a women's forum to launch an innovative advertising campaign. The online ripple reverberated globally when Facebook COO Sheryl Sandberg[32] posted about the campaign, prompting Procter & Gamble, the makers of Pantene products, to announce that it would bring the Philippine-born campaign to the West.

We created Rappler at the time when Big Data was transforming our world. That gave us an early advantage, using both structured and unstructured Big Data before the social media platforms and other entities began shutting down access to it. Like during my ABS-CBN years, one of the most crucial areas was elections.

During the May 2013 elections, Rappler moved ahead of our Western counterparts when we signed an agreement with the Philippine Commission on Elections and published the full data set of automated voting results in a friendly user interface. It was the first time globally that granular details of voting results were available in real time.

We created a real-time reporting template that broke the results down into exactly how many people voted for whom in each of the 92,509 clustered precincts, in what was then the largest and fastest electronic vote count in history.[33] Now people no longer needed to wait for a television anchor to announce the results they were waiting for. They could search—and go back in time—instantly. That made reporting transparent and countered the old allegations of bias or "trending" when reporting election results.

In 2013, we would also see what an anti-corruption campaign on social media looked like.[34] After all, it was the golden age of social media empowering citizens to demand reforms from their government. Among the first to have posted their demand for better governance on Facebook? The Occupy Wall Street protesters in New York in 2011.

By then, Cory Aquino's son, Benigno Aquino III, had been elected president. The same old Marcos-era corruption problems persisted, including pork-barrel politics, the practice of appropriating public money for local projects in Congress. When the well-connected businesswoman Janet Lim Napoles was charged with working with more than a dozen congressmen to siphon off $232 million in public funds intended for farmers, public anger erupted against the Aquino government.

The advertising executive Peachy Rallonzo-Bretaña had never led a protest before, but she and her friends were so angry about the corruption that she posted about it on Facebook. It triggered the first social media–organized mass protest in the Philippines.[35]

Watching it come together in the virtual world was fascinating. When the idea for the protest was first floated, it took seven days, from August 17 to 25, to get up to ten thousand mentions on Twitter. Then, the day before the protest, the number increased exponentially.

By 11:00 a.m. on August 26, 2013, protestors were arriving in Luneta Park in the center of Manila. By that time, we were recording five tweets per second.[36] Since there was no central organization, people at the protest didn't really know what to do: there was no central stage, no program. People arrived and walked around in groups. Some families set up picnics. Peachy Rallonzo-Bretaña's Facebook post ended up bringing

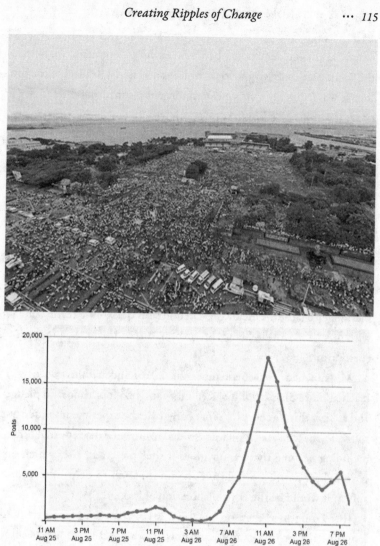

out eighty thousand to a hundred thousand people. The hashtag was #MillionPeopleMarch.[37]

We at Rappler marked it as the first time individuals recognized us as an organization. People came up to our field teams to greet us. Of course, the protestors were our audience; it was a digitally fueled action for social change demanding better from the government. We mapped the social media activity to look for hubs and nodes, leaders of the protest. It was a quickly shifting community map mirroring the activity in the real world.

Our last anti-corruption crowdsourcing initiative was on August 10, 2016, and was called #NotOnMyWatch.[38] Rappler's MovePH worked in tandem with two government agencies, the Civil Service Commission and the Office of the Ombudsman. They had told us that one of every twenty Filipino families paid bribes, and of those who paid, only 5 percent would report doing that. So we decided to make it easy to report corruption by using an online form and a Facebook messenger chatbot. One of the catchphrases our young team came up with was "Talk to the Hand!" to express a zero-tolerance approach to corruption.

We launched it on September 24, 2016, and within two days, it reached more than 2 million accounts[39] and had four thousand pledges and at least thirty reports.[40] What had made the experiment unique was the real-time feedback loop we provided to citizens who reported bribes, including keeping them anonymous if they preferred, after which our government partners would use the information to demand accountability. It would be the last collaboration of its kind.

Three months earlier, on June 30, 2016, a lawyer, prosecutor, and longtime mayor of Davao City named Rodrigo Duterte had become the president of the Philippines. He gave one of his first one-on-one interviews from Malacañang Palace to Rappler, and, as we wrapped up, he agreed to do a public service announcement about #NotOnMyWatch. He good-naturedly put on the giant hand—as in "Talk to the Hand!"— and supported the campaign.[41]

"One of the promises I made to the people is that I will stop corruption in government," he said. "I cannot do it alone. You have to be aware of what I'm doing, and you have to help me. You can help just by being assertive of your rights."

While still with CNN in the late 1980s, I did a story on a vigilante mayor who was cleaning up his city. Because the justice system was moving too slowly, he condoned vigilante killings. It wasn't a favorable story. That was the first time I met Rodrigo Duterte, and when we met again nearly three decades later when he was a presidential candidate, he asked me about our previous interview good-naturedly. Or so I thought.

If he won as president, he said forcefully, three things would happen. He then counted them on the fingers of one hand: "I would stop corruption, stop criminality, and fix government."

What made him different was that he repeatedly said he was willing to kill to make that happen.[42]

"When I said I'll stop criminality, I'll stop criminality," said one of the Philippines' longest-serving mayors. "If I have to kill you, I'll kill you. Personally."[43]

I held his gaze to see if he meant what he said. He did.

In 2016, Duterte ran against candidates from old political families. He said what he thought and was prone to offensive, off-color jokes and flashes of cruelty, as well as crudely nationalist and populist rhetoric. He compared himself to Adolf Hitler[44] and joked about not getting the chance to rape an Australian missionary who had been gang-raped and killed in the Philippines.[45] When criticized, he cursed then president Barack Obama and Pope Francis, calling them "sons of whores."

He would also be the first politician to successfully use Facebook to win our country's top post, changing politics in the Philippines forever.

On the day of his last campaign rally, Duterte said, "Forget the laws on human rights. If I make it to the presidential palace, I will do just what I did as mayor. You drug pushers, holdup men, and do-nothings, you better go out. Because I'd kill you. I'll dump all of you into Manila Bay and fatten all the fish there."[46]

Duterte won with 39 percent of the vote. Within hours of his inauguration, the first killing happened a short distance from where he had vowed to protect the Constitution. We had no idea then how bad things would get.

Chapter 7

How Friends of Friends Brought Democracy Down

Think Slow, Not Fast

Police gather materials retrieved from a dead body with covered face and sign board saying I AM A DRUGLORD, found on a street in Tondo, Manila, on July 28, 2016. (*Rappler*)

What an amazing view of Singapore harbor, the busiest in the world! I was gazing through floor-to-ceiling windows on one of the top floors of a gleaming building in Southeast Asia. I was in the offices of Facebook.

It was August 2016. The Duterte administration had just come to power, along with about six thousand political appointees, whom Duterte had proudly announced he had installed because of their loyalty. Local officials along with law enforcement and military personnel from Duterte's tenure as mayor of Davao were taking the top jobs in the capital. At first, I thought the question would be about their competence. If they couldn't do their jobs, I assumed, they would be held to account.

More worrying were the daily reports of deaths: bodies found in the streets of poor neighborhoods, eyewitnesses whispering about killers descending upon homes in the night. Duterte's drug war had begun turning Manila into a real-world Gotham City, without a caped crusader.

Rappler had one reporter and a production team assigned to work the overnight shift. They soon began reporting as many as eight dead bodies every night, dumped on the sidewalk or in the street, their blood pooling on the pavement. They were gruesome murders: some hogtied, their heads wrapped in duct tape, a cardboard sign on top: DRUG DEALER, *HUWAG TULARAN*: "Don't become like me."

I was relieved to be in Singapore, a world away from the violence. When I stepped into that top-floor cafeteria with dazzling views of the bay, I tried to calculate how much the perk of free food must cost the company. Rappler had considered giving our employees a free, nutritious lunch to keep our team in place, a benefit we knew they'd like but would also be tax deductible for us. Still, the spread in front of me, stretching as far as the eye could see—Indian, Chinese, and American cuisine—was a display of wealth beyond anything our little startup could imagine.

The purpose of my visit was to deliver a warning to our Facebook Asia–based partners, the people with whom I coordinated many of Rappler's partnerships. Among them were Ken Teh, who among other things handled news groups in the Philippines from the company's Singapore office; Clare Wareing, who headed Asia-Pacific Policy Communications; and Elizabeth Hernandez, who was in charge of public policy for the Asia-Pacific region. I had first met Elizabeth when she was working at Hewlett-Packard. I thought that having a Filipino in that critical position at Facebook would be good for the Philippines. It turned out that it wasn't.

Rappler's relationship with Facebook had begun on a promising note. Ken Teh had contacted me in early 2015, tasked with building partnerships with news groups in the Philippines. Rappler was a logical choice given that we fused online journalism with social network theory.[1] By the time Facebook was staffing up in Southeast Asia, the United Nations–based World Summit Award had already chosen Rappler as one of forty "best and most innovative digital innovations."[2] Facebook had even showcased Rappler at F8, its annual conference for developers, in San Francisco in 2016.[3]

When Facebook opened its first office in the Philippines that year, it released startling statistics: that Filipinos spent 1.7 times more time on Facebook and Instagram than watching TV. Filipinos had 60 percent more Facebook friends than the global average, and they sent 30 percent more messages than the global average. Out of the 65 percent of Filipinos who accessed Facebook every day, the mobile app was used 90 percent of the time. Filipinos spent one out of five minutes online and one out of four minutes on mobile. "The Philippines is a highly engaged mobile-first nation," said Facebook's VP for Asia Pacific at the time, "filled with people who are creative, entrepreneurial and have a strong sense of community."[4]

Part of why Rappler had started outperforming legacy news organizations so quickly was our use of Facebook. We had embraced the platform early and knew its performance in the Philippines better than Facebook itself did, often surprising its executives with what we had discovered in our daily data-monitoring operations. I even secretly entertained the idea of actually working for Facebook. It struck me that, like CNN for my generation, Facebook was determining the flow of information for this one.

I always eagerly awaited what Facebook would come up with next.

In 2015, it launched an application and website called Internet.org, intended to facilitate easy, free-of-charge internet access to a variety of websites, including Facebook, in developing nations. It used the Philippines as a prime test case. Mark Zuckerberg's argument was that its service, which eventually became known as Free Basics,[5] was good for the people and good for its telecommunication partners, who essentially paid the bill. Facebook partnered with Globe,[6] then the smaller of the two top mobile companies in the Philippines; Rappler was a partner with both, in part because of our crowdsourcing initiatives. Within fifteen months, Globe overtook its rival with the incredibly popular lure of free access to Facebook.[7]

When Facebook asked the top four Filipino news organizations to try another new product, Instant Articles, they asked the television networks ABS-CBN and GMA-7, the *Philippine Daily Inquirer*, and Rappler. Unlike the other three, Rappler went all in, deciding to place all our stories on Instant Articles, rather than our website, to give us clear metrics—before and after. But Instant Articles failed miserably, and we soon stopped. Facebook acknowledged that it had a lot of work to do for news companies. Its "Move fast, break things" mindset meant that it asked companies and people to join new projects before thinking them through.

Mark's pitch for Internet.org and its supposed advantages for developing countries used the same tactic he still uses today: the parsing of information in supposedly independent studies that would sway public opinion. "There was this Deloitte study that came out the other day," he told a mobile industry conference in Barcelona in February 2014, "that said that if you could connect everyone in emerging markets, you could create more than 100 million jobs and bring a lot of people out of poverty." It was a nice story. What he didn't say was that the Deloitte study had been commissioned by Facebook and been based on data provided by Facebook.[8]

But back then I continued to drink the Kool-Aid. And even though

I had come to Singapore that day with serious concerns, I was doing this in good faith. It was my old mantra again: trust until they prove they can't be trusted. I was only beginning to see how fragmented Facebook was as a company. In some ways, that made sense; it was a sprawling, global startup that grew as it adapted. But that meant that the group that, say, showcased short films of Rappler for Internet.org and Free Basics[9] was different from this team in Singapore, which was different from the product and investigating groups for violations in Menlo Park that would later be called the Integrity team.

Which meant that no one had the complete picture.

After choosing my lunch from the lavish buffet spread, I followed Ken, Clare, and Elizabeth to a long table and sat down to eat. "What we found is really alarming," I proceeded to tell them. "I've never seen anything like this, but it's clear how dangerous this can be."

What I was there to convey had a history.

A former colony of the United States, the Philippines' nearly 113 million people[10] boasted of an English-speaking, often college-educated, labor force familiar with Western culture. That's one reason why our country has long been a source of cheap labor for the West. In 2010, the Philippines overtook India as the world's top call center, business process outsourcing (BPO), and shared services hub.[11] More significantly, we became a prime source of internet scams, from the days of Hotmail and email spam. Many foreign businesses experimenting in gray areas came to the Philippines because it had few or no internet regulations, and what regulations it did have, it didn't enforce.[12] Some parts of the Philippines developed a reputation for services euphemistically known as "onlining" that spammed email addresses around the world.[13]

Our country was also where the hate factory 8chan, later 8kun, best known as a forum for violent extremists, was based and later linked to

QAnon: the American father and son suspected of creating it had been living on a pig farm south of Manila.[14]

A lot of that changed after a global crackdown between 2010 and 2012, when internet security researchers and law enforcement agencies dismantled spambots and technology evolved to control them. So when those involved in that homegrown industry looked for new business opportunities, they turned to social media.[15] Well before the 2016 presidential elections, the stage had already been set in our country for three converging trends that helped the government shamelessly consolidate power: click and account farms, information operations, and the rise of political influencers in the grayer areas of the advertising industry.

As early as 2015, there were reports of account farms creating social media phone-verified accounts, or PVAs, from the Philippines.[16] They would become a global phenomenon. That same year, a report showed that most of Donald Trump's Facebook likes came from outside the United States and that one in every twenty-seven[17] Trump followers online was from the Philippines. When the influence economy took off, some shady companies that sold Twitter likes and followers had offices in the Philippines.[18] Political marketing by now had evolved into "networked disinformation." When Filipino politicians began to experiment with social media, many outsourced their operations to advertising and PR strategists who pulled together a spectrum of content and distribution accounts, from digital influencers to community fake account operators. They gave shape to the disparate elements already in the Philippines that operated in a gray area of law and ethics.[19] Supply met demand, and disinformation became big business.

The Philippines was also a fraud hub. By 2019, it was the global leader of online attacks,[20] both automated and human, followed distantly by the United States, Russia, the United Kingdom, and Indonesia. A report at the time pointed to three reasons: "sophisticated tools, cheap manual labor, and good economic incentives associated with online fraud." (Forty-three percent were human, i.e., not bots.) The Philippines also has a higher-than-average number of unlicensed software installations,[21] often seeding malware into PCs to turn them into botnet platforms for automated attacks.

Uncomfortable questions came up for the Filipino advertising community, as it soon would in nations all over the world: How many of them were "freelancing" in that gray area? How many were working with "influencers" around the world and in emerging markets now known as creators of fake accounts and likes? How were they defining the line between influence and fraud when working with multinational clients? The design of social media platforms encouraged all of that behavior, so the technology platforms were having a corrupting influence on the values of our younger generation, especially those roped into working in the industry.

And what about the politicians who betrayed their commitment to the public by exploiting what had once been a marketing tool and shamelessly and insidiously manipulating the public they allegedly served?

It was all about power and money.

This evolution in the Philippines had begun in 2014, when online fans began using social media to support their stars, and political operatives discovered the potential of this kind of engagement.

One day, we invited a dozen kids with big digital footprints to our office, none older than fifteen years, who were so powerful that Twitter had singled them out. What they did became known as the AlDub phenomenon.[22] AlDub was a play on the names of the Filipino actors Alden Richards and Maine "Yaya Dub" Mendoza, who appeared on a popular afternoon TV show about two lovers who never got to meet in person. Their fans began lobbying for the two to finally meet, to the point where their social media followings smashed Twitter's global record for the number of tweets about one subject. As the BBC noted, the previous record holder had been during FIFA's World Cup final in July 2014, when Germany had defeated Brazil.

The young fans had time to experiment and crack the code. Building fan groups helped create what were then the harmless precursors of what Facebook called "CIB"—"Coordinated, inauthentic behavior." They organized to artificially make hashtags trend higher, at times hijacking whatever else was trending. Those young people told us that all you had to do was organize people "to tweet seven thousand times per minute" to make a hashtag trend. The groups became so large and successful that it was only a matter of time before corporate marketing seized on their tactics.

Then fandom turned into politics.

Let me show you how easily those shifts happened through the experience of a young man I'll call Sam. In his early twenties, Sam, who was working for a friend of mine, came to the Rappler office in jeans and a tight shirt, his hair spiked with streaks of blue. He told us he was the one who had pushed Duterte's drug war to the national consciousness, helping move it from the eighth most important national concern to number one during the campaign period. He said he had helped a candidate win a presidential election.

"It made me happy to control people," he told us. "Some people now call it evil, but imagine, I'm like a god. I can make them do what I want them to do."

With boundless energy, he described how he had started creating pages when he was still in school, starting with an anonymous page that focused on romance. He had begun conversations by asking about people's hottest date or their worst breakup. He had grown one of his communities to more than 3 million followers. He was only fifteen years old when he began developing groups, tapping into what he thought were topics that appealed to Filipinos: one page was about joy, another about mental strength. About a year later, corporations began to ask him to mention their products. By the time he was twenty years old, he claimed to have at least 15 million followers across several platforms.

That was when he shifted from advertising to politics: he joined a team working for Duterte's campaign. He claimed he had built a series of Facebook groups in different cities using their local dialects. It had started innocently enough with pieces on tourist attractions and local news. Then every now and then he would drop in crime stories. The group had started sharing one story every day at peak traffic time. Then he and his friends would write comments that connected the crime to drugs. That was, in part, how Duterte's "drug war" became seen as something necessary in Philippine life.

That was the tactic Facebook didn't pay attention to. What we now call "astroturfing"—the fake bandwagon effect—however, was extremely efficient.

Replicate the story of Sam numerous times, and you'll see the evolution of Duterte's campaign machinery. Sam is today running his own digital company. He's traded in his boy-band look for a corporate suit, and he is offering his services to political candidates and corporations.

In 2016, Rappler began tracking people who shifted the discourse as Sam did and all of the networks of disinformation. Our research arm wanted to understand the phenomenon. We were one of the few media organizations doing so in the world, which was another reason I had been eager to tell the Facebook Singapore team what we had found.

I laid out how Rappler had charted three stages of the degradation of the online information ecosystem and political life in the Philippines. One was the early experimentation and buildup of campaign machinery in 2014 and 2015. The second was the commercialization of a new online black ops industry. The third was the consolidation of power at the top and the spread of political polarization across the country.

Chances are that you've seen some version of this if you live in a democracy. These phases have been enabled by global decisions and realities far from the Philippines; more than ever before, what's local is global, and global is local.

In the beginning, it was hard to know what was even happening. Since Rappler and I lived on social media, we felt the shifts more than we understood them. In the run-up to the 2016 election, we began seeing new distribution and messaging techniques for candidate Duterte on social media platforms. In one instance, his supporters created a Facebook page calling for the death of a student who had asked a question critical of Duterte.[23] That was a new form of inflammatory behavior, prompting our first editorial on this topic entitled "#AnimatED: Online Mob Creates Social Media Wasteland."[24] When we called the campaign team, they asked their supporters "to be civil, intelligent, decent, and compassionate."[25] Those were early days.

In that same election, Ferdinand "Bongbong" Marcos, Jr., the son of Ferdinand Marcos, was running for vice president.[26] We observed over social media a distinct push to change the history of his family's past, efforts to redefine and cleanse the Marcos family record. And we witnessed the strong presence of an "us-versus-them" worldview, which inspired anger and hate and helped polarize the electorate.

The second phase of degradation had to do with the commercialization of a new black ops industry that was capitalizing on an underground digital economy long operating in a legal gray zone. As early as 2014, before bots and fake accounts became notorious around the world, particularly in Ukraine, Rappler discovered information operations during the country's telecommunication wars. In a story we called "#SmartFREEInternet: Anatomy of a Black Ops Campaign on Twitter,"[27] we showed how a company could use three types of accounts to influence public perception.

The Philippine Long Distance Telephone Company and its mobile provider, Smart, were fighting for users with Globe Telecom and its own mobile subsidiary. Smart was running a promotional campaign on Twitter and Facebook using the hashtag #SmartFreeInternet. Rappler chronicled how a combination of bots and fake accounts had suddenly shut down the entire #SmartFreeInternet online campaign: when someone used the hashtag, it would signal to a bot or fake account to automatically message you something negative.

That drew on an old strategy popularized in the computer industry in the United States in the 1990s—mostly by computer companies like IBM and Microsoft targeting their competitors—known as "fear, uncertainty, and doubt," or FUD. The disinformation campaign spread negative information and lies to fuel fear. The conversation we mapped online reminded us of the Communist strategy "Surround the city from the countryside": it effectively cut off Smart's Twitter account from its targeted millennial audience. "Some corporations, interest groups, and governments are mobilizing fictitious social media resources at scale to disrupt other legitimate uses of these platforms," we wrote in the article. "Left unchecked, practices like this could turn a platform like Twitter into a wasteland, discouraging people from participating and limiting the potential power of the crowd for good."

And, indeed, just two years later, we saw FUD transfer to politics and propaganda. It shouldn't have been a surprise because the people who had experimented with it in 2014—such as Sam—were among the ones who turned to politics and rolled it out for Duterte in 2016.

I showed Ken, Clare, and Elizabeth how we had first discovered the shift to politics: by investigating a network that was attacking Rappler and ABS-CBN.

First, Chay and her team meticulously recorded the attackers' Facebook accounts, their "friends'" accounts, and the groups the accounts belonged to on a spreadsheet. One chart compiled all twenty-six accounts, along with what the accounts claimed were their "facts": where they worked, where they went to school, their jobs, where they lived. We took every column on that sheet and assigned a reporter to verify those details. Every single claim was a lie.

Those twenty-six accounts behaved differently than most users did: they belonged to more Facebook groups than they had actual friends. One example was the account of Mutya Bautista, who described herself as a "software analyst" at ABS-CBN. Bautista's public friends list showed that she had only seventeen friends, but she was a member of more than a hundred groups, including those campaigning for Ferdinand Marcos, Jr., overseas Filipino communities, and buy-and-sell groups. Those groups had members ranging from tens of thousands to hundreds of thousands.[28]

It took our team at least three months to manually count the reach of those individuals' messages in those public groups. They charted how one fake account on Facebook can reach 3 million to 4 million others,[29] proving the exponential reach of a lie. I believe Rappler was the first to quantify this.

I also showed the Singapore Facebook team how systematically those black ops players had weaponized social media by focusing their tactics according to demographics: the Philippines' tiny upper class, the middle class, and the mass base.[30] They had created content that would then be amplified through the distribution networks. Though Facebook was a key vector of distribution, the effort was across all social media platforms.

What we were seeing was a kind of asymmetrical warfare online, except in this case it was Goliath using the tactics of David; it was the platforms and larger powers using the surreptitious tactics of a rebel group. Anyone who stood up to the lies spreading over pro-Duterte and pro-Marcos disinformation networks was gaslit, or told they were crazy. What the bad guys were doing, they ascribed to the good guys.

The same process was happening in other democracies around the world. Facebook was becoming aware of that but felt it was in a bind. In the United States, more lies were being spread among far-right and alt-right groups on its platform, and Facebook had the data to prove it, but it did nothing (independent researchers would expose those cover-ups much later) for fear of alienating Republicans. That meant that the public, its users—the targets of those information operations—were left completely vulnerable, with few defenses available against what seemed like normal flows of information. Donald Trump flagrantly, delightedly lied all throughout his presidential campaign and into his presidency, and all of his lies took off through bottom-up social media operations similar to those in the Philippines. Both Trump and Duterte changed what their populaces thought and how they behaved.

We at Rappler began to think about how we could create a database to monitor our information ecosystem—a kind of Interpol for disinformation networks. We needed to build technology to understand the technology. We started automating data collection to see what kinds of content were spreading and which networks were spreading them. Mapping information was built into Rappler's DNA. In the beginning, we had been trying to answer this more positive question: How does an idea spread through communities to galvanize civic action? For example, by studying the formation of online communities, we tried to assess whether the Philippines had real political parties based on ideological lines. Now we got our answer: no, we didn't have real political parties based on ideology; we had personality-driven political parties.[31] Though the journalists knew that qualitatively, it was different to have data back it up.

Those were the origins of the database we called "Sharktank."[32] We used fact-checking to identify lies, then monitored which networks repeatedly shared the lies. We learned to organize the data so we could monitor public information cascades throughout our country. And we made all the information publicly available.

Over the coming years, as I stood up to the most powerful officials attacking us, people asked me how I found the courage.

"It's easy," I would often reply. "I have the facts."

I shared those discoveries with Ken, Clare, and Elizabeth at lunch, urging them to provide more of their own data to verify what we had found. Where did they think this could lead?

"You have to do something," I remember exclaiming, "because [if not] Trump could win."[33]

We all laughed because that didn't seem possible, even in August 2016.

By the end of our meeting, the others looked disturbed; I suspect it was because it was the first time they had dealt with anything like that and they didn't know what to think. Frankly, Rappler understood the internet and data better than they did. At the very least, though, I thought Facebook would want to make a statement about our findings. As an alpha partner of Facebook, I wanted it to stop the insidious manipulation we were seeing so I could report what had been happening and what the company had done to stop it. I was so alarmed at that point that I thought it was more important to fix what was wrong than to just do the story.

But after our meeting, I heard nothing back from Ken, Clare, and Elizabeth. I waited through the rest of August and September.

On Friday, September 2, 2016, at 10:00 p.m., an explosion hit a night market in Davao City, Duterte's hometown.[34] The bombing killed more than a dozen people and injured dozens more. Unfortunately, this kind of violence is not uncommon in the Philippines. But the new government's reaction marked a draconian change.

The morning after the explosion, Duterte declared a nationwide "state of lawlessness."[35] The justification for the declaration included Duterte's pet concern: illegal drugs. My thought bubble? Preposterous. "These are extraordinary times," Duterte said. ". . . There is a crisis in this country involving drugs, extrajudicial killings, and there seems to be [an] environment of lawlessness, lawless violence."

He stopped short of declaring martial law or a nationwide curfew, but he did call for a greater presence of soldiers all over the country. The government set up more checkpoints. Online, Duterte supporters began to justify the declaration. Public support was necessary because in the past, bombings like this rarely brought such strong measures.

When I sat down to breakfast that Saturday morning, I turned on my computer and was alarmed by what I saw. I immediately called our social media head, Stacy de Jesus, and our head of research, Gemma Mendoza. Within an hour, I called my cofounders and alerted them. I had never seen anything like this before.

A nearly six-month-old article, "Man with Bomb Nabbed at Davao Checkpoint," was our number one story in real-time Google Analytics.[36]

Boy Hugot
19 hrs · 🌐

Buti nga sa kanya. 😞🤬💬

Man with bomb nabbed at Davao checkpoint
The suspect claims he carried the improvised explosive device in his backpack upon orders of the New People's Army
WWW.RAPPLER.COM

This Facebook account was the first to tweet this old article in the first information operation discovered by Rappler in 2016.

Originally published on March 26, 2016, five months before the bombing, it had now been trending at number one for more than twenty-four hours. It would stay in the top ten stories for more than forty-eight hours.

That was the first time we became aware of a real-time, clumsily executed information operation to manipulate public opinion. Anonymous and fake accounts, meme pages, Duterte fan pages, and dubious websites[37] worked hand in hand to make it appear that our "man with bomb" story from March was a breaking-news story, seeming to justify Duterte's declaration of a state of lawlessness. Filipinos were duped into sharing a lie.

That was how the state's "coordinated, inauthentic behavior," as Facebook would belatedly call such operations, began in the Philippines. It was also the opening salvo in what would be open online warfare meant to tear down the public's trust in the independent media, and specifically Rappler.

The old story had generated 32 page views (largely from Google search), but the day after the information operation began, the story catapulted to more than 105,000 page views—an exponential increase of more than 3,281 times!

Perhaps the operation would have worked even better if the operators had not inadvertently alerted us. Some users shared the link directly, and the websites that had repurposed that old story linked back to Rappler. That signaled that the creators were either former journalists or editors with attribution practices ingrained into their habits. That also stopped as soon as Rappler published what we had found.

Three key websites took the entire Rappler story and republished it out of context and without our permission: News Trend PH (newstrendph .com), SocialNewsph.com, and Pinoy Tribune (pinoytribune.com), all of which were created days after President Duterte took his oath of office. All three were taken down soon after we exposed the operation.

Though some Facebook pages shared the Rappler story directly, several pro-Duterte pages, among them Duterte Warrior (@dutertewarrior),

President Duterte 2016 (@DigongDuterte2016), and Byaheng Duterte, shared the repurposed web pages with the old, dated story within minutes of one another and with the same alarmist captions. All three generated hundreds of comments and thousands of shares and likes.

The operators manually altered the date and time stamps of their posts, apparently to make it appear that they had been published on Thursday, September 1, earlier than the bombing.

To warn the public that that old story was being used to mislead perception, we decided to publish a warning post on our Rappler Facebook page. "Rappler asks our community to verify sources of information, and stop sharing the dated article," we posted on Facebook on Sunday, September 4, 2016, at 6:18 p.m. "If you see it on your feed, please let others know this happened on March 25, 2016." We also added a short editor's note on the story page on our website, which would be the first sentence any reader would see: "This story was published on March 26, 2016."

But we decided not to do a full story about the operation on Rappler because we didn't want to amplify the disinformation. In general, we struggled early on with how to balance getting out the information about manipulation, correcting the disinformation, and trying to limit its reach. We became better at this in the coming years, deciding that radical transparency, including publishing full geeky maps of the accounts taking part in disinformation networks, was the way to go: give as much information as the most detail-oriented reader might want.

We continued our investigation of the case for many years.[38] We found that the "man with a bomb" online network was connected to the core manpower of the Duterte campaign. In August 2021, I discovered that the URL of one of the three key disinformation websites, newstrendph.com, had disappeared. In its place was a Chinese online betting site, linked to a controversial Duterte initiative, the Philippine Offshore Gaming Operation (POGO),[39] which suggests that those three pro-Duterte websites might have been connected to Chinese information operations. The "man with a bomb" story led to the Duterte administration's links to China, Duterte's new ally.

I also shared all the information we had with Ken, Clare, and Elizabeth. It was clear that not only was Facebook ill prepared to handle those types of operations, but even when confronted with the data and the facts, its executives didn't entirely grasp what was happening on their platform. I have no doubt that they ran our case "up the flagpole," but nothing was done in those early days. Timely action could have maintained a trust system that Facebook instead exploited; early action could have prevented the anarchy and chaos that encouraged and rewarded information operations in the coming years.

Months later, our Facebook post, which had warned our followers about that attempt to mislead the public, was taken down by Facebook itself. Our social media head, Stacy, sent me Facebook's reason for deleting our post: "This message was removed because it includes a link that goes against our community standards."[40]

When we complained, Facebook restored the post, but when I looked again a few months later, it had been taken down again. So we complained again. There was no response.

As of August 1, 2021, the link was dead. It's almost as though Facebook didn't want its users to know it had ever happened.

———

That was the beginning of my growing disillusionment with the company that had initially opened up such exciting possibilities for Rappler. Today, I'm beyond disillusioned. I believe that Facebook represents one of the gravest threats to democracies around the world, and I am amazed that we have allowed our freedoms to be taken away by technology companies' greed for growth and revenues. Tech sucked up our personal experiences and data, organized it with artificial intelligence, manipulated us with it, and created behavior at a scale that brought out the worst in humanity. Harvard Business School professor emerita Shoshana Zuboff called this exploitative business model "surveillance capitalism."[41] We all let it happen.[42]

Facebook today favors moneymaking over public safety. Its company lobbying efforts enable it to bend and break the often lax content rules it sets itself. It rarely prioritizes safeguards for the nearly 3 billion users on its platform, which in 2020 had revenues of $85.9 billion. In 2021, the revenues were $120.18 billion, an increase of 40 percent.

It was Sheryl Sandberg[43] who brought surveillance capitalism[44]—which treats human data as commodities to be bartered and traded in markets[45]—from Google to Facebook after Mark Zuckerberg hired her as his second in command in 2008. Sandberg created and fine-tuned Facebook's business model, as well as ran its policy and integrity groups. What happens if a media organization needs to publish something that goes against the company's interests? In a news organization, there's a metaphorical wall between the head of editorial and the head of business because of that inherent conflict of interest; the editorial head always ends up fighting the business head, which was how old media struggled but survived. At Facebook, Sheryl collapsed the two functions together, meaning that every decision was politicized. Every decision became about making a profit and protecting Facebook's interests.

In 2011, Sheryl hired Joel Kaplan, a former Harvard classmate, to lobby and court the conservatives and the American Right. By 2014, he was Facebook's vice president of global public policy, running government relations and lobbying efforts in Washington, DC, along with determining its content moderation policy around the world. Other companies, including Google and Twitter, keep public policy and lobbying efforts separate from the teams that create and implement content rules. Several employees who resigned from Facebook demanded that those teams be separated, but to this day, that hasn't been done. An internal Facebook memo, "Political Influences on Content Policy," stated that Kaplan's group "regularly protects powerful constituencies," starting with then candidate Donald Trump in 2015.[46]

This is partly why the company has consistently allowed politicians to lie, why it hid the truth, then blunted its announcement, about Russian disinformation and information operations, and why it allowed extremist groups to grow and seed metanarratives that led to its wake-up call: the violence on Capitol Hill on January 6, 2021, when Donald Trump exhorted thousands of Americans to attack the US Capitol building in protest against his election loss. That was when Silicon Valley's sins came home to roost.[47] Recent surveys show that up to 40 percent of Americans still believe that Trump won, including 10 percent of Democrats.[48]

There are three assumptions implicit in everything Facebook says and does: first, that more information is better; second, that faster information is better; third, that the bad—lies, hate speech, conspiracy theories, disinformation, targeted attacks, information operations—should be tolerated in service of Facebook's larger goals. All three ideas are great for Facebook because they mean that the company makes more money, but none of them is better for users and the public sphere.

The dangers of "more" and "faster" have led us to dystopia: the suffocation of our minds by junk, a loss of clarity of thought and a lack of concentration, and the empowerment of individual over collective thinking. There is a reason why executives and leaders needing to make complex decisions ask for executive summaries: atomized information often leads nowhere. Even worse, when supercharged with emotion, it becomes a fire hose that destroys rational decision making.

Lies repeated over and over become facts in this online ecosystem. As a journalist, I know that we are only as good as our last story and any error must be accounted for, fixed, and publicly announced. That's why we have correction pages. We report the facts because that creates our shared reality. The splintering of life into billions of Truman Shows began with Facebook's idea of separate, individual feeds: that your "news" feed is different from mine and if you see a lie about you, you can just "mute" it—yet another idea introduced that was good for its business while concealing its social impact. The reality is that lies, left unchecked, create and sustain flat-earthers, QAnon, Stop the Steal, and a rabid anti-vax movement, to mention a handful of the most noxious conspiracy theories.

Mark Zuckerberg's decisions prioritizing company over country,[49] of growth above all, added to the fact that lies are prioritized over facts, and have destroyed the information and trust ecosystem that gave birth to Facebook. When he accepts 1 percent disinformation on his site, it's like saying it's okay[50] to have 1 percent virus in a population unchecked. Both can take over, and if not eradicated, they can ultimately kill.

I have tried to understand how Zuckerberg could come to those decisions, and the best that I can see is that it's baked into the iterative process of software development. When you build technology products, there's a prioritization process. Like when building a house, you have to break it down into the elements: nails, cement, tools, wood. Then you build in phases, what tech calls "agile development," a breakdown into tasks that allows quick shifts depending on what has been accomplished.

So how do you prioritize what to build? As you saw with Rappler, what you choose to prioritize reflects your values and your goals.

In Facebook's case, one of Mark's choices early on reflected what a young man would think but not what an experienced responsible corporate executive would do, like giving every Facebook engineer unlimited access to users' data. In that upside-down world, that became a Facebook recruitment tool; he offered tech engineers a workplace without bureaucracy so that engineers could test and build with user data, unimpeded by the real-world concerns of other companies.

By the time someone[51] actually looked at what that choice enabled and brought it to Mark's attention in September 2015, a total of 16,744 Facebook employees[52] had access to our personal data—from our posts to the way the company's advertising algorithms cluster us (based on our politics, for example) to the messages we send to our exact location at any given moment (which, in many people's cases, could be a security concern). Some Facebook engineers even tracked their dates and love interests.[53]

Another harmful decision that has been made by every social media platform is to grow its business through algorithms that recommend friends of friends. Executives at those companies have realized that that's the most efficient way through what's called A/B testing, which tests the impact on users of any two things on the internet—real-time experimentation on real human beings, treating us like Pavlov's dogs. We click and grow our individual networks, and by extension the platform's, more when we're served friends of friends.

So in 2016, after Rodrigo Duterte used Facebook to help him get elected, this "friends of friends" algorithm, along with his divisive us-against-them rhetoric, further radicalized Filipinos. If you were pro-Duterte and you were getting recommendations for posts from friends of friends, you moved farther right. If you were anti-Duterte, you moved farther left. And over time, the chasm between the two sides grew. This has been a global theme; substitute Narendra Modi, Jair Bolsonaro, or Donald Trump for Duterte, and you get the point.

Algorithms serve up content that radicalizes us. If you click on a borderline conspiracy theory, for example, the next content a platform serves you is even more radical because it keeps you scrolling.[54] Groups like QAnon spread from the darkest corners of the web onto Twitter and Facebook (and have links to the Philippines), until they were suspended and banned.[55] It took years to get to that ban. In the meantime, what happened to the people who were swayed to believe in the conspiracy theories? What about their cognitive bias, which may lead them to see the bans as yet another evidence of a conspiracy?

Those technical decisions fed the surveillance capitalism model: increasing the companies' growth with friends-of-friends recommendations and increasing the time you spend on a site by serving you ever more emotive, radical, and extremist content. The model bypassed our rational, logical mind, what Daniel Kahneman called "thinking slow,"[56] and instead tapped our "thinking fast" brain: quick, instinctive, largely unconscious emotional reactions lodged in the amygdala. The late biologist E. O. Wilson called these our "paleolithic emotions." If you read something that makes you emotional and prone to share or act, slow down; think slow, not fast.

Our ability to slow down, though, is limited because over time, Facebook knowingly created a disastrous and extremely harmful feedback loop: the more time you spend on Facebook, the more data the company gets to trick you into spending more time on Facebook. Your emotions, triggered by hormones and neurotransmitters like dopamine, are elevated; you feel as though you're doing something, but in the end, it becomes a time suck, siphoning your energy away from real-world action and accomplishments. Think the Matrix, powered by human batteries. And what were we doing? Performing in our own Truman Shows.

This is only one of the numerous side effects of algorithms created by big-data companies; they often build in the biases of whoever coded them—largely young white men—and the data sets they're fed. This has had adverse effects on education, finance, crime reporting, and democracy in the United States; US platforms like Facebook and YouTube spread those biases to the rest of the world.

Facebook is changing our behavior, and it is using its global user database as a real-time laboratory. It changes individuals and societies, just as the sociological experiments on group dynamics showed. On a large scale, this kind of behavioral change exerted by large groups is emergent behavior, and no one can predict the organic change from the individual parts. I saw that happen slowly in the real world in Indonesia while studying the way the radical ideology of terrorism spreads. Today, online, it's on steroids, crippling societies by destroying trust globally.

Comparisons to the lies and tactics of Big Tobacco in the twentieth century are wholly justified. Facebook, and the politicians benefiting from it, know full well the harms they are unleashing on the public. Facebook is the world's largest distributor of news, yet studies have shown that on social media, lies laced with anger and hatred spread faster and farther than facts.[57] The very platforms that now deliver the news to you are biased against facts, biased against journalists. They are, by design, dividing us and radicalizing us—because spreading anger and hatred is better for Facebook's business.

In the United States, the surge in extremism has become a full-blown crisis. The United Kingdom and Europe are still reeling from Brexit, the Syrian refugee crisis, and the rise of right-wing nationalism. Similar experiences have been replicated in Brazil, where social media, largely YouTube, moved Jair Bolsonaro and his supporters into the mainstream. In Hungary, Viktor Orbán's savvy promotion of anti-migrant toughness has enraptured voters. In India, the world's largest democracy has fallen prey to the ugly Bharatiya Janata Party (BJP) machinery of Narendra Modi. Everywhere in the world, societies are being fed a steady diet of online violence that turns into real-world violence. Versions of white replacement theory are sparking mass shootings from Norway to New Zealand to the United States, powering the rise of "us against them" or, in a word, fascism.

This is anger and hatred that coalesce into moral outrage that then turns into mob rule.

In 2016, Rappler launched a #NoPlaceForHate campaign[58] to try to alert and protect the public we served by introducing more aggressive comment moderation standards. "We have zero tolerance for comments that curse, trash, degrade, humiliate and intimidate," we wrote on Rappler and on all our social media accounts. ". . . Freedom of speech does not mean license to smear reputation and ruin credibility. . . . Freedom of speech is the recognition of the right of anyone to speak his or her mind, and to express a contrary view without being objectionable. We are reclaiming our space. . . . No one should be afraid to write or speak what he or she thinks."[59]

This is the power Facebook should have exercised. The world would be so different today if Mark Zuckerberg had not stuck to his ignorant, self-serving interpretation of US Supreme Court justice Louis D. Brandeis's aphorism that the way to counter hate speech is more speech.[60] Brandeis said those words in 1927, long before the time of abundance, the time of Facebook, when a lie can now be delivered a million times over. His formulation also worked only if there is something of a level playing field, not what Facebook algorithms created. The company's choices gave a bullhorn to hate speech, disinformation, and conspiracy theories—emotive content that keeps you on site and scrolling, bringing in more revenues for the platform. If Facebook had taken its gatekeeping responsibilities as seriously as the journalists they took them away from, the world would be in a far better place today.

Faced with the same decision at Rappler, alarmed by the information operations designed to justify the drug war and incite hate that were dividing our world into "us against them," we acted quickly. Our course of action was simple if we wanted to protect our users, the public sphere, and democratic debate.

We saw how the comment threads were being controlled by Duterte supporters spewing hate and attacking anyone questioning the drug war. A few users fought back, but over time, most real people chose silence. So the attacks succeeded, and the narrative that won followed Duterte's arguments for killing, dulling the public reaction to the dead bodies dumped on sidewalks every night and creating a bandwagon effect for more killings. My last straw was when five-year-old Danica May Garcia was shot and killed coming out of her bathroom in her home during a police drug operation that targeted her grandfather.[61]

That Filipinos would condone and even support killing drug addicts and pushers is shocking to me because the Philippines was one of the first signatories of the United Nations' Universal Declaration of Human Rights. I didn't think our values had changed.

The images of dead and tortured Filipinos began gaining worldwide attention. For those of us living in the country, a sense of terror seemed to grow every day. Rappler decided to publish a series on the three-part weaponization of the internet. I wrote two parts,[62] and Chay wrote the third.[63] Like the discovery of the "man with a bomb" information operation, it was all new territory. We could see what was happening, connect the dots, but we didn't yet know why. We had to find words to describe what we were living through.

I sent one last email to Elizabeth, Clare, and Ken, asking for a statement.

Before we published the series, Glenda and I ran the stories by our board and received their full approval. We would roll out the series starting October 3, 2016. I had no idea what exposing the weaponization of the internet would mean for me and Rappler; no one then could have thought that the groundbreaking series would lead to criminal charges against all of us.

But I have no regrets. I would do it all over again.

Chapter 8

How the Rule of Law Crumbled from Within

Silence Is Complicity

Mark and I on the sidelines of the F8 conference in San Jose, California, April 19, 2017. (*Photo courtesy of Facebook*)

I t was the day after my birthday, October 3, 2016. Silence from Facebook. Nevertheless, we were resolved to publish the first part of the series on the weaponization of the internet that day.

I spent the morning putting the finishing touches on the pieces.[1] I went over the data, starting with our forensic investigation of the "man with a bomb" story. Then I included the viral picture of a dead girl that at the time had been shared by Duterte's campaign spokesman, Peter

Tiu Laviña, perhaps as a way of showing why drug dealers should be killed. He had implied that the dead girl was Filipino, but the photo had actually come from Brazil—another incendiary lie.

I reviewed my introductory piece for the series one last time. In it, I argued that the government's anti-democratic "death by a thousand cuts" strategy was using the strength of the internet and exploiting social media's algorithms to sow confusion and doubt. Our series was intended to take apart this new phenomenon: the paid propaganda taking over social media, the weaknesses of the new, easily exploitable information ecosystem, and their impact on human behavior. We also detailed a network of the twenty-six fake accounts on Facebook that had ultimately influenced at least 3 million other accounts.

Our office had an open floor plan. There was a center bridge—a circular raised command deck à la *Star Trek*—for the folks on editor duty. The people they managed sat at desks that spread from the bridge like sun rays. Clusters of large TVs hung on some of the walls, and more meeting rooms and offices, all separated by glass, which was usually covered in multicolored notes, messages, charts, and numbers that Rapplers had scrawled during brainstorming sessions, took up the rest of the loftlike industrial space. Around one corner were the *manang*s' and managers' desks, with my office farthest in the back, surrounded by windows on one side and sheathed in glass walls on the other, on which I also scrawled numbers and dates. Sitting on the other side of the glass were Glenda and Chay; Beth sat on the other side of the newsroom, overlooking our studio and control room. The newsroom thrummed with energy. Plus, I had just finished three Coke Zeros.

I walked to Chay's desk and started reading over her shoulder. After she finished, she looked at me. We had done that at least three times now.

"It's good," she said and moved her cursor over the final box. "Ready?"

"Go!" I said, and she clicked and published.

It was 7:00 p.m. I ran to the bridge, where our social media head was working, along with the editors on duty. "Stacy, it's out. Please share?"

"Okay," she said and pulled up the just-published piece, scrolling through it. She posted it on our internal Facebook page and Slack, alerting other Rapplers.

"We'll megashare!" she said as her fingers quickly typed alerts and prepared Rappler's post of the story to go out on our social media feeds. "Megashare" had been our call to action since 2012, when Rappler's distribution numbers had depended on the networks of our original twelve employees.

I noticed that Stacy was dressed up. "Hey, you look nice! What's the occasion?" I asked.

"I was depressed, so I dressed up," she replied, laughing.

"Is it the attacks?" I asked. Stacy was handling our #NoPlaceForHate campaign. Launched to stop the chilling effect of attacks on our page, it had opened a Pandora's box of further attacks that we hadn't anticipated. We understood the innate rhythm of organic sharing because we lived on Facebook. But what was happening this time was different.

"They're so fast, Maria," she replied, flipping tabs to show me how she was moderating our Facebook page. "We post something, and within seconds, they're commenting—but very simple and repetitive." She showed me several posts and the barrage of pro-Duterte comments that had arrived seconds after Rappler had posted.

"Do you think they're using bots?" I asked. "Maybe they have a bot alert and then the first posts are programmed?" That made sense: when Duterte's name is mentioned in any post, they could have set up an automated response, then followed up with more responses by their "keyboard warriors."[2] "But that's way more sophisticated than where they were."

I thought back to a month earlier, when Rappler had conducted its final interview with outgoing president Benigno Aquino[3] in the presidential palace. After we had finished, Aquino had pulled me aside. "These attacks," he had asked quietly, "they come so fast. Are they real?"

"I think so, Mr. President. They're real," I'd responded.

In fact, Nic Gabunada, Duterte's social media campaign manager, later described to us how he had started the campaign's online army with five hundred volunteers organized geographically into four clusters: the main islands of Luzon, Visayas, and Mindanao and the OFWs, referring to the 10 million to 12 million overseas Filipino workers.[4] Nic, a former top media and advertising executive, would become the first private individual in the world whom Facebook exposed and took down for "coordinated inauthentic behavior."[5]

I had initially dismissed Aquino's comment about the speed of the online attacks. Now that it was happening to us, I began to understand what he had been trying to tell me; you don't really know the extent and impact of scale until you're attacked.

Like the difference between Big Data and an Excel worksheet, the volume and frequency make the attacks something completely new, allowing only the target to see the pattern and at first only intuitively. The impact of the attacks at first is psychological, something also only the target feels—uncertainty and fear. The second is the impression it leaves on the audience, the impact of "astroturfing," as "Sam" had done during Duterte's campaign for his drug war, a fake bandwagon effect that shifts public perception of an issue or problem. The tactics, in fact, were evolving with each day.

We wanted to see the government and public reaction to the first piece in our series before we published the second and third parts. By the end of the week, we published part two, "How Facebook Algorithms Impact Democracy,"[6] which highlighted the case of a pro-Duterte campaigner named Mocha Uson, and part three, "Fake Accounts, Manufactured Reality on Social Media."[7]

It was the first time anywhere in the world, including the United States, that data and anecdotal evidence had been marshaled to show Facebook's corrosive effects on democracy.

I don't think the government officials knew what to make of the first piece. Usually, they took their time to process and formulate a response, much as they had with the "man with a bomb" incident. So, perhaps naively, we prepared for a straightforward government response, as had happened in the past, before Duterte. After all, I thought, they couldn't argue against the facts and the data. I assumed that the government would admit its role and curb its online army, or "the bloggers," as it called them.

What I didn't know was that the government had been developing a new strategy for dealing with facts and journalistic exposés. It needed to, because the Philippine news media was portraying its sinister drug war for what it was: systematic murder.

Every night since the June 2016 election, an average of thirty-three dead bodies had been found on the streets and in the poor neighborhoods of Manila.[8] Several news organizations began publishing lists of victims. The top newspaper, the *Philippine Daily Inquirer*, had started a page titled "The Kill List";[9] its first entries appeared just hours after Duterte took his oath of office. ABS-CBN also published an interactive map of the killings.[10]

Rappler was among the first to publish deep profiles of the people killed: "The Impunity Series"[11] gave names and faces to the numbers and detailed the police involvement in the killings. The dead were usually from Manila's most benighted neighborhoods; many were teenagers and kids. We carefully tracked the growing death toll and how the police tried to change the numbers. We made the drug war—in reality, a war against the poor[12]—our focus.

All three news groups would be targeted in the coming months by President Duterte himself. Since taking office, he had appointed nearly six thousand government employees, chosen, he himself said, because of their loyalty, not their competence. They became the foot soldiers in his drug war, which added to the general atmosphere of impunity. Duterte's men and women know that they could commit corrupt acts, whether financial or legal. They could be physically abusive, even murderous, and get away with it. Duterte assured them all immunity. "Pardon given to Rodrigo Duterte for the crime of multiple murder," he once said, "signed Rodrigo Duterte."[13]

When he had been mayor of Davao, Duterte had ruled with the force of his personality, giving haphazard directions in a weekly radio and television program. He replicated that modus operandi when he moved to Manila. Mass communication, in fact, was at the center of his leadership style, and he embraced terror-inducing and violent rhetoric: "Hitler massacred three million Jews," he once said. "Now, there is three million drug addicts. I'd be happy to slaughter them." His language was false (Hitler murdered 6 million Jews, and the presence of 3 million drug addicts in the Philippines was unlikely) and incendiary, but his statement took off on Facebook and social media.

During the crucial transition period after Duterte took office, Mocha Uson, an entertainer, became the center of the government's offensive. Uson's popular Facebook page at first had consisted mostly of sex advice and sessions in the bedroom with her all-girl band, the Mocha Girls. It soon exploded with venom against journalists and anyone else questioning the Duterte administration. Her daily posts featured conspiracy theories about coup attempts and CIA plots. The Duterte campaign seized on her social media power and even later appointed her as a government official.

The explosive growth of Uson's page, as well as her evolution from sexy dancer to political blogger, propagandist, and government official, was a prime example of how Facebook's algorithms enabled the government, already powerful with state resources, to further abuse its power.

In August 2016, Uson had introduced a meme with the term

"presstitute"[14]—a portmanteau of *press* and *prostitute*—to describe the mainstream media's "negativity." Her narrative was clear: journalists were corrupt. They would write whatever they were paid to write by their funders—people who wanted to take down Duterte. The state narrative, which spread to the general populace, became "us against them," but for a while the journalists had no idea what was happening. As the seeded metanarrative went, the media were "biased"[15] against Duterte, who was often painted as the underdog challenging the elites and oligarchs in "imperial Manila." Like the social media–generated attacks on the fracture lines of American society during the 2016 election, particularly on gender, race, and identity, the attacks in the Philippines were fundamental ones: rich versus poor, rural versus urban, elites versus everyman.

The data mapping in Sharktank, our internal database, showed a surge between 2016 and March 2018 of the use of certain words: *bayaran*, or "corrupt"; *dilawan*, or the Aquino family's yellow color, which was portrayed as elite and out of touch with the lives of ordinary Filipinos; and "bias." At its peak, Uson and others' online bromides deployed the word "bias" in thirty thousand comments in a single day. Within the groups and pages Rappler monitored, nearly fifty thousand posts and more than 1.8 million comments used the term *bayaran*.

Rappler was already being targeted because of our #NoPlaceForHate campaign, but the reaction to our weaponization of the internet series showed me how much our information ecosystem had been fundamentally corrupted. I was beginning to grasp that journalists were no longer the gatekeepers of facts and information. The new gatekeepers, the technology platforms, had put into place rules that give the equivalent of nuclear weapons to digital populists and authoritarians to turn our society and democracy—all around the world—upside down.

After we released the weaponization of the internet series, the attacks on Rappler began in full force. On October 4, 2016, they came as first a trickle, then a flurry, then a tsunami when, on October 8, Thinking Pinoy, the Facebook page of a blogger named RJ Nieto, began calling for Duterte supporters to #UnfollowRappler.

A day later on Sunday, October 9, around 9:00 p.m., Mocha Uson joined in, releasing an hourlong Facebook Live video full of propaganda about the Duterte administration's first hundred days and how its "enemies were working 24/7" to bring Duterte down. The title of her post was "My reaction to Rappler's accusations about me," but it expanded into a rant about "mainstream media," Rappler, and myself, full of lies, distortions, and innuendo. It's unclear whether those were intentional, plain ignorance, or a combination of both.

"While we are quietly working," Uson said in Filipino, "there are those who attack us. I no longer read mainstream media."

In the meantime, the number of comments on her Facebook page surged, partly fueled by fake accounts. (Facebook would take them down two years later.) That night, Duterte's social media onslaught accomplished what the designers of the propaganda machine wanted to portray: a groundswell of support for Uson and for Duterte, also aimed like a machine gun at me and Rappler.

Five years later, after US citizens stormed the Capitol building, terms for such behavior would at last become standardized after Facebook finally rolled out a policy on "brigading," or coordinated abusive online behavior. The attacks break down into several categories. There are "sock puppets," or fake accounts that attack or praise; "mass reporting," or organizing to negatively impact the targeted account; and "astroturfing," or fake posts or lies designed to look like grassroots support or interest.

"They want to take out Duterte," Uson alleged on Facebook. "All we are asking for is fair news coverage. They drown out what's important in negativity. . . . I guess our entire nation wouldn't go to social media if journalists were doing their jobs. They just don't appreciate the good things Duterte is doing."[16]

"Rappler, were you hurt when we said 'presstitutes'?" Uson asked. "Why are you sensitive? Maybe you shouldn't have focused on it—unless, of course, you are presstitutes." That was an example of the false, often incoherent conclusions she jumped to—as well as a redeployment of online misogyny—but the simplification was exactly what her audience wanted. She distilled the data and questions of the three-part series into one sentence. She was playing to the egos of both those watching and those fueling conspiracy theories.

"Maria Ressa said we are bots, trolls, fake profiles. . . . Are you guys fake?" she asked her online audience. ". . . She called us 'pro-Duterte propaganda'—now it's propaganda to be nationalistic! And if you're a patriot, you're a troll. Isn't Duterte the president? Shouldn't we show him respect?"

With those dog whistles, she rallied supporters against me and Rappler, quoting the repeated attacks of Nieto, aka Thinking Pinoy, who was posting lies about Rappler as many as five times a day—all of his attacks amplified by Facebook. What Facebook gave one individual's posts or one entertainer's videos was the high level of distribution that had once belonged to television broadcasters. Rappler and I were defenseless. Duterte's propaganda machine was taking advantage of Facebook's tyrannical algorithmic design.

Mocha Uson's post on March 12, 2018, read "Maria Ressa, Rappler, your news shouldn't only be gossip." In it, she compared her Facebook page and that of Thinking Pinoy with Rappler's. The Tagalog in red reads, "Because no one believes in you, you call the followers of other pages 'fake account.' Don't be bitter, and stop blaming Facebook for your low engagement."

Operatives like Uson boasted that they were beating mainstream media traffic; they even posted their page view metrics. In the process, they tore down the credibility of journalists and news organizations.

There's a word in Filipino that describes this action: *talangkaan*, the behavior of crabs crawling on top of one another to get to the top. Duterte's minions were changing our information ecosystem in plain sight. That continued nonstop for years before Facebook took any action.

This is how information operations work everywhere. Lies that are repeated over and over exponentially change the public's perception of an issue, something that world powers have always known about propaganda but that gained new meaning and pitch in the age of social media. As Facebook then reached more than 3 billion people around the globe, world leaders found a way to play power politics through individual social media users.

What happened in the Philippines in 2016 is a microcosm of every information operation launched in democratic countries around the world. The combination of bots, fake accounts, and content creators (real people like Mocha Uson) infected real people like a virus, but often those unsuspecting citizens didn't even know they had been infected. Looking back, we can see that the metanarrative of a tragic event had always been seeded years earlier through toxic internet narratives. In my case, Uson and Nieto seeded "Journalist equals criminal" and "Arrest Maria Ressa" years before my first arrest; they softened public acceptance for legal cases that later became a reality.

Mocha Uson's live video attacking me and Rappler contained a perfect mix of interactivity, vitriol, "us against them," and easy engagement—exactly what Facebook algorithms reward. Nearly five years later, that attack video remains on Facebook, with more than 3,100 shares, 12,000 comments, and 497,000 views.

The personal attacks against me came in her comments section, the worst posted by men, or by accounts pretending to be men. This is behavior that has been repeated everywhere Facebook operates around the world; the platform actually rewards behavior that women and other vulnerable groups globally have spent decades fighting. All of it was something we flagged early on for Facebook because it was in the comments where we saw a lot of astroturfing happen. Typically, Mark Zuckerberg didn't take the comments into account when he claimed that disinformation composed only 1 percent of the site.

The attacks on my own Facebook page also increased. I tried to respond, but my feed was inundated with comments. Midway through Uson's live broadcast against me, I started counting the attacks. By midnight, I had reached an average of ninety hate messages per hour. I was angry, and my heart was pounding. I stood up and walked around my apartment, trying to understand what was happening, debating how exactly I should try to fight back.

I couldn't respond to the triumvirate content creators, Uson, RJ Nieto, and Sass Sasot, a Filipina trans student living in the Netherlands who wrote a blog called "For the Motherland." Responding would legitimize their rants to the demographics they catered to, and even then I knew I wouldn't reach their audiences. Yet I saw real people being persuaded to change their minds about my long journalistic track record, which no longer seemed to matter. It was like drunk frat boys coming together, and just like that, the credibility I had built up during my entire career crumbled. I watched it happen in real time.

So I did what I had learned to do while in war zones: I took five deep breaths in a row, pushed my emotion to the pit of my stomach, and decided on a course of action. I decided to take the abuse that was sent to me directly, which only I could see on my Facebook page, and post it publicly for everyone to see.[17]

I would document the attacks.

That night, the impact of Uson and company's campaign on Rappler's Facebook page was immediate: twenty thousand accounts unfollowed Rappler, the highest ever in a single day, and the attrition continued in the coming days. In a month, we lost 44 percent of our weekly reach and 1 percent of our total followers, a little more than fifty

 **Peter Ian Tabar**
View Profile

8:30PM

die stupid bitch! If you don't like our president, leave our country!!!! WHORE!!!!!!

This was one of the many attacks that came via private message in the days following the publication of the propaganda war series. I posted this, along with other "creative attacks," after midnight, October 10, 2016. Peter Ian Tabar is a medical doctor who admitted that he used to believe in me but now he "hates" me.

thousand accounts. It was, in essence, a new and insidious form of state censorship that was taking advantage of Facebook's algorithms. Twenty-five percent of our page views from Facebook disappeared. My credibility, built story by story over the past thirty years, was trashed, even as public trust in Rappler, our fledgling media company, was being tested.

No self-respecting journalist would do what those so-called bloggers did to take over our country's information ecosystem, which meant that in the beginning, most journalists like me chose not to respond to what seemed like kindergarten antics and bullying. Then the viciousness began, followed by government attacks. It was only in retrospect that the cycle became clear. We had standards and ethics manuals; we upheld freedom of expression. We were fighting a war in a new world using old-world paradigms, thinking that doing the journalism was enough.

We didn't grasp that Facebook, the website that millions of people still believed fostered community and connection, had supplanted traditional media. We didn't realize that those "content creators," with their crude, sometimes lewd, manipulative posts, now passed as political pundits, even as journalists reporting "facts." Those accounts were at the core of a propaganda machine that bullied and harassed its targets and incited its followers to violence. The same thing happened with Stop the Steal in the United States, anti-Muslim riots in India, the invasion of Ukraine by Russia, and many other events around the world. Facebook didn't only provide a platform for those propagandists' speech or even only enable them; in fact, it gave them preferential treatment because anger is the contagious currency of Facebook's profit machine. Only anger, outrage, and fear led to greater numbers of people using Facebook more times a day. Violence has made Facebook rich.

It was only in 2018, after the Cambridge Analytica scandal, the Brexit referendum, the 2016 elections of Donald Trump and Rodrigo Duterte, and more, that Facebook began high-profile post takedowns in the Philippines and around the world, which included limiting the reach of Mocha Uson's page and taking down the network built by Duterte's social media campaign manager.

By then, of course, it was too late.

The year 2016 had been the target year for Rappler to break even—about half the time of a traditional news group—and we were on track to do that—until we published our weaponization of the internet series and Duterte's propaganda machine tore us apart.

For two years, Facebook largely ignored the data we gave it, because we were in the Philippines and not the United States. Those years, with information operations functioning with impunity around the world, were characterized by systematic, large-scale manipulation that distorted facts, changed the public narrative, and destroyed public trust.

Within six months of Duterte's taking power in the Philippines, the checks and balances of the three branches of government—executive, legislative, and judicial—collapsed through a system of patronage, blind loyalty, and what I started calling the "three C's": corrupt, coerce, co-opt.[18] If anyone refused what the government desired or offered (often privately and often linked to business opportunities), they were attacked.

That happened in two ways. In the first, indiscriminate, repeated online attacks created a chilling effect, curbing online conversations and speech. A climate of fear settled on the virtual world, mirroring the violence and fear that the drug war was creating in the real world. Then the administration targeted high-profile individuals in specific sectors: business, politics, and media. Duterte needed to make highly visible examples of what happened when anyone challenged his power.

In business, the first cautionary tale was that of the tycoon Roberto Ongpin,[19] whom President Duterte targeted with not only withering public attacks but charges of securities violations in August 2016. Ongpin was one of *Forbes*'s fifty richest Filipinos in 2015, with a net worth of $900 million. So the government's narrative pandered to populist sentiment: the people, led by Duterte, were going up against the "oligarchs." The government would use that same narrative repeatedly in the coming years to make businesses do what the administration wanted them to. And the propaganda campaign worked. Duterte's public statements moved markets: in that first year, the share price of Ongpin's publicly listed company, PhilWeb, fell by 46.3 percent.

Simultaneously, however, Duterte's shock-and-awe tactics resulted in rewards for the "new tycoons," like Dennis Uy, a businessman from Davao and a longtime Duterte friend and supporter.[20] In 2016, the best-performing stock was Uy's Phoenix Petroleum, whose price gained 92 percent. Uy's empire, which was highly leveraged,[21] noticeably expanded during Duterte's administration.

In politics, the cautionary tale that showcased the scope of Duterte's vast power was Senator Leila de Lima. A former justice secretary and former head of the Commission on Human Rights, she had investigated charges against Duterte of extrajudicial killings while he was mayor of Davao.

When Leila became senator, she launched a Senate investigation;

the public heard explosive testimony from credible witnesses who had allegedly carried out Duterte's orders to kill. The most vocal of Duterte's critics then, Leila was fearless. In August 2016, she delivered a speech decrying the extrajudicial killings in the brutal drug war. Some of what came out then is now included in the charges human rights groups brought against Duterte at the International Criminal Court in 2021.

A week before her public investigation started, Duterte launched a scathing and tawdry personal attack on her, accusing her of having a "driver and lover" who accepted money from "Muntinlupa," referring to money from drug lords at the New Bilibid Prison, located in that area of Manila.

"Here is an immoral woman . . . a woman who funded the house of her lover," Duterte said in a televised speech. "Whose money came readily from drugs," he went on. In conflicting sentences, he said he had no proof that Leila had drug money, yet concluded, "By the looks of it, she has it [money]." He then said he had a sex video of Leila.[22]

Like the later accusations against alleged coup plotters, this story was an egregious lie. But the government bureaucracy managed to turn the lie into reality. Like a mafia boss, Duterte publicly tried to intimidate Leila into silence by threatening to release what his allies would later claim was a sex video—a video that didn't exist. Duterte's people claimed that they had something they did not have and did not show the public. The president's speech was another dog whistle, a signal to his online supporters to attack. Memes and photos started appearing on social media as if on cue; as Duterte attacked Leila publicly, vowing to take her down, the propaganda machine swung into full force, publicly shaming and humiliating her.

The videos, supposedly shot in 2012, claimed to show Leila and her former driver-bodyguard Ronnie Dayan in sexual acts. Leila dismissed the video as "nonsense." Justice Secretary Vitaliano Aguirre II echoed Duterte's salacious and shocking personal attacks on Leila, repeating the sordid allegations of her affair. The fake videos went viral—even physical DVD copies popped up on the streets.

Rappler struggled with how to report the misogynistic attacks and their aftermath. Not wanting to spread them further, we chose not to do certain stories, but that didn't stop their spread and may have isolated Leila further. Leila could see online all the attacks designed to break her spirit, but few others could. The public didn't understand why she was often so emotional.

Pushed into a defensive position, Leila admitted she had previously had a relationship with her driver[23] but said she had not paid for his house, never mind paying for it with drug money. Dayan, Leila argued, was now being intimidated into following the government narrative.[24] She denied that she was in the sex tape, and Rappler's research team verified her claim.

Nevertheless, Duterte's allies in the Senate stripped Leila of her committee leadership. The senator who took over her chairmanship, Richard Gordon, promptly closed the investigation into Duterte's drug war, as well as the alleged killings years earlier in Davao.[25] In a further act of retaliation, the House of Representatives, dominated by Duterte allies, launched an investigation into Leila's supposed role in the illegal drug trade within the national penitentiary in Muntinlupa; the allegation was that Leila had received drug protection money. It was a ludicrous accusation.

In a public congressional hearing, most of the key informants were convicted drug lords. Congressmen feasted on their sordid stories of Leila's affair with her driver, laughing and jeering like boys in a locker room.[26] It was a real-life misogynistic pile-on.

"When did you reach climax?" asked a congressman in a televised public hearing.[27] One of the inmates called to the witness stand claimed that Leila had supposedly "pole danced"[28] for another prisoner. News organizations were careful; they reported that all such details were unverified and, perhaps more important, came from convicts, the implication being that they might easily have been used by the government. But the allegations spread like wildfire on pseudonews websites.

The next year, Leila de Lima would be arrested on drug charges. She is now in her sixth year in prison.[29] Amnesty International calls her a prisoner of conscience. Human Rights Watch, the European Union, the United Nations, and US legislators have repeatedly called for her immediate release.

In the past, when a government focused so much of its resources on something, part of me would follow the trail with an open mind, thinking that where there is smoke, there may be fire. I thought it would be crazy if the story weren't to some degree true. That was because in the past, in the Philippines, despite the weaknesses of our institutions, such brazen power plays, such cruel pettiness, rarely ever happened. None of what happened to Leila de Lima in 2016 and 2017 was normal for us.

It is hard to always see the thousand cuts in real time. Looking back, it should have been obvious that the checks and balances of our democracy were collapsing. Here was our president, successfully jailing an opposition politician who had fought to expose his crimes, with the support of the people and institutions that should have kept him in check. Duterte, like Facebook, benefited from the system of trust that they both destroyed. The weaponization of the internet had evolved into the weaponization of the law.

It was only a matter of time before the government came for us. Before Leila's arrest, Rappler received a tip: that Solicitor General Jose Calida was pushing the Securities and Exchange Commission, which is under the executive branch, to open an investigation into our company. Despite all that had gone on in the previous months, it was still hard for me to take such an outlandish idea seriously. For all the corruption that I'd witnessed over the years in my country, the use of the government levers for this kind of retribution against the press seemed so strange and unlikely.

By 2016, Rappler had been breaking even as planned, its reach and revenue on track. I had three key hires from the United States for disciplines that still didn't exist in the Philippines: a Silicon Valley CTO, a UX/UI (user experience and user interface) designer, and a data analyst. A year earlier, we had opened a small bureau in Jakarta. We had also raised more money from investors.

Our existing Filipino shareholders wanted more shares, but I wanted Rappler to have the golden seal from the global community and to attract investment leaders in two areas: journalism and technology that enabled civic engagement. In 2015, North Base Media, founded by former newsroom leaders like Marcus Brauchli, a former executive editor of the *Wall Street Journal* and the *Washington Post*, had announced that it would invest in Rappler.[30] At a time of dramatic change for journalism, I believed that that would fortify our brain trust and extend our global reach. Soon after, the Omidyar Network, created by eBay founder Pierre Omidyar, also announced its investment.[31] Both North Base and Omidyar called Rappler a pioneer in both our journalism and our reader engagement model.

Less than a year later, I was watching my reputation—and Rappler's—ripped apart online. We responded to the attacks the way responsible journalists do: by examining whether the attacks on our coverage of Duterte had any basis in fact. In 2017, we submitted ourselves to an external independent audit by GMT Media, led by former BBC World Service director Jerry Timmins, that compared Rappler to the main Filipino news organizations as well as global news standards. It found that we had treated the government fairly. In other words: we were doing our job well.

Still, I felt helpless in dealing with the online attacks, which continued unabated. My anger was building. I funneled that anger into more investigations, more data. I told anyone who would listen exactly how we all were being manipulated. We were not going to be intimidated into backing off of our hard-hitting coverage of the new administration.

We did not relent, nor did Duterte and his online army. In May 2017, we published a transcript of a call between Duterte and US president Donald Trump during which Duterte called North Korea's leader a "madman," which understandably caused great embarrassment for the administration. In response, RJ Nieto posted a video calling me a "traitor" who had made the Philippines a target of North Korea. By November 2017, the video had eighty-three thousand views and encouraged comments such as "#ArrestMariaRessa" and "Declare Rappler & Maria Ressa as enemies of the Filipinos."

I followed the serenity prayer: to accept the things I could not change, find the courage to change the things I could, and have the wisdom to know the difference.[32] Despite the churning in my stomach, I learned to embrace my fear and change what I could. We gathered data, monitoring the evolution of tactics as well as the growth and messaging of disinformation networks. Then we published stories that forecasted what might happen in other democratic countries.[33]

We knew we were wading into dangerous waters. By then it was clear that online violence led to real-world violence:[34] reports had detailed the way social media groups had fueled the fury of white supremacists in the United States.[35] We prepared for the worst-case scenarios and increased our security. By 2018, we had increased our security six more times.

But we worried about the impact of those virulent attacks on our young team. Not by design, Rappler is 63 percent female, and the employees' median age was twenty-three years. We encouraged our staff to talk to us about what was happening to them online and offered counseling to any member of our team who needed help. They weren't afraid as long as we weren't; first they gained courage from us, and then, when we got tired, we gained courage from them.

Palace insiders told Rappler that starting in September 2016, money had been released to "groups" that maintained online support[36] for Duterte, so we knew that the attacks would only get worse. Our social media team devised an online system where anyone targeted would be protected by other members of our team.

In early 2017, RJ Nieto's Thinking Pinoy, one of Duterte's earliest hatchet men, began seeding the idea that the government should take legal action against Rappler's newly expanded board. Nieto posted all of Rappler's financial filings from 2011 to 2015, omitting 2016, the year we broke even, because it didn't fit the meta-narrative he was building: that not only was Rappler failing but we hadn't paid taxes on our investment Philippine Depositary Receipts (PDRs, a kind of security), and the company owed the government 133 million Philippine pesos. Nieto predicted that Rappler would close down in 2018.

In April, I flew to San Jose, California, for the F8, Facebook's annual developer conference. Facebook had asked me to attend, meet with its officers and partners, and talk about our work at Rappler.

A year earlier, Facebook had featured Rappler and our crowdsourcing efforts during disasters[37] at F8. #ProjectAgos, the crowdsourcing platform we had built for typhoons and disasters, had been included in the rollout of Facebook's Free Basics, the low-bandwidth app available on mobile phones for free.

But my feelings about the company had changed in the intervening year. My warnings to our Facebook partners in Singapore the previous August had been entirely ignored. By the time I got to San Jose after Duterte's assault on Rappler, Roberto Ongpin, and Leila de Lima, I was ringing the alarm even louder.

At the F8, I was invited to a small founders' meeting with Mark Zuckerberg to give him perspectives about how we use Facebook from around the globe. I was the only journalist in the room. A Facebook employee next to me held down the top of my computer when I was about to open it and take notes.

When it was my turn to speak, I first invited Mark to come visit the Philippines.

"Well, thank you so much," he replied, "but as you can see, I'm find-ing out how little I know my own country, so that's what I plan to do this year."

He was referring to the election that November of President Donald Trump. In response, Zuckerberg planned to spend 2017 traveling to all the states in the United States because he wanted to "get out and talk to more people about how they're living, working, and thinking about the future."

Fortune had recently named Zuckerberg businessperson of the year. He was about to turn thirty-three years old. It dawned on me how much power that young man had.

"It may take me a while to get to the Philippines," he went on, "espe-cially since we just found out that my wife is pregnant with our second daughter!"

"Congratulations," I replied, "but you have no idea how powerful Facebook is in the Philippines."

For the second year in a row, it was calculated that Filipinos were the global citizens who spent the most time on the internet and on social media (2021 would be the sixth year in a row). Despite slow internet speeds, Filipinos had also that year uploaded and downloaded the larg-est number of videos on YouTube since 2013.

As a Filipino and the only journalist in the room, I wanted to warn the group how social media was fundamentally changing journalism and our information ecosystem.

"Ninety-seven percent of Filipinos on the internet are on Facebook, Mark!" I exclaimed, hoping, in part, that that tidbit might entice him to visit. Perhaps then he would better understand the problems we were beginning to see: how journalists were coming under attack and how the government had hired social media "influencers" to wage its propa-ganda war.

Mark was quiet for a beat. Maybe I had been too pushy. "Wait, Maria," he said, looking directly at me, "where are the other three percent?"

I wasn't the only one speaking out. Numerous people, from presidents to civil society to journalists all around the world, began warning Facebook that it was ravaging our democracies. If Facebook had acted then, so many people speaking truth to power would have been spared persecution: journalists, human rights activists, politicians. Conspiracy theories would have been kept where they belonged, on the fringes of society—not driving mainstream politics as we see today.

The next politician the Duterte administration targeted was the leader of the opposition, Duterte's vice president, Leni Robredo. (Though presidents and vice presidents often run together, they are elected separately and can be from different political parties.) It was a new phase in Duterte's attacks: using state resources to do information operations against the top opposition leader.

Calm, pragmatic, honest, and with a bias for social action, Leni is a lawyer who was a force behind the political career of her husband, Jesse Robredo.[38] A member of the Aquino cabinet, he died in a plane crash in 2012. Like Cory Aquino in 1986, Leni took up her husband's legacy and went on to beat Bongbong Marcos in 2016 in the vice presidential race by just about two hundred thousand votes.

The information operations against Leni took off in January 2017. The same three content creators led the charge against her: Sass Sasot, RJ Nieto, and Mocha Uson. By that time, all three had appeared in photos of palace gatherings; Mocha was now a government official, working for various Duterte administration entities, including his communications office, while RJ Nieto was a consultant for the Department of Foreign Affairs. They accused Leni of working with US groups to oust Duterte. It was laughable,[39] yet Facebook gave their wild statements mass distribution. Again, that was Facebook's call.

In 2018, the data, and our work that identified that the attacks were coming from government officials and groups close to Duterte,

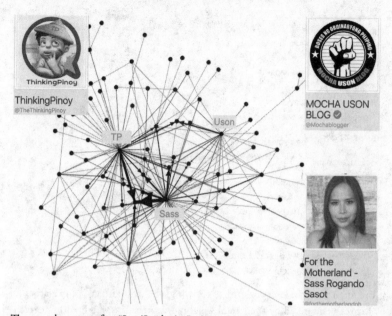

The attack vectors for #LeniLeaks in January 2017. Leni Robredo was a favorite of the propaganda machine, attacked nearly daily, with a direct impact on statistical popularity survey ratings. This is the same network that attacked me, other journalists, and the top news organizations.

proved to us that it was state-sponsored hate.[40] Three years later in 2021, the Commission on Audit would find that the government office that had disseminated the hate attacks (#LeniLeaks was the main hashtag for the attacks against Robredo) had hired some 375 contract workers,[41] 260 percent more than its regular staff. It had cost $1.4 million.

But in 2016 and 2017, we didn't yet know all that; all we knew was that there was something wrong. At first, it seemed as though otherwise obscure bloggers were overtaking and overwhelming traditional news organizations and journalists based on the algorithmic design and distribution of Facebook. The full extent of the ties to the state—how the new online propaganda process worked—was still not clear to us.

label	Group Name	weighted indegree	weighted outdegree	weighted degree
294969194202067	Sass Rogando Sasot	17	143	160
567419693405138	Thinking Pinoy	5	118	123
969295043116670	Lapu-Lapu	47	13	60
319779186521	MOCHA USON BLOG	9	39	48
1145212948834290	VOVph	12	34	46
110296245691141	Showbiz Government	19	4	23
1444892222391240	CRUELTY OF NOYNOY "ABNOY" AQUINO AND HIS GOVERNMENT	20	0	20
1031317600238250	Kasama Ng Pangulo sa Pagbabago - National Chapter	0	19	19
240711942975412	President Rody Duterte Facebook Army	19	0	19
156249678052611	Maharlika	3	14	17
1376086699270700	BongBong Marcos United	15	0	15
1632962006934810	Freedom Society (Original)	15	0	15
192588367599737	Crabbler	7	7	14
408328902693628	OFW4DU30 Global Movement	13	0	13
288218004888308	REAL PHILIPPINE HISTORY	12	0	12

The data for the network map showing the top fifteen propagators of #LeniLeaks, ranked by their total weighted degree. The weighted in degree is the number of posts it shared from other channels; the weighted out degree is the number of times other people shared from that channel. You can see that some pages are clear influencers (zero in degree, high out degree), while the ones closer to the bottom primarily distribute the content. This shows the content creation and distribution network behind the attack against Leni Robredo in January 2017, demonstrating the anatomy of an information operation.

We should have flagged that more for the public, but, as with the attacks against Leila de Lima, we still didn't realize that the technology platforms had fundamentally switched the gatekeeping rules and were rewarding lies over facts. Plus, Rappler and I had been one of the best recruiters for social media. Having that powerful force, which had so empowered our organization, suddenly being used against us and others was a confusing development.

I was naive, too. I was facing a situation that I couldn't have imagined from my decades in journalism. I had always been taught to let my work, and therefore Rappler's work, speak for itself. As the attacks rolled in, I didn't respond to any of them publicly, determined to just keep going.

As the leader of Rappler, I felt the pressure to be strong all the time, but a part of me felt helpless.

Until a fateful dinner in Durban, South Africa.

I feel like a punching bag," I said.

It was June 2017, and I was having dinner at a conference in Durban with Julie Posetti, the head of the Journalism Innovation Project at Oxford University. She had been a reporter, an academic, and a researcher, and she understood the rhythm and the problems of daily news on the internet. With Julie, I was finally in a safe space, without having to worry about the impact of my words.

"They're lies," I said, referring to the people attacking me day in, day out. "But if we respond, then we give them a bigger platform, and they wind up using us. But if we don't respond, then everyone thinks what they're spreading is true."

"Maria," Julie said, "you have to consider speaking publicly about what you're going through." She had studied sexism in the news business and had a far more nuanced understanding of how attacks on journalists worked.[42] "I'm working on something now that I think you should be part of."

At that point, I was one of the first journalists to name the threat we faced: the platforms themselves. Far too many of us were still operating on past paradigms. But I didn't know if I wanted to open myself up to more scrutiny. Julie was working on a UNESCO study about freedom of expression and told me that online attacks targeted female journalists three times as often as male journalists.[43] She wanted to interview me for the publication.

"Tell me what that would look like, Julie," I said to her.

"You'll have to share some of the worst things you've been going through, because I guarantee that this isn't just happening to you," she said.

I told her that my reputation was being tarnished in front of me. But my instinct was still that if I responded and tackled the problem head-on, it could get worse.

"But if you don't, then it will also get worse," she said.

Julie had a bias for action, while I perhaps had developed symptoms of learned helplessness from the attacks. I needed an outside perspective from someone who had been in the media trenches and knew what journalists had to deliver every day, while understanding how the new world we were operating in was fundamentally different from anything we'd experienced before.

I decided then to participate in the UNESCO study.[44] The book the organization eventually published and presented at a UN Conference was titled *An Attack on One Is an Attack on All*, showcasing the risks journalists face and offering creative solutions to the problems.

It was one of those pivotal moments when I chose to trust—and I am so glad I did. By sharing my fears with near strangers and getting an outside perspective, I was able to see a bigger picture outside myself. I learned how what I was living through fit into the larger global landscape, and it helped me embrace my fear.

And it reminded me that people are good. As I had at the pajama party, I opened the car door and walked out. Instead of laughing at me, people came to help. The many friendships I nurtured with people like Julie grew from our work: our common values around journalism and speaking truth to power.

In the following years, Julie continued to ask questions about what we were doing at Rappler in response to attacks. Her feedback helped me bridge the gap between what we were doing and what Western news groups were doing. She was one of the few people who realized that Rappler was, by necessity, slightly ahead of the curve in the discovery of the problems and solutions journalism was facing, and she continued writing about us. In the following years, Julie would enlist computer scientists from the United Kingdom to help analyze nearly half a million social media posts attacking me. Nearly five years after the attacks began, the first-of-its-kind big-data analysis[45] would explain why and how: 60 percent of the attacks had focused on tearing down my credibility, while the other 40 percent had been extremely personal and virulent attacks, aimed at crushing my will to keep doing my job. It helped to see data produced by people outside Rappler. Sometimes you need an external validation of your reality.

She and her colleagues[46] were also among the first to question the basic assumptions of technology platforms, seeing the way that Filipino, South African, and Indian newsrooms were evolving to confront increasing threats and the death of trust. At one point, she and her team would do a deep dive into how three news organizations from the Global South were evolving their operations because of these new forms of attacks.[47] She spent at least a week each at the *Daily Maverick* in South Africa, at the *Quint* in India, and in Rappler's newsroom.

If she had stayed at Rappler a day longer, she would have been in our newsroom the day I was first arrested.

In July 2017, President Duterte attacked Rappler in his second annual State of the Nation address, claiming that it was violating the Constitution by having, as he claimed, foreign ownership—an easy way to whip up nationalist resentment. The bottom-up lies seeded on social media now began to come from the top down. "Rappler, try to pierce the identity and you will end up [with] American ownership," he said about thirty minutes into his speech attacking us in a mix of English and Filipino. "If you are a newspaper you're supposed to be 100% Filipino and yet when you start to pierce their identity, it is fully owned by Americans."[48]

None of what President Duterte told the nation was true, but that didn't matter. Earlier that month, he had threatened an exposé of faulty tax payments by the family that owns the *Philippine Daily Inquirer*, the largest newspaper in the Philippines,[49] and two weeks later, the family announced that it would sell its stake in the paper. In April 2017, Duterte had threatened to block the franchise renewal of my old network ABS-CBN, still the largest broadcasting network in the country.[50] A congressional committee would shut it down in May 2020 for the first time since Marcos had done the same when he had declared martial law nearly half a century before.

Duterte's threats against the media didn't just cause a chilling effect on freedom of speech in the Philippines; it became Siberia.

Rappler was live on Facebook, YouTube, Twitter, and our own website when Duterte attacked us in his State of the Nation address. I was the coverage anchor along with three analysts seated around the table in our office. No one got scared that day. Despite the speech's being live, we stood up straighter.[51]

I immediately wrote a public response that I wanted to tweet and messaged the *manangs*' Signal group. We were still listening to Duterte. I looked at my cofounders in the room, and each of them nodded. Within minutes, I tweeted, "President Duterte, you are wrong. @rapplerdotcom is 100 percent Filipino owned. Any leader should vet his information."[52]

Let me tell you one more thing that happened that year, when I met with a woman named Camille François, the principal researcher for Google's think tank, Jigsaw. Rappler had joined Camille's research project with about a dozen other groups around the world. Camille had a strong background in public policy and technology (she had been special adviser to the chief technology officer of France) and gender studies, as well as human rights. Titled "Patriotic Trolling: The Rise of State-Sponsored Online Hate Mobs," the resulting paper gave a big-picture view of patriotic trolling: "the use of targeted, State-sponsored online hate and harassment campaigns leveraged to silence and intimidate individuals."[53] It featured more than fifteen case studies in which governments, to varying degrees, were using online hate to inundate and overwhelm a truth teller and change the public narrative. More than anything else at that time, the report captured the scope of the global disinformation crisis. It was to be released in August 2017, but it kept getting delayed.

In October, Camille and I had lunch at Chelsea Market in New York, just below the Jigsaw offices. It was the first time we were meeting, but we had been working together for more than a year. Friendly and speaking English with a slight French accent, Camille was having a salad; I was having a burger and onion rings. She said she had something to tell me. "I'm sorry, Maria," she said, "but I don't think we'll be publishing the study."

She was digging her fork into her salad; then she put it aside. We had submitted a final draft in August. It was nearly two months later.

"It's really important that this study be published," I said.

"Unfortunately, there's really not much more I can do," she said.

Google was not going to allow its publication.

If it had been released, I am certain the ripple effect might have prevented so much of the worst that we have lived through. I pushed Camille to fight back, but I noticed how diplomatic she was. I wasn't surprised when, a few months later, Camille announced that she would be leaving Jigsaw.

Until today, I don't know what made Google kill the report. But it brought home to me, again, the lesson I was learning: silence is complicity.

Just because others compromise doesn't mean you do. Just because they're silent doesn't mean you have to be.

A little more than a week after Duterte's nationwide attack, we received our first subpoena. Multiple investigations into Rappler began, alleging criminal acts in three large buckets: foreign ownership, tax evasion, and cyberlibel.

We had to hire lawyers, and the ones who accepted our cases knew that there might be repercussions against them, too. Within six months, about a third of our operating expenses would be siphoned away by our ballooning legal fees. It was the beginning of fourteen investigations against us.

If there was one upside, it was that the brazenness of Duterte's attacks on us began attracting worldwide notice. In October, Bloomberg News investigative reporter Lauren Etter[54] came to the Philippines to spend time with us. In December, Bloomberg Businessweek ran her cover piece with the title "How Rodrigo Duterte Turned Facebook into a Weapon—with a Little Help from Facebook." To help protect me (and to show you how uncertain the times were), the online title was changed to "What Happens When the Government Uses Facebook as a Weapon?"[55]

It was the beginning of what would become a rush of international attention on the Philippines, Rappler, and me.

PART III

Crackdown

Arrests, Elections, and the Fight for Our Future

2018–Present

Chapter 9

Surviving a Thousand Cuts

Believe in the Good

At the Rappler office, shortly after we received an unprecedented shutdown decision from the Securities and Exchange Commission, January 15, 2018. (*Leanne Jazul/Rappler*)

We had known since 2016 that the solicitor general, Jose Calida, had ordered the Securities and Exchange Commission (SEC) to conduct and file the mother case against Rappler, alleging foreign control and ownership.[1] During the intervening months, our sources would give us occasional updates on the progress of the government's investigation, but it remained unclear to us what the endgame was. Deep down, I still could not quite believe that the government's outlandish behavior would result in real consequences. All that ended in January 2018, when the SEC revoked our license to operate.[2]

I had to ask our lawyers what that meant.

It was simple: the government wanted to shut down Rappler. "The SEC's kill order revoking Rappler's license to operate is the first of its kind in history—both for the Commission and for Philippine media," we wrote in our statement reacting to the decision. "What this means for you, and for us, is that the Commission is ordering us to close shop, to cease telling you stories, to stop speaking truth to power, and to let go of everything that we have built—and created—with you since 2012."[3]

Of course, we didn't stand for it. We knew our rights. You feel the fear; then you bust through it.

The *manang*s rallied. Glenda immediately made arrangements to fly home from Boston, where she had been doing a fellowship at Harvard. Beth, Chay, and I stayed close together as we fielded and made calls. Even separated by geography, the four of us were running down parallel paths, each with a task to finish, each checking back in regularly so we could see the picture taking shape.

Midmorning, we called a company meeting, what we call a general assembly, and told our folks that we would fight the charge. I stood on the *Star Trek* bridge in the middle of the office and reassured them that we would get through it—even as I was wrapping my head around our government's unprecedented act. Despite it all, the team was in good spirits, and the photo we took afterward showed all of us smiling broadly.[4] We knew what we had to do.

When the SEC formally announced the decision and reporters came to us for interviews, we decided to hold a press conference. We had nothing to hide. Our lawyers objected, asking for time to study the decision before we spoke publicly. Well, too late. We had already released our statement,[5] which we then realized we had forgotten to run by our lawyers. I suppose it helped that the *manang*s had done this before: we had experience; we knew the lines we couldn't cross. We knew how egregious the move was for the government, and we couldn't stay quiet because silence is consent.

As I had learned throughout my career: don't let anyone else tell your story in the golden hour.

Beth made arrangements for live coverage of a news conference in time for the prime-time newscasts at 6:30 p.m. Chay and I would each give an opening statement before answering questions. We had nothing prepared. Instead, we quickly compared the notes we were writing. Then we jumped off the cliff.

"Thank you very much for coming here," I started, smiling at the journalists. "We're not closing down! I guess first of all I'm going to say that right up top. The speed at which this has happened, and the kinds of attacks that media in general has gone through, shows the very political nature of this decision. We will be challenging this in court."[6]

I described the crux of the SEC decision. It was absurd. That small administrative body was claiming that our Philippine Depositary Receipts (PDRs), a kind of security, owned by investors outside the country constituted foreign control and violated the Constitution. I told the press that PDRs were legal according to our Constitution, and we had submitted our documents to the SEC in 2015.

Judging by the online attacks, I knew that I needed to simplify the legalese. Otherwise, it would be so easy for the government propagandists to mislead and lie, as they were already trying to do.

"Somebody who puts money on a PDR is like the person who bets on a horse at the racetrack," I explained. "It doesn't mean that you can dictate what the horse will eat or who the jockey for the horse will be. You don't have any control over anything, but you bet on a horse. If the horse wins, great, you get something. If it doesn't win, you get nothing."

I also warned that the impact of the SEC's decision would affect not only the Philippines but also businesses invested in the Philippines: in this case, the Omidyar Network and North Base Media. The implication of the SEC's case was that foreign firms controlled Rappler. But Omidyar Network and North Base Media's PDR holdings were both below 10 percent, and those derivative financial instruments by design gave them no control. They didn't even own shares.

"The people who have the majority and who dictate the course of Rappler are the journalists," I said. "That's us."

I was shocked that the government was willing to take such a huge risk with the business community. A high-profile public decision like this was a bad signal for business and the rule of law—something the journalists understood but apparently the government either did not or was arrogant enough to think wouldn't matter.

Chay spoke next. She has a deep, mellifluous voice and TV reporter roots, and she spoke in deliberate tones. "This is going to be business as usual," she said. "No changes. Our marching orders for our reporters are still pursuing and writing stories and reporting as aggressively as they are wont to do—as you, as media, are wont to do. And we will continue to hold power accountable, and we will continue to tell the truth, no matter what.

"This has been a continuing wave of harassment since last year," she went on. "And we've been anticipating this decision by the SEC, and finally it's come. So now it's out there in the open. We know how to deal with it."

In a strange way, it was a relief to have what had been a low-intensity conflict with the state now out in the open.

"Assuming that there is rule of law in this country," Chay continued, "we will go through the process.... We will even go to the Supreme Court because this is clearly a constitutional case ... this is a press freedom case."[7]

The SEC had not even followed the rules of procedure. As an administrative body, it would normally flag what it saw as potential problems. Assuming that there was anything wrong, the company involved would have up to a year to fix the alleged problem. The largest telecom provider, for example, the Philippine Long Distance Telephone Company, actually once had a foreign president. It was given a year to bring in a Filipino president and it did. But in our case, the SEC hadn't gone through due process: it had issued an order to shut us down without giving us an opportunity to respond to the special panel's decision. Based on an obscure technical interpretation, it claimed that Rappler had ceded control to foreigners, which was a fantasy.

It was the weaponization of the law, happening before our very eyes. And we weren't the only ones. Senator Leila de Lima was still in prison on charges that should never have made it to court, and the state had recently used outlandish legal procedures to oust Supreme Court chief justice Maria Lourdes Sereno.[8]

Less than a month after the government tried to take away our license

Author and cofounder Chay Hofileña during an impromptu press conference in the Rappler newsroom, January 15, 2018. (*Leanne Jazul/Rappler*)

to operate, Rappler's Pia Ranada, who reported on Duterte and the executive branch, was prevented from entering Malacañang Palace.[9] As we had drilled with our team just days earlier, she took out her cell phone and went live on Facebook and Twitter, asking the soldier on duty why she couldn't enter the presidential compound. She was scared but relentless. Her hands were shaking, in part because she was angry. "I didn't want them to get away with it," she said.

The order had come from the vindictive Duterte,[10] we were told, partly in retaliation for Rappler's hard-hitting investigative piece exposing corruption around naval purchases linked to Duterte's assistant Bong Go.[11] Duterte's palace ban included me and would later be expanded beyond the presidential compound to anywhere Duterte traveled around the world.[12]

Along with more than forty other journalists, activists, and academics, we would challenge those arbitrary moves, clear prior restraint that violated the Constitution,[13] in the Supreme Court. But the death by a thousand cuts continued, and we had no choice but to weather it.

That's when you realize how powerless you are. Each day brought new challenges, new lows.

During that time, Mark Zuckerberg announced that Facebook would be overhauling its news feed.[14] The changes would be a puny response to the growing public outcry over the disinformation it had allowed to run rampant. It would now be prioritizing what friends and family shared[15] over content from publishers and brands (even the idea of lumping news and advertisers together like this is fundamentally flawed). In effect, it further weakened journalists and news organizations, significantly reducing traffic[16] and causing a drop of 20 to 60 percent for smaller news groups[17] around the world. That meant that facts reached fewer people. And if there are no facts to counter the lies that make their way to family and friends from information operations, disinformation spreads further exponentially.

Facebook's decision to deprioritize news[18] was an absurd way to address issues of "fake news." It claimed that it wanted to drive engagement through comments and discussion, not shares and likes. Like the whole idea of providing a personalized feed or muting and blocking posts instead of removing them, it said that "meaningful interaction" would now come from family and friends. Research showed that most of us are predisposed to share what our friends and family tell us. The predictable end result of designing the algorithms to suppress news?[19] More hate, toxicity, and "fake news."[20]

Which was exactly what happened.

Three months later, the Cambridge Analytica scandal broke. Good journalists see a hanging thread; then they begin to pull it, and they follow the trail. Carole Cadwalladr, a Pulitzer Prize–nominated reporter and feature writer for the *Observer*, the sister publication of the *Guardian*, had collaborated with the *New York Times* to expose how the political consulting company Cambridge Analytica had illicitly harvested data from millions of Facebook accounts to better target voters and advance political campaigns, including Brexit and Donald Trump's successful 2016 presidential bid.[21] The country with the largest number of compromised accounts was the United States.

The second largest? The Philippines.[22]

Cambridge Analytica did the same during the Brexit referendum and, we would discover, in campaigns in the Philippines.[23] All of those had been corrupted, and what enabled it was Facebook.

Partly because of Carole's tenacity, the US Congress called Mark to testify. The Federal Trade Commission then fined Facebook $5 billion, the largest penalty ever levied against a tech company. Carole said it wasn't enough. Even though we knew so much more about what had happened in the 2016 elections, no one was able to hold anybody to account.

By that time, Old Power, like governments and news organizations, still had no idea how much New Power—technology platforms— had eroded the established structures that had once, at least somewhat, maintained order and stability around the world.

That hit me in June, when the Atlantic Council gathered fifteen of us in Berlin to study disinformation and its impact on power. Among the other participants were Madeleine Albright, former US secretary of state; Carl Bildt, former prime minister of Sweden; Steve Hadley, former US national security advisor; and representatives from Facebook and Microsoft.

Old Power and New Power tried to find a language to bridge the monstrous gap between them. There was one fundamental conflict: government officials moved at glacial, consensus-building pace, mapping out downsides and including public discussions as part of their process. Technology firms moved fast, often removing safeguards, and had no qualms about breaking things they didn't understand or care about.

I learned a lot that week from Madeleine Albright, who had recently published her book *Fascism: A Warning* about the rise of authoritarianism around the world.

The use of that word hadn't occurred to me before, but it stayed with me. I began to reexamine everything we were living through. Journalists could pinpoint a problem but rarely found solutions. My role in this fight was changing: I tried to imagine what we could do to prevent a dystopian future.

In September, I went to Paris to join the Information and Democracy Commission, a group trying to establish the principles and values that should rule the internet.[24] Once again, my perspective on our struggles in the Philippines started to broaden. Overseas trips like those allowed me to put our experiences into context: Was anyone else going through what we were? What were the root causes? How could we strengthen the fabric of our democracy?

At the commission's formal launch, I felt my role expanding. I was now the journalist, the target, and the researcher, both reporting on the commission and participating in it.

"Free speech is being used to stifle free speech," I told the audience.

Our task in Paris was to begin to draft the International Declaration on Information and Democracy, which would serve as the foundation of a partnership among governments, private-sector companies, and civil society to protect democracy. Two years later, the group would publish a report I cochaired with a dozen structural solutions and more than 250 tactical steps to fight what we called an "infodemic."[25]

Still, what I remember most vividly from that week in September was the bright sun as I was standing outside the Élysée Palace, the residence of the president of France, along with Iranian Nobel Peace Prize laureate Shirin Ebadi and Turkish journalist Can Dündar as we waited for our audience with French president Emmanuel Macron.

It was the first time I realized that my world could change drastically.

In 2003, Shirin was the first Muslim woman and the first Iranian to receive the Nobel Peace Prize for fighting for democracy and human rights, especially for women and children, in Iran. Can, the former editor in chief of *Cumhuriyet*, an opposition newspaper in Turkey, had fled to exile in Germany after he had been convicted of espionage for publishing a story about Turkish arms shipments to Syrian rebels.

Both Shirin and Can were now living in exile away from their homes and families. Shirin had lived in exile in the United Kingdom since 2009, though her family still lived in Iran. Can lived in Berlin, but the Turkish government had taken away his wife's passport, banning her from travel.

"Where do you live?" Shirin asked me. "In Manila?"

"In Manila," I responded.

We spoke about what it was like to live separated from family. I played it down. I explained that my family was scattered all over the United States and the Philippines anyway. I suppose I was rationalizing. "I don't want to go into exile," I told them.

I was still thinking that the Philippines was not Turkey, which at one point had jailed more than seventy thousand people, or Iran, which had long been repressive toward journalists, activists, and political opposition.

I had chosen to build my life in the Philippines and I wanted to stay the course, whatever the consequences. Not long before, my cofounders and I had jokingly made a pact for what each would bring me (food, sheets, a fan, books) if I were thrown into jail.

The world was taking even more notice of what Duterte was doing: the violence, the creeping dictatorship, the weaponization of the law. By then there were fourteen ongoing investigations into Rappler. One carried the truly ridiculous charge of "cyberlibel." The government was trying anything to silence us.

At the same time, Rappler was gaining global recognition. One important event took place in November, when we received the International Center for Journalists' Knight International Journalism Award in Washington, DC, in a ballroom filled with five hundred people. "We battle impunity from the Philippine government and Facebook," I told them. "Both seed violence, fear, and lies that poison our democracy. Those lies on social media formed the basis of the government's legal cases against us."[26]

I knew I needed that Beltway audience to care about my faraway country, where tactics to manipulate them were being tested.[27]

"Why should you care?" I asked. "Our problems are fast becoming your problems."[28]

The events of 2018 reinforced for me that as much as I've learned my craft and wielded some power, there was much more that was beyond my control. The rule of law can be an illusion and can vanish in an instant—a lesson I had first learned in Indonesia as a young journalist. That night in the ballroom, I appealed to my fellow journalists to stay the course in holding governments and Big Tech accountable for eroding democracy in their quest for more money and power. I ended with what has now become our global rallying cry: "We are Rappler, and we will hold the line."

That was the genesis of #HoldTheLine: the line in our country's Constitution that defined our rights. Using fear and violence, the holders of power were trying to force us to step back and give up our rights. In my mind, we linked arms to hold the line at any attempt to violate them. And we would never voluntarily give up our rights, no matter the danger.

As an exhausting year was coming to a close, I was faced with the discouraging realization that despite everything I was saying privately and publicly, it wasn't enough.

Clearly the international recognition was antagonizing the Duterte government. While I was receiving an award from the Committee to Protect Journalists in New York at the end of the year, the Department of Justice in the Philippines issued a press release saying it would indict me and Rappler,[29] without sending us any legal documents.[30] That was what I got for accepting these awards and speaking my mind.

I flew back to Manila the next day. Since an indictment was pending, my lawyers at ACCRALAW, one of the best law firms in the country, were worried that an arrest warrant might have already been issued against me, so it sent lawyers to meet me at the airport in case of an arrest. Our reporter Paterno Esmaquel II met me as I left the plane, and Beth joined us at the baggage claim after I cleared immigration. But luckily, nothing happened.

So much fuss for a few days in Manila. I was going to be home only for the weekend, for a few meetings, but I began to wonder how much of a psychological toll—and how much money—the fear of an arrest was going to cost us.

So I kept going. I wanted to live my life as though nothing had changed. I went to London first, and then to Paris. While I was packing in my Paris hotel room to take a flight back to Manila, I heard protestors outside. It was the "yellow jackets" or "yellow vests" protests, triggered by fuel price increases to help France deal with climate change.

I didn't even think: I picked up my coat, tripod, and camera and went out into the streets. It was cold and raining, but it felt good to be a reporter again—to talk to people on the streets and do a walk-and-talk for Rappler.[31] Those protests were the strongest and most violent challenge so far to Macron, when the Left and the Right found common ground against an unpopular move.

The French police said that about 136,000 protestors were out that day, with 268 people arrested. Those protests were different because the people behind them were decentralized: organized on social media—largely Facebook, according to my interviews—where disinformation was misleading and fueling past grievances, many of which might have been legitimate but now had been amplified to the point of encouraging violence. When I left for the airport, I could hear the water cannons still firing, the sirens wailing.

On one phone, I was watching cars burning in Paris. On the other, I was texting back and forth with the *manang*s and our lawyers, who told me that an arrest warrant had been issued for me—this time apparently for something related to securities and tax evasion. I got a brief sinking feeling. But then I absorbed it and focused on what would happen next. From my long-ago war-reporting days, I had been trained for this kind of crisis. I wouldn't allow myself time to wallow in my fears and anxieties, despite how overwhelming they might seem.

My flight from Paris was scheduled to arrive in Manila at 9:40 p.m. on Sunday, December 2. My family asked me not to go back to Manila. That was not an option; I had a company to run and people who trusted me to do my job. My anger was growing at the injustice the government was propagating, redefining and breaking the rule of law. I planned to see the conflict through and hold the government accountable.

One of our lawyers asked if I would delay my flight home. I thought about it, but it would have taken too much trouble and money. I preferred confrontation because it would bring resolution. I wasn't going to go out of my way to bend to the government's intimidation tactics.

As I arrived at Charles de Gaulle Airport, I prepared myself for the worst, including spending the night in jail. I opened my suitcase and took out pajamas, a toothbrush, and a change of clothes, all of which I packed into my carry-on. Then I went into the airport, checked in, and boarded the flight. I was so tired that I slept for much of the twenty-hour trip.

My homecoming involved a lot of people: a half-dozen lawyers from ACCRALAW and a team of at least six from Rappler. It was the second time we were doing this. Imagine the disruption to our operations and our lives. I didn't know whether to be angry or afraid; I was both, I guess.

Hours before my plane landed, ACCRALAW's Francis Lim, a former president of the Philippine Stock Exchange and our lead counsel,

Arriving at Ninoy Aquino International Airport in Manila on Sunday, December 2, 2018. (*Rappler*)

issued a statement: "Fervently hoping that Maria Ressa will not get arrested upon her arrival in Manila tonight. It is not common for warrants of arrest to be served on Sunday nights. Doing so will just give more weight to the well-founded perception that our government has been unduly rushing cases against the officers of Rappler because of its fearless reporting on the true situation in the Philippines."

After nearly twenty hours of travel, my plane landed in Manila. I turned on my cell phones, and a stream of messages came flooding in. From our *manang*s chain, I got a text briefing of what had happened and what to expect. My sister Michelle texted that she had her hands full preventing Mom and my aunts from going to the airport. I made a mental note that maybe my parents should go back to the United States, a major shift since they had just decided, with my nudging, to move their primary household to Manila.

I walked out of the jetway to see airport police waiting to pick me up.

Close behind them were two of our lawyers and our reporter Paterno Esmaquel. While we were walking to immigration, they explained that they just wanted to help me get through quickly. Phew. There didn't seem to be any sign of arresting agents. As we exited the arrivals area, there was a bank of television cameras and reporters. Lights came on, and questions came fast.

"I don't know what to expect," I said after thanking airport security. "Here's what we know. We know that an arrest warrant has been issued. I don't know exactly what that means, right? I mean, imagine if an arrest warrant is issued for you. I will do what I need to do to face all this."[32]

"Do you know what will happen with the cases?" another reporter asked, referring to the tax evasion cases.

"I can't really tell you," I responded. "All I know is that we filed a motion for reconsideration, but the cases were filed before our motion for reconsideration was even considered, so I'm going to challenge the process. And I'm going to challenge the charges. The charges are reclassify-

At an impromptu press conference late Sunday evening, December 2, 2018, at Ninoy Aquino International Airport in Manila. (*Rappler*)

ing Rappler as—and this is a direct quote—'a dealer in securities.' We're obviously not a stockbrokerage agency, right? I'm a journalist. I've always been a journalist. So bring it—and I'll face it."

"How do you feel about possibly being arrested?" a reporter asked.

"Well, number one, I'm going to hold my government accountable for publicly calling me a criminal," I responded. "The second is, obviously, it makes you feel vulnerable." I was horrified when I felt my voice crack.[33] "But I think that's the point, right? The point is for the government to actually make you feel its power and that it can do what it wants to do."[34]

I preemptively posted bail on the arrest warrant the next day, and a day after that, we filed a motion to dismiss the charges because, among other things, the court that had issued the warrant didn't have jurisdiction over the case.[35] The whole thing seemed like a farce.

I was back in court a few days later, when the judge accepted our motion and postponed my arraignment.[36]

We had bought some time, but each day brought a possible new worst-case scenario. Simply doing my job was tough enough, given the changing technology landscape that was directly impacting the survival of news organizations, their distribution and advertising business model. The government's attacks meant that I also had to do crisis management, with me as the target. We were spending money on legal fees and wasting our time in endless meetings with our lawyers. Some weeks, I spent 90 percent of my time with different lawyers. A few Sundays, I remember sitting at a table with more than half a dozen lawyers for hours. I felt sorry for them and for me, for what had become of our lives for the most absurd of reasons.

O ne morning in December, I woke up early to go to the Court of Tax Appeals and post bail yet again—this time against four more tax evasion charges.

I headed to the office after that and by noon was totally exhausted. By 6:30 p.m., I was having dinner below our office, trying to shake off the shadows of the day, when I saw an announcement on Twitter that I had been named one of *Time* magazine's People of the Year. I actually called our social media head to check whether it was real, and then my phone rang. It was CNN asking me for a reaction to the *Time* cover.[37]

My stomach churned. My first thought was that the exposure would only lead to more attacks. In retrospect, maybe that was PTSD. In reality, the honor created a protective shield around Rappler.

"What's your reaction?" asked Kristie Lu Stout, CNN's prime-time Asia anchor.

"It's bittersweet," I responded. My speech was halting and disjointed. I later saw on CNN's video that my face was weary and lined. "We know it's a tough time to be a journalist, but I think what strengthens all of us is that there is probably no better time to be a journalist because this is when we live our values and we live our mission."[38]

"Tomorrow is the one-year anniversary of the conviction and detention of the two Reuters reporters in Myanmar," Kristie said. Wa Lone and Kyaw Soe Oo had been arrested for reporting on the murders of Muslim men in Myanmar's Rakhine State. I might never have been asked that question by an anchor in the United States, for whom the Myanmar reporters' fate might not even have registered as relevant to American audiences or concerns. "What is your message to the two Reuters reporters and their families in the fight for justice?"

"We have to keep fighting," I replied. "We need to stay principled. We need to make sure that we continue to challenge every time authorities anywhere around the world move backwards. I think Myanmar also shows the same things happening in the Philippines, which is the impact of social media and how social media can be used to incite hate, to tear down the credibility of journalists around the world."[39]

On New Year's Eve, I was in New York City. It had been a long year—one in which I had realized how much we take our freedom and our rights for granted. I hadn't been sure that the court would give me permission to travel, so to be walking around New York City with my sister Mary Jane was unimaginable bliss.

The Times Square Alliance had invited nearly a dozen journalists to honor our work and help it count down to the ball drop for 2019. I looked at my cell phone while we were being called onstage, and my sister Mary Jane, by now at home with her family, was asking which channel they should watch. My sister Nicole in Los Angeles texted that she was already watching, while my parents and Michelle in Manila texted that they were watching on Rappler.

We began walking up the stage, but the rain started pouring, so I pulled the hood of my hoodie over my head. I wished I could pass that energy and anticipation to the journalists like me who were having to find hope to power through each difficult moment. All I could be was thankful.

The pop star Bebe Rexha was introduced to perform John Lennon's "Imagine." There was a moment of silence, and then her powerful voice began to take the familiar song and fill Times Square as well as households around the world. It was fitting that an American singer whose parents are of Albanian origin was transforming John Lennon's words, giving them new context and meaning, nudging us again to imagine a better world.

It was T. S. Eliot all over again: the present transforming the first moment I had heard John Lennon sing it and vice versa. We began to sing along to the familiar lyrics: "You may say I'm a dreamer, but I'm not the only one. I hope someday you'll join us . . . and the world will be as one."

I wiped tears from my eyes. "Happy New Year, everybody!" yelled Bebe. And a rousing cheer rose from the crowd. Then the one-minute countdown began.

We all screamed the final ten seconds, and 2018 was over.

Chapter 10

Don't Become a Monster to Fight a Monster

Embrace Your Fear

Arrested and detained overnight, I arrive at court to post bail, February 14, 2019. (*Alecs Ongcal/Rappler*)

It was February 13, 2019. The sun was streaming in through my office windows, and, as I often do, I stopped to marvel at the colors of the sunset across the Manila skyline. I was about to head into a meeting with Facebook's new team from Singapore, one that would be working on tracking information operations. This time, they had come to us.

It was their first time visiting the Philippines. What struck me about them, as it had about Mark Zuckerberg, was their youth. But I had learned to trust their supervisor, who was a former FBI investigator. Gemma Mendoza, who heads our disinformation research, was joining me to take the Facebook team through the tactics and methodology of the attack networks we had discovered.

It was my second-to-last meeting of the day, and I would be getting on a 6:00 a.m. flight to Malaysia the next day to interview Prime Minister Mahathir Mohamad. I wanted to download my thoughts to them quickly, leave the Facebook team with Gemma, and confirm my interview with Mahathir before giving a speech at the University of the Philippines and heading home to pack.

In the glass conference room, with my back to the newsroom, I launched into my presentation. At some point, Beth suddenly entered the room. Somewhat surprised, I stopped and introduced her to the Facebook team. "Hey, Beth, meet the new team working on disinformation networks at Facebook," I said. "Guys, this is one of the founders of Rappler, Beth Frondoso."

"Maria, don't turn around," Beth said tersely. "They're here to arrest you."

Of course, I turned around immediately. Over my shoulder, I glimpsed Glenda on her cell phone and Chay speaking to a group of what appeared to be plainclothes officers. Others were scattered around the newsroom. Then I looked down at my cell phone, which I had muted, and saw a slew of messages from journalists, including one from Alexandra Stevenson at the *New York Times*.

"Our reporters are livestreaming it, Maria," Beth continued, her face strained. "Glenda's calling our lawyers. Chay is holding them back."

"Okay," I replied, pushing my emotions down. "Everyone, look at me."

Two young faces across the table from me tightened.

"Gemma, find a way to bring these guys out quietly," I instructed as I turned to our Facebook partners. "You don't want to be here if this gets worse. Well, you see what we go through to do our jobs, so please help us." I tried to keep it light. They began packing their things. "Let's just catch up later," I continued. "Maybe we can have dinner at your hotel. Just not sure how long it will take me to post bail. Anyway, you guys want to get out of here fast."

While all that was going on, one of our reporters, twenty-four-year-old Aika Rey, was livestreaming the whole thing on Facebook, despite being intimidated by one of the plainclothes officers of the National Bureau of Investigation, our FBI.[1] "Be silent, or you're next," the agent told her.

Aika stood her ground. She was terrified and her hand was shaking, but she remembered the lessons from our team drills and knew the importance of continuing the livestream.

A senior officer joined in, his voice firm but adamant. "Can you stop what you're doing now?" he told Aika. "Is that okay? And say this to your colleagues: if we see our faces on the net, you'll be sorry. You'll be sorry. We'll go after you."

Aika ignored him and kept livestreaming. In response, he took out his cell phone and began shooting video of her doing the livestream. You could hear their whole conversation on Rappler's Facebook Live. You could also see at least two other plainclothes agents shooting cell phone videos of the Rappler office, while most of our staff continued doing their work. Sofia Tomacruz, who had come into Rappler around the same time as Aika, was also taking video of the officer trying to intimidate Aika.

Aika and Sofia were our third-generation reporters. It was only a year before that Pia Ranada, part of our second generation, had taken out her cell phone and livestreamed officials trying to ban her from Malacañang Palace. No matter what the government does to me or to Rappler, the next generation of journalists is here, imbued with a mission adapted to this age and possessing the key characteristic good journalists all around the world have always needed: courage.

The dozen or so agents of the National Bureau of Investigation (NBI) waited until our lawyers arrived. I was still in the glass conference room when one of the arresting officers read me my Miranda rights: the right to remain silent, the right to an attorney. Part of me was still in disbelief that it was actually happening. Then they ushered me out.

Outside, we were besieged by journalists and cameras. I didn't know what to say except that I was going to NBI headquarters as the arresting officers demanded. I didn't want to say anything that would allow them to take away any more of my rights.

There were at least two irregularities in the arrest: they had arrived right before the courts closed with a defective warrant that contained no amount for bail. But as I had already scoped out the worst-case scenarios, I knew that there was a night court that didn't close until 9:00 p.m. and could address our case. Even then, I was still thinking that I could make my 6:00 a.m. flight to Malaysia.

My cell phone kept buzzing with inquiries from reporters. In retrospect, I should have been speaking to the press that entire time. Why voluntarily gag myself when the state was doing something so egregious? But I did, and part of the reason was that I didn't want the officers to take my phone away.

When I arrived at NBI headquarters, accompanied by Glenda, Beth, and our lawyers, we were made to wait in the conference room. After twenty minutes, I looked at the clock and realized that the officials there were delaying so that the night court would close and they would be able to detain me for the night. So we decided to ignore the "Do not enter" sign on the door and burst into their office, where we found the arresting officers having dinner.

That moment was as close as I got to raising my voice. They knew what they were doing. But despite our protests, they kept stalling, and by 8:30 p.m., it was clear that I wouldn't be able to post bail.

Their plan succeeded. This government wanted me to stay in jail that night to harass and intimidate me. That firsthand experience of how petty it was and how far it would go only strengthened my resolve to #HoldTheLine.

I got angry again when the arresting officers said I needed a medical exam after they booked me. Rappler had a plan in place for the booking procedure, with photos ready to bypass the mug shot, which we knew the government could distribute to propaganda bloggers. Glenda and I left our lawyers to negotiate with them, and we went back to the conference room.

On the way, I was stopped by a breathless Dr. June Pagaduan-Lopez, an acquaintance from an award we received, The Outstanding Women in the Nation's Service (TOWNS), a group of women high achievers. She had come to the NBI office as soon as she'd heard I was arrested because she didn't want me to be alone for the medical exam, when you are forced to take off your clothes and are at your most vulnerable. She knew that I could bring my own doctor with me, so she asked me to declare her my physician, which I did.[2]

I was overwhelmed by that act of kindness—because no matter how much you plan ahead, you can't think of everything. My eyes misted: June cared so much, powered by her knowledge of what can go wrong in such instances. The kindness of strangers would be a recurring theme in the coming years, strengthening my faith in the goodness of human nature.

Outside, we could hear chanting: "Free Maria Ressa!" I couldn't believe it: youth leaders from the Akbayan Citizens' Action Party, Millennials PH, and other groups came to protest my arrest.

Then Beth began updating us on the annual gathering at the University of the Philippines, where I was scheduled to speak that evening.[3] In my place, Beth had sent Patricia Evangelista, who had reported the Impunity Series[4] on the drug war. She told the thousands of students gathered what had happened and read our statement:

If this is another of several attempts to intimidate us, it will not suc-
ceed, as past attempts have shown. Maria Ressa and Rappler will
continue to do our jobs as journalists. We will continue to tell the
truth and report what we see and hear. We are first and foremost
journalists. We are truthtellers.[5]

Beth showed us a video of the speech as it was happening. At one
point, the open field was engulfed with thousands of lights[6] as far as you
could see when the students held up their lit cell phones and chanted,
"Defend, defend, defend press freedom!"

The day I was first arrested—my first of ten arrest warrants in less than
two years—transformed me. And it made clear that the government was
opening a new phase in its war against press freedom and against me. I
could even hear one officer talking on his phone to someone in the palace, reporting their every move.

Glenda and Beth stayed the night with me, which relieved some
stress. We tried to sleep on chairs when we could, but most of the
time, we worked (at least we were allowed laptops). The next morning,
the bail negotiations began early. It would be the sixth time I had posted
bail in about two months. It was the largest amount so far, 100,000
pesos, or about US $2,000. But I was smiling as I reeled off the details
for the press as I left the courtroom.

I was smiling because I was so angry. You see only a hint of that anger
when a reporter asked me to react to a statement by Secretary of Justice
Menardo Guevarra, who had said that my arrest was Rappler's own fault.

"Let me turn it around," I spat, then paused for control. "DOJ secretary Guevarra, who was, I thought, a professional. These are your actions. The ripple effects are what we feel in society, but you don't want
to be known as the secretary of injustice. I also have the right to hold

you accountable. I am a citizen of this country, and you cannot violate my rights."

That night, when my government took away my freedom, they drew the line of repression directly to me. It was the moment when my rights were violated, when I went from being a journalist to being a citizen. If they could do this to journalists with some power, in the glare of the spotlight, what would they do to vulnerable citizens literally left in the dark? What recourse did a poor person have in a dark alley?

"For me, it's about two things: abuse of power and the weaponization of the law," I told the assembled reporters. It was the first time I had spoken so harshly in public; every time the government did something draconian, it radicalized me. "This isn't just about me, and it's not just about Rappler. The message that the government is sending is very clear, and someone actually told our reporter this last night: 'Be silent, or you're next.' So I'm appealing to you *not* to be silent, even if—and especially if—you're next!"

Press freedom is not just about journalists; it is not just about Rappler; it is not just about me. Press freedom is the foundation of the right of every Filipino to have access to the truth. Silence is complicity because silence is consent.

"What we're seeing is death by a thousand cuts of our democracy," I continued. "And I appeal to you to join me. . . . I've always said that when I look back a decade from now, I want to make sure—"

My voice broke then, so I repeated the sentence. "I want to make sure that I have done all I can. We will not duck. We will not hide. We will hold the line."[7]

No surprise—arresting me didn't make me miraculously shut up or force Rappler to stop reporting on corruption and abuse of power. So the Philippine government arrested me again a little more than a month later. Part of me wondered whether getting arrested every month would become my new normal. I accepted it.

By that time, I had tightened my security, at times having another car follow me when we had received tips of potential threats. That went hand in hand with increasing security around Rappler and vulnerable Rapplers as well. The whole process changed our lives. At one point, it became too expensive for me to be in Manila at all.

As a result, I began to accept more international speaking invitations. After all, I could work anywhere, and time differences allowed me to pack my days more. Speaking abroad was also an effective way of raising the alarm to the global community: If this is happening to us, it is also happening to you. If not today, then soon enough.

As the arrest warrants and cases against me increased, so did the number of courts that needed to grant me permission to travel. From December 2018 to March 2020, I had to get thirty-six permissions to travel.

On Wednesday, March 27, 2019, a little after 10:00 p.m., I was waiting at San Francisco International Airport, having just checked in for a thirteen-hour direct flight back to Manila.

My phone started filling up with alerts. Feeling a now-familiar wave of panic, I looked at the group chat between the *manang*s and our lawyers at ACCRALAW, which by now was being pressured by the government to drop our cases. The lawyers warned me that they were anticipating an arrest warrant to be issued for me shortly—my seventh. One outlined the worst-case scenario. This is the exact text:

1   Law enforcers will enter the plane and get Maria before passengers are off-loaded;

2   After arrest, Maria will not go through immigration and will be taken out of the airport to a detention center;

3   Arresting officers will confiscate her phone, and she will not be able to communicate with any of us;

4   Maria will be detained indefinitely and will have no access
     to us.

After I read the messages, I had to stop, take a breath, and lean against the wall. Once again, the government was upping the ante with its tactics. Was the Philippines becoming North Korea?

The *manang*s were already updating me on the status of their preassigned tasks: Glenda was just about to get into the car so she could go to court to post bail. Beth was handling the media and security, and she was starting to ask our lawyers questions so she could brief our drivers and guards. Chay was asking for all the documents so she could begin to frame our story on Rappler.

Me? I had to deal with my fear.

In the past few months, I had gotten used to preparing for worst-case scenarios. I kept bail money in my purse and a "go bag" in my car in case of another arrest; in it were clothes, a towel, a toothbrush, even a pillowcase. I had imagined being arrested in an airport while leaving Manila, and I had acquired a second, newer computer with fewer documents on it in case my electronic devices were confiscated.

This time, though, I was unprepared. I scrambled around the airport to find an open store where I could buy a change of clothes should I actually be arrested and jailed upon my return. Mostly, I needed to clear my head. I eventually headed to the airport lounge and sat down in a chair in the corner. I took out my laptop and began deleting the most sensitive documents.

When rats desert a sinking ship, it's a sign of danger.

I had felt that before, when I had led the negotiations for the release of our journalists with the terrorist group Abu Sayyaf when I was at ABS-CBN. When you are part of a huge corporation, politics can dictate how people avoid personal risk. At the most crucial moments, those concerned with power wash their hands of responsibility, pulling their support away at a time when it matters most.

To a much lesser degree, the filing of criminal charges against Rappler's board of directors in 2019 had that effect as well.

Our directors were the best in their fields, as well as my friends. The criminal charges they faced—and their arrest warrants—came because they believed in me and Rappler. But it wasn't a surprise—even if it was also disheartening—that those who were the most successful in business distanced themselves from us, the journalists.

That was the situation that Glenda described on the phone while I was waiting at the airport. At a restaurant near the court, she was sitting with our lawyers strategizing, while at an adjacent table, three of our directors were discussing the case with their own lawyers, despite our offer to consolidate our defenses. While in the past we stood united, we all had differing responses to the legal attacks. One of our directors never posted bail and simply avoided returning to the Philippines, a great sacrifice since his family was here. Another, a former IBM Philippines president, posted bail later in the day.

"I am so worried that their divide-and-conquer strategy will work, Glenda," I said.

"You can't do anything about it, Maria," Glenda said.

"I can call them," I said. "What deals can the government offer? Do you think we have to worry about this?"

The government's ability to sow distrust is staggering. I'm not naive; I'd spent my career observing our country's behind-the-scenes deals. Still, I had always avoided corruption. Now my friends—successful, upstanding citizens—were being catapulted into a situation in which they were being personally attacked, their businesses threatened. I felt guilty for having brought them to this crisis.

By now the four *manang*s were well versed in dealing with government intimidation. When a crisis hit, we were one step ahead of our attacker, the four of us making quick decisions aligned with our values and infused with our experience. We huddled on a four-way call, with Glenda giving an update of what the lawyers were saying: the charge, the amount of bail. Chay was asking questions to help draft the story for publication.

I asked them all the question that was burning through my gut: What was their reaction to the worst-case scenario from our lawyer? I even raised the specter of the 1983 assassination of Ninoy Aquino, who had been taken from a plane and shot on the tarmac.

They laughed, releasing my tension. Each gave a measured, thoughtful response to my question. Those are the fears they never tell you about: that you can imagine infinite worst-case possibilities and, especially if you are the target, that you need a reality check at key moments. Rapplers had each other's backs.

An announcement over the airport intercom interrupted the call. It was time to board. I said good-bye, packed up my things, and walked to the gate. When I got to my seat on the plane, I stowed my bag and asked for orange juice.

It was after 4:00 p.m. in Manila, less than an hour before the courts would close. There was still no arrest warrant for me. Maybe the worst-case scenario would remain in our imaginations. I sipped my drink and began to feel better.

The plane door closed. That was when I got a text that kept me awake for most of the thirteen-hour flight home: "The judge issued the arrest warrant. Prepare to be arrested."

My adrenaline was pumping when we landed. Thankfully, the plane wasn't stopped at the runway. Gathering my things, I ran through my plan of action step by step, setting up my two phones so I could just push a button to go live on Rappler's Facebook page, willing my intentions into muscle memory.

After the plane door opened, I was first up. As I exited, I turned on Facebook Live on one cell phone, the other primed in my back pocket. As soon as I stepped off the jetway, police officers approached me, two women in the lead. One pulled me aside and began reading me my Miranda rights. There were at least six other officers lurking close by, including a man who seemed to be their supervisor.

They asked me to put my coat over my hands. I asked why. Their protocol called for them to handcuff me, but they must have found it strange or difficult for some reason. I waited as they tried to find a compromise. The subtle dissension within their ranks showed me something: individuals in a country that is sliding toward autocracy don't lose their personal agency in one day; they make choices every day whether or not to comply with the autocrat's demands.

I told them I wasn't going to pretend to be handcuffed. An ACCRALAW lawyer stepped in when my voice started to rise. After a short discussion, the group escorted me through immigration and baggage claim, my hands uncuffed.

Waiting inside their van were six officers in SWAT gear, fully armed. I guess to a lying government, a journalist is a terrorist, setting off bombs that blow up their lies.

When one of the women officers held my head as I entered the van, I pushed back. Somehow that hand at the back of my head symbolized every wrong that I was subjected to.

Then I remembered: Pull back. Suppress your emotions. Find clarity of thought.

Again I posted bail and kept going.

The month after that arrest, I went to New York City to attend the formal launch of TrialWatch, a system of observing court trials around the world, that had been created by the Clooney Foundation for Justice.[8] The Philippine government still allowed me to leave the country, but as usual, before each trip, I had to go through the arduous and enraging process of seeking court approvals. It took both time and money to file the necessary legal documents, and every time I had to wait through the uncertainty and then post bond, I wanted to assert my rights even more.

I was also exhausted. When I don't get enough sleep, it shows in my skin. I have atopic dermatitis or eczema, extremely dry skin that erupts—the skin literally breaks open when I'm stressed. Through years of dealing with this, I have learned that my mind and emotions play as much of a role as the medicines my dermatologist prescribes for me. But I had been ignoring the latest outbreak for weeks—weeks that had now turned into months. It was so bad on the plane that a friend took me to the doctor soon after.

It was cold and windy the morning of the TrialWatch launch, which was being held at Columbia Law School. I went to the back row of the auditorium and set up my tripod and camera. I was going to livestream the event on Rappler. When I took the stage, I looked out over a who's who of human rights activists, lawyers, tech types, and journalists. George and Amal Clooney were in the front row.

The panel discussed how the law had been weaponized against journalists all around the world and why it was so important to have international court observers. There was no better example than the three of us onstage: to my right was the Canadian Egyptian Mohamed Fahmy, jailed in Egypt for 437 days;[9] on my left was the Iranian American Jason Rezaian, jailed in Iran for 544 days.[10]

Listening to them, I realized two things: one, I had not yet been jailed beyond the one night to scare me, so it was probably going to get worse, and two, having a dual identity such as Filipino American might help when it did.

After the panel ended, I whispered to Fahmy, "So what advice would you give me?"

"Get Amal as your lawyer," he said.

After the panel finished, I was ushered into one of the offices upstairs. Shortly after, Amal and George walked in. The door closed, and Amal sat behind the desk. "I've been thinking about what's important," she began, "and I think you have a choice in how you want me involved."

Then, rapid-fire, she began to lay out exactly what would happen to me, offering her own experiences in different countries with various journalists as examples. I took out my notebook and began scribbling furiously.

Amal outlined two ways she could be involved: either as the head of TrialWatch, sending observers to my court trials, in which case she would have to be more circumspect about my case; or she could represent me, in which case she would be my advocate.

Well, that seemed like an easy choice. She summarized some of her lessons from cases she had worked on, pulling up references from numerous countries like Azerbaijan and Egypt and her ongoing negotiations for the release of the Reuters journalists Wa Lone and Kyaw Soe Oo, who had been jailed in Myanmar. She expected that they would be released within the next two weeks on a presidential pardon.

"Didn't Myanmar just take another hardline position last night?" I asked.

"You have to give governments like that room to save face, Maria," she replied. "There are things that happen publicly, and there are things that happen behind the scenes. A lot of my work I can't ever talk about."

Then she asked for specifics about my cases: Who else aside from Duterte could act on my cases? Would it be possible for me and Rappler to get a fair trial? I told her that so far not one decision on those ridiculous cases had come down in our favor.

And once a state files a criminal case against you, people look at you differently—much as I once had with Leila de Lima. It isn't "You're innocent until proven guilty" as much as "Prove your innocence." Somehow our instinct is still to trust that a state won't use its power in an absurdly vindictive manner—that is, until the evidence of it becomes overwhelming. I appreciated that even though Amal said she would have to study our cases, she treated me like few did at the time—innocent until proven guilty.

She asked why I wouldn't just stay in the United States, given that I was a dual citizen and my family was here. It's a question I get a lot, and my response has always been the same: I run Rappler; I am responsible for a company. If I get scared and leave, who will bear the brunt of all the attacks? That would betray everyone who believes in Rappler's vision and those who support us.

But talking to Amal showed me how poorly prepared I was for even the best worst-case scenario that I had imagined. I knew so little about international law, UN processes, and what I might face in the coming days.

I hate feeling unprepared because that's when I get scared. And I did.

A little less than two weeks later, Wa Lone and Kyaw Soe Oo walked out of a Myanmar prison after more than five hundred days in jail, part of the seven-year sentence they had received for allegedly violating the Burma Official Secrets Act. They were among the 6,620 prisoners released under a presidential amnesty, just as Amal had predicted.

The news reinforced a painful realization: I couldn't tell our editorial team that Amal predicted this; I could no longer add context to breaking news because my main task now was fighting for my rights. Such irony for a reporter: the more you find out, the less you can tell.

Amal agreed to be my legal counsel and to help Rappler. As we worked together, I began to realize how unique she is:[11] she pays extreme attention to detail and has a strategic mind that, like my own, prepares for the worst. Her focused public messages show the influence of her journalist mother. I joke that I have a flashlight to shine the light, but Amal has massive klieg lights. Though she first focused on human rights, succeeding years have seen her fighting for journalists and independent media. She works for change both in the trenches, at the micro level, and in the halls of power on the global stage.

Amal assembled a brilliant international legal team, all of them familiar with the dangers of being a journalist. One of them, Caoilfhionn Gallagher, was the lead international counsel for the family of the murdered Maltese journalist Daphne Caruana Galizia, and had worked on many cases involving journalists at risk around the world.[12]

I learned so much from listening to how they all worked and what they did. Above all, I came to see how international law needed revamping because of the root cause: the changes in our information ecosystem. After all, facts lie at the heart of the rule of law.

"I do feel pressure when I work on cases like yours," Amal told me. "To some degree, your case does keep me up at night, and so it should. . . . Your foe is the most powerful person in the country."[13]

There are times when I joke that I have to thank President Duterte for attacking us. I wouldn't have needed such help: neither my lawyers nor the thousands of people who contributed to our legal defense fund, everyone who helps us hold the line.

In February 2020, I was in London for a packed three and a half days. Little did we know that in about a month, a virus would lock down the world.

In Manila, there were daily protests outside ABS-CBN, demanding that its franchise be restored. There was much uncertainty as the Philippines prepared to celebrate the thirty-fourth anniversary of People Power.

I was trying to get some work done, but the heat in my room was stifling. I had gotten at least an hour of good work in, but I felt off-kilter, unbalanced. I was so tired, my mind so cluttered, my skin agitated, telling me I needed to sleep.

Amal was adamant that I come to her house for dinner during the trip. She said we needed to talk about the concerns she'd had from the beginning and about the full range of risks that I faced—a conversation we could have only in person.

It was one of those go/no-go moments, like the feeling right before I plunge into war zone coverage, trying to anticipate everything that could go wrong. What if I don't go back to Manila, take the safe route, and stay where I am? But it was an option I couldn't seriously consider. I just had to embrace my fears. These discussions with my lawyers, as it turned out, would trigger one of my biggest crises of confidence about the road ahead.

At Amal's home that evening, she raised the case of Daphne Caruana Galizia. Caoilfhionn Gallagher had talked to me a lot about Daphne, including showing me some of the online abuse, which had grafted her head onto animal parts. I had also showed Caoilfhionn some of the dehumanizing memes being used against me.

I told Amal that two of Daphne's sons had already spoken to me. "Matthew and Paul made it a point to tell me that they were worried about me. Matthew took me to lunch and said, 'You are following in my mother's footsteps.' That made me stop, Amal, because he was in the kitchen when the car bomb exploded and killed his mom."

At one point, Daphne's family took what they were telling me privately and issued a statement:

> *Over the years, we watched the former Prime Minister of Malta Joseph Muscat and his cronies pursue increasingly deranged attacks on Daphne. . . .*
>
> *This targeted harassment, chillingly similar to that perpetrated against Maria Ressa, created the conditions for Daphne's murder.*
>
> *The government of the Philippines is creating the possibility of a violent attack against Maria and other journalists.*

Its targeted legal harassment of Maria identifies her to Duterte's officials and supporters as an enemy, implicitly granting them permission for further attacks.[14]

"It's very volatile, Maria," Amal said, "and you're at their mercy."

I tried to listen and stay open to Amal's thoughts. I knew I needed to hear what she was telling me. That dinner began two days of intense doubt and self-questioning. It made me afraid. And it was the first time in a long time that I felt alone. So I imagined taking different paths and carried them out in my mind.

Early the next morning, I touched base with the *manang*s. Glenda, Beth, and Chay were just finishing a protest march outside ABS-CBN. They huddled in the parking lot as I laid out my concerns. Could it be that we weren't seeing the forest for the trees? Were we the frog in boiling water? Do victims of state suppression and killings know when it's time to leave? I reminded them that on the day *Washington Post* journalist Jason Rezaian and his wife, Yeganeh, had been sent to jail in Iran, they had postponed plans to leave the country.

It proved to be a difficult conversation because it was a rare instance when our personal and professional interests diverged. They knew I was scared and that if I acted on that fear, the cascading failures would fall on them. By now you know that I love the *manang*s: they are the best example of the goodness of human nature, of how we fight our worst demons and take the right path for the public good. I didn't want to be the deserting rat, triggering a stampede that would ultimately sink the ship.

So my cofounders reminded me that in times of crisis we have always taken a step back, assessed it, and carefully calibrated our response to it. "Look at history," Glenda said. "We know where this is headed. We've always known what we're doing, and nothing has changed." She and Beth pointed out that the government attacks were legal in nature, coordinated by Jose Calida, the solicitor general; that the Duterte administration's weapon of choice, at least for us right now, was lawfare.

"We do have to keep track that that doesn't change," Beth reminded us. "And we are. We have enough sources so we will know if that changes."

But as more purges happened inside government, law enforcement, and the military, those who were professional and competent and had a track record that we could rely on as sources were gradually opting out—either retiring or just shutting up while third-string appointees took over. It was a disastrous combination of incompetence, arrogance, and impunity.

"Maria, you'd be jumping bail," Chay reminded me.

"I know, and I can't give them that satisfaction," I responded.

Even though the government was making a farce of the rule of law, I abided by the principles of the law. But would I be breaking the law if I didn't comply when illegally charged? It was a point Amal was reinforcing all the time, the slippery slope of what happens when those charged with keeping strong the rule of law bend and break it. There is nothing left.

The next morning, the day I was supposed to board a flight to Manila, I met Caoilfhionn for breakfast. She began laying out the next steps, and like Amal the other night, forcefully expressed her concerns about the risks I was facing. She was deeply immersed in the legal and advocacy work of helping journalists and human rights activists in some of the most difficult places around the world. She had the courage to visit countries other lawyers would stay away from. I trusted her, too.

But I was back on firmer ground emotionally. When I walked her to the hotel entrance, we embraced.

"You're getting on the flight, aren't you?" Caoilfhionn asked.

"Yes, I am," I said. "It's where I have to be and what I have to do."

Since 2019, I've invariably been asked by interviewers why I choose to come back to the Philippines, and my response is simple: there is no other choice.

Over time, you get used to fear. It diminishes. You accept that bad things may happen, and if it does, what will you do? I can almost clinically take apart the worst-case scenario. I know I can survive it. There are always upsides to even the worst events. If I were to go to jail, I could sleep, for one.

In those last months of 2019, and certainly by the covid lockdowns of March 2020, I was so exhausted that I was starting to break down. The Duterte propaganda machine had been attacking me not just with visceral sexist and misogynistic posts for almost four years but also with metanarratives about my so-called criminality to help set the stage for the government's future acts against me. As the cases piled on, I had to seek court approvals to travel outside the Philippines, which were, at that point, granted. Perhaps the government wanted me to jump bail. But, as the *manang*s maintained, that would have made their lie a reality. Jumping bail would mean that I would break the law. I would be a criminal.

It all became clear to me: no one can make you do anything you do not want to do. All the government's actions—the online attacks, the president's threats, the legal cases it filed against me—all of them were meant to frighten me, to make me so afraid that I wouldn't be me. The people in the government wanted me to act like them.

Except: I'm. Not. Like. Them.

The term *gaslighting*—in which an abuser avoids accountability by either claiming the abused is crazy or turning it around and accusing the victim of what the abuser is doing—took on new meaning in the age of social media, where abuse is exponential and creates a bandwagon effect. So although the repeated lies likely convinced some people that I was a criminal, they also convinced me that the administration was willing to break the law in order to consolidate power. I had firsthand experience. Proof.

That gave me two insights, one about them, the other about me.

Let's start with the political operators and others who so lack a moral compass that they are willing to manipulate the law and government agencies to punish a journalist. Lackeys not only repeatedly break the law; they then use their power to excuse themselves. The implicit values in the Duterte administration's words and deeds[15] were like those of the Mafia: use your power for yourself; get away with whatever you can. It works in patronage-driven feudal politics, and it works when you're building a nationwide kleptocracy.

All those are big words, societal problems caused by the way those we elect exercise their power, quick financial gains (otherwise known as corruption) anchoring all of it. Over time, it becomes imperative to retain power because all that has been done for money would be exposed if power transferred hands.

The closer we got to the next presidential elections, which would be held in May 2022, the more desperate Duterte's allies were to keep power. They took increasingly bold measures, from changing the Constitution to escalating violence to prevent others from running for office to bribing the military and police with increased benefits and pensions. Duterte admitted it: he leads with violence and fear.[16]

That was why I kept coming home and why I will stay and fight until the end: I believe that the way to fight back is to expose every single abusive step in what the government is doing to me, Rappler, other journalists, human rights activists, and Filipino citizens.

There's a great quote from Ursula K. Le Guin (who used "boy" and "man" in this paragraph, but I will use "girl" and "woman" instead): "You thought, as a girl, that a mage is one who can do anything. So I thought, once. So did we all. And the truth is that as a woman's real power grows and her knowledge widens, ever the way she can follow grows narrower: until at last she chooses nothing, but does only and wholly what she *must do*."

While social media hammered the fracture lines of society, playing on our insecurities, the path forward was simple: we must cut through the noise.

You always have the choice to be who you are. I choose—as I always have—to live by the values that define who I am. I will not become a criminal to fight a criminal. I will not become a monster to fight a monster.

You value life most intensely when you are living with the threat of its end, and you fight every step, moment by moment, to find meaning. That's the biggest lesson Twink taught me.

By that time, her first marriage had been annulled, and she had finally found the love of her life and given birth to a son named Juancho, to whom I was an absentee godmother, or *ninang*. After we started Rappler, she became the Bloomberg TV Philippines channel head, a *Philippine Star* columnist, and a TV5 anchor. But we stayed close, catching up over lengthy, memorable dinners and early-morning, rambling, hours-long conversations that bridged the different worlds we now lived in.

Back in 2016, her cancer, which had been in remission, had returned with a vengeance.[17] It had not only come back but had metastasized in her lower back and was now at stage 4. There is no stage 5.

"How do you fight a disease that doesn't play fair?" Twink asked her cancer support group after receiving the news. "Why do you fight when fighting is futile; when fighting won't cure you: when losing is inevitable and the only reason to fight is just to 'not go down without a fight'?"

Whether we are cancer survivors, patients, or totally healthy individuals, we actually die a little every day, they told her. Each day lived is also another day never to be repeated. Now all we ask is to spend our remaining days with significance.

Twink took that to heart.

When I felt as though I was in the fight of my life, pushing back against a government that was abusing its powers, Twink put things into perspective for me: my trials paled compared to hers. And despite what she was going through, she was always there to help. When the online attacks and lies escalated, she notified me. When I felt inundated by them, she began answering them. She always wanted to know what was happening, how I was feeling, trying to give me strength, cursing others for me when I couldn't.

She helped me track a lie started by a former journalist, who tweeted that my parents were Indonesian. His social media posts were amplified by the Duterte propaganda machine.

Twink responded aggressively to the tweets. Her posts gave me great energy. Mine never quite had the same punch.

Despite the grimness of the diagnosis, all along I assumed that she would beat cancer like she did the first time. Until the end, I was in denial.

Her physical changes should have alerted me in 2019: the total hair loss, the body brace; at one of our last lunches alone together, she had to use a cane. I offered to come over to her place, but she countered that she would meet me in the office. By that time, she had to wear a surgical mask

---

Malcolm Conlan @MalcolmConlan · Jul 18, 2019
How is she a Filipino? Both her parents are Indonesian, it was down to pure luck that she was born in the Philippines, so acquired Filipino Citizenship.

   27   ⟲ 2   ♡ 12

Twink Macaraig @twinkmac · Jul 18, 2019
Both her parents are Filipino. Her father died & her mother married an American. But NONE of her parents is Indonesian. I know bec I was her classmate from ages 4-9 in a Mla school. Her 1st degree relative is Filipino pianist, Raul Sunico. Cite YOUR sources, you malicious prick.

   12   ⟲ 66   ♡ 464

Maria Ressa ✓ @mariaressa · Jul 18, 2019
Thanks, Twink!

   2   ⟲ 2   ♡ 79

Twink Macaraig
@twinkmac

Replying to @mariaressa @MalcolmConlan and @FlamingPie30

Don't mention it. Happy to debunk even just 1 of the countless lies abt u being wantonly spread. Be safe 😊
#holdtheline #DefendMediaFreedom

9:05 AM · Jul 19, 2019 · Twitter for Android

for fear of catching a disease, and she asked me to walk with her to help steady her.

Despite all that, I assumed that her strength of will would ultimately prevail over the disease. I suppose that's a fundamental belief I should reexamine: that you can shape the world you live in with your mind.

In December 2019, Twink's health took a turn for the worse, and Cheche and I visited her at the hospital. She waved off her frailty and started making plans. She wanted to see the fireworks on New Year's Eve, so I offered my apartment, which has a fantastic view of the skyline. She, her husband, Paulo, and Juancho would stay the night. Since her immune system was compromised by the cancer treatments, I canceled the party I had planned.

When they arrived on December 31, it was already dark outside. Paulo was pushing Twink in a wheelchair; Juancho took their things into the guest bedroom. Twink was relieved that she was coherent. The doctors had now prescribed fentanyl for her, and even a quarter of the dosage made it impossible for her to write or think clearly. Early in his term, and again in 2019, President Duterte had admitted to taking fentanyl. Twink was adamant that Duterte couldn't be coherent with the far larger doses he was taking.

Paulo wheeled Twink into the living room and left us alone. It was clear that Twink wanted to talk. After about fifteen minutes of catching up, she said she was starting to get tired. It broke my heart to see her so frail.

"Maria, when I die, I don't want a wake," she said.

"Oh, c'mon, Twink, stop that. You're going to beat this," I said. "What can I do? Let's plan your next steps."

"Remember when I told you I want a party when I die?" she asked. "I haven't changed my mind."

In 1986, soon after I had returned to the Philippines, I'd often get to her place around two in the morning. I would sleep over, and when we woke up, we would shoot the breeze talking about life and love. During those moments, as we were just starting our lives, we talked about how we wanted to die. Twink had explained to me that Filipinos stayed for days and nights in front of the open coffin of someone they loved, one of the most uncomfortable customs I was learning about. A wake, or *lamay*, would last from three to seven days, sometimes longer.

"I don't want people looking at me," she'd told me back then, "when I can't look back at them. So definitely no wake. I'd rather my friends all have a party to celebrate me."

I had, of course, been horrified, and we had debated it over the years. When you cover death and destruction, as we did, there is plenty of time to do that.

As I got older, I realized that the wake isn't for the dead; it's for the living.

"Promise me that you will have a party," she told me now, holding my hand before the fireworks exploded for 2020. I don't remember if I promised. I didn't have to, because, of course, I would follow her wishes.

In the early-morning hours of January 14, 2020, before a pandemic would force all of us to wear surgical masks as she already did, Twink died. That she was gone didn't really hit me until her birthday on May 9, when she would have turned fifty-six.

New Year's Eve fireworks, December 31, 2019, with Paulo Alcazaren and Twink Macaraig. (*Photo by Patricia Evangelista*)

By then a global lockdown had forced us all into quarantine at home, allowing me to pull out our old photos and a column she had written in 2019. I know how hard she had worked on that because she had sent drafts to me before it was published. In it, she had accepted her mortality, but in doing that, she had issued a call for battle, comparing her cancer to our nation's fight for democracy. She wrote:

I look at this world I'm struggling to stay in and feel only despair. The despot Filipinos elected to the presidency has infected the populace with a malignance unmatched by the deadliest of cancers. . . .

Both suppress your freedoms. By dint of my disease, my movements have been severely curtailed. I will never run, do a Surya Namaskara, play tennis or cover a news event again. My immune system is so compromised that venturing into a crowded room is a roll of the dice. I cannot stand or sit up for long periods and my double-

vision makes writing difficult. In short, practicing journalism, the profession I devoted most of my adult life to, is no longer viable. In a much larger context, Duterte has enfeebled our institutions by populating them with minions who share his low regard for human rights, due process and what words really mean. These institutions that form part of our nation's immune system should have ensured that our freedoms were protected. Instead, they're party to repressing dissent, demonizing the opposition and preventing scrutiny by a critical press. The Constitution, the last bastion of our democracy, and also a key component of the collective immune system, is in the process of being dismantled. When that goes, all protections, all the freedoms it guarantees go too.

So where is the outrage? Where is the resistance?

A weary voice in my head says, Don't look at me. I'm dying. I should be excused.

I've long made peace with my demise. . . . My last will and testament—handwritten amidst many tears—is in the safe. . . .

I could Give Up. Succumb. Surrender. But I won't.

No matter how many times I read this, I cry.

. . . Because not fighting would ignore the very real option that still exists: the handful of brave, honorable souls putting their lives on the line on the firm belief that the Filipino people can get better; can choose to get better; deserve better. They represent, if not a cure, the lone path to a cure too late for my benefit, perhaps, but for the next generation.

While family and friends, their family and friends, keep praying rosaries for my healing, or send chakras and incantations my way;

While my husband continues to move me with his sweetness and my son doesn't run out of silly jokes, magic tricks, and funny anecdotes of his daily exploits;

While the very heart of me—that chamber that stores my conscience and conviction, love and dreams, memory and self-respect—remains unbreached, I will fight.[18]

I will, too, in Twink's memory.
Rest in peace, my friend.

Chapter 11

Hold the Line

What Doesn't Kill You Makes You Stronger

Rey Santos, Jr., Ted Te, and I answer questions from the press after our conviction, June 15, 2020. (*Rappler*)

One of the last dinners I had before the pandemic was in London with Carole Cadwalladr in February 2020. Carole was the *Observer* reporter who, along with reporters at the *New York Times*, had broken the Cambridge Analytica story. The businessman Arron Banks, the largest Brexit campaign donor in Great Britain, had filed a case against her the previous year for libel.[1] In response, Carole had turned around and filed a case right back against him.[2]

Throughout the pandemic, Carole and I would compare notes about the line between journalism and activism: how the online attacks against us affected our work, how we dealt with our ongoing legal cases. Both of us needed to confront antiquated definitions of the two because of the attacks against us. Carole's challenges were immense; she didn't have an organization supporting her. In order to pay her legal fees, she had benefited from a successful crowdsourcing campaign but had still had to mortgage her home. During the worst of times, we checked in with each other.[3]

The attacks on her groundbreaking reporting put Carole into a predicament similar to my own. Carole put it to me this way: "In Britain, where I was looking at this erosion of democracy and the tech platforms' role in that and the use of bad actors, it positioned me in a cultural war. So instead of it being like 'This is defending the rule of law, it's defending our national security,' it's different. And I was seen as a rampant anti-Brexiteer . . . and that fed into this language of misogyny and abuse. . . . I found myself targeted and smeared. It's had an impact because it stopped me from doing the job that I once did because now I'm seen as . . . a partisan, controversial figure when I was literally just trying to do my job."[4]

Similarly, the targeted online attack campaigns painted me as anti-government or pro-Aquino, politicizing my reporting, something neither I nor Rappler ever did; the Philippine political landscape and media had previously not been as ideological as that in countries like the United States and the United Kingdom. But the attacks against me had started to affect my work, including my ability to interview government officials. After one of my chats with Carole, I called the *manang*s, and we began discussing a timetable for me to ease out of editorial. We agreed that I would continue to run our tech, data, and business operations, but I would no longer be executive editor. Effective November 2020, Glenda Gloria took over Rappler's top editorial post.[5]

I was entering into a new phase of my life. I went from being the researcher to the one taking action. I also had nothing to lose. I was in lockdown, I was facing trials that could put me into jail for life, but by that year Rappler's new business model was working. That gave me the energy to try something new. I had realized that journalism wasn't the only part of the solution. Journalism enabled facts to survive. But it was communities that must respond. Globally, we needed a new model of civic engagement.

For a few years, starting in 2016, I still went to Facebook executives in the hope that our data and my arguments would encourage them to change certain aspects of their platform. By 2018, I realized that Facebook wouldn't do anything substantive. And in 2020, I started to think that Facebook was the bad guy. That year, Carole also asked me to join her brainchild, what we later called the Real Facebook Oversight Board.[6]

Mark Zuckerberg had recently announced the creation of Facebook's "Supreme Court," an oversight board[7] designed to take content moderation to an independent court-style setup. That board addressed the wrong issue: content, which had never really been the problem. The first problem was the company's distribution model: an oversight board on content could never match the speed of the dissemination of information online.

The Real Facebook Oversight Board consisted of experts demanding that Facebook change the policies that were destroying our world. One was Shoshana Zuboff, the academic who had coined the term "surveillance capitalism." The others were Roger McNamee, one of the first Silicon Valley investors in Facebook; Rashad Robinson, the president of the civil rights nonprofit Color of Change; Derrick Johnson, the president and CEO of the NAACP; and Jonathan Greenblatt, the CEO of the Anti-Defamation League. I learned that activists were crucial in such an endeavor; academics and journalists could spin themselves in circles, but activists provided a road map for action points.

The Real Facebook Oversight Board launched a little more than a month before the 2020 US presidential elections. With so much at stake, we thought it was time to puncture Zuckerberg's persistent deflection of criticism, as well as our collective learned helplessness before Facebook's unimaginable power.

"Our group has come together for one purpose," Shoshana said. "We demand comprehensive action to ensure that Facebook cannot be weaponized to undermine the vote and with it American democracy."

We decided that instead of making broad, lofty demands, we would focus first on quickly actionable points,[8] especially given the tight timeline and Trump's increasingly unhinged behavior. We distilled them down to three demands of Facebook: to enforce its own policies and remove posts inciting violence; to ban ads that seek to delegitimize election results; and to take measures to prevent disinformation and misinformation about the election results. It was a sign of the times that within twenty-four hours, Facebook acted on all of them.

It never admitted it, though. Instead, it attacked our members. In those months, much of what Rappler had discovered about Facebook and social media based on our own data and research, as well as many of our suspicions, was slowly being confirmed by reporters, whistleblowers, and even the companies themselves.

A mong the first was Christopher Wylie, the Cambridge Analytica whistleblower, whom I managed to meet twice—once as a journalist interviewing him and the second time when I joined him for *Studio B: Unscripted*, an Al Jazeera program[9] taping in London. I had wanted someone to verify many of Rappler's findings. He not only verified our data but offered me his analysis of the processes and products he had helped build.

Chris had learned data and targeting in the Obama campaign, taken it to Canada's opposition, had taught himself to code, had gone to law school at the London School of Economics, and had been getting his PhD in fashion trend forecasting when he had gotten the idea for Cambridge Analytica's "psychological warfare mindfuck tool,"[10] as he would call it. When we talked, he was also able to fully explain the relationship between Cambridge Analytica and the Philippines.

"When the Cambridge Analytica scandal broke," I said to him at our first meeting, "the most number of compromised Facebook accounts was in the US, but the second most . . ."

". . . was in the Philippines," he replied right away.[11]

The company Chris worked for was a company called SCL (Strategic Communications Laboratory) Group, the parent company of Cambridge Analytica, which had a relatively long history of working in Filipino politics. Later, when he worked for Cambridge Analytica, staff from the company would visit the Philippines. Chris's main message and lesson learned from Cambridge Analytica was "Colonialism never died, it just moved online."

"The way SCL—and later Cambridge Analytica—would make money is they would go into countries with relatively underdeveloped regulatory infrastructure or questionable rule of law," Chris explained, "where it was easy to get away with things and create propaganda and support politicians who would be willing later to pay back favors."[12]

Chris had learned that even if Western powers had officially left a country, a certain kind of influence did not. "It just became more discreet. And so SCL was the company that specialized in doing that," he said, "It did work in the Philippines. When you look at countries in the developing world or the Global South, there are certain countries that stand out with a much higher rate of internet penetration and social media use. So the Philippines is one of those countries where you've got a lot of people online and a lot of people using social media. So when you've got that kind of setup, it's an ideal target."

"Target as in a place to experiment?" I asked. Former digital managers of products with companies like Yahoo and startup founders had told me the same thing: if you want to test a digital product for the West, you try it out first in the Philippines.

"Yes," Chris said. ". . . Whether it's manipulating voter opinion or disseminating propaganda, it's more difficult to do that in countries like the US or Britain or Europe where there is robust regulatory action, there's robust law enforcement. . . . In countries . . . where corruption is rife, it creates an ideal petri dish type situation where you can experiment on tactics and techniques that you wouldn't be able to do as easily in the West. And if it doesn't work, it doesn't matter, you won't get caught. If it does work, then you can then figure out how to port that into other countries. The company worked in a lot of places in Southeast Asia and in Africa as well as the Caribbean to play with ideas and to try to develop technologies before it would then port it onto the West."

"Is it fair to say that the trial and error, the petri dish in the Philippines, paved the way for Brexit and Donald Trump?" I asked.

He paused. "Okay, so if you look at the Philippines—" He paused again. I thought he might be weighing how to navigate potential legal land mines.

"Recently, Filipino politics kinda looks a lot like the United States," he continued, rolling his eyes and gesturing with his hands. "You've got a president who was Trump before Trump was Trump, and you have relationships with people close to him with SCL and Cambridge Analytica. And you had a lot of data being collected—the second largest amount of data after the United States being collected in the Philippines. Also if you look at how SCL and Cambridge Analytica operated in a lot of countries . . . one of the things they talk about is that they use . . . they don't go into a country as Cambridge Analytica. They don't go into a country as SCL Group because it's too obvious. So you use local partners—"

"Proxies," I clarified.

"You use proxies," he continued. ". . . They're on camera admitting this. They go into countries, set up bullshit companies that are just fronts and they send in staff. It makes it very difficult for regulators or opposition parties to actually identify what's happening. And as they also have admitted, once an election is done, they just get out. So they're in. They're out. They've got their guy in, and then you know they can come back and ask for favors."

"Okay," I interrupted, "Alexander Nix [the Cambridge Analytica president] came to the Philippines at the end of 2015 before the campaigns began, and there was a photo of him—"[13]

"Yeah, he met with people there," said Chris.

"—the staff of Duterte," I finished.

"Yeah! What do you think he was doing there?" Chris asked.[14]

Each new revelation about Facebook practices—from the Cambridge Analytica scandal to the *Wall Street Journal* series covering the documents leaked by the whistleblower Frances Haugen—validated everything Rappler had long said and much of which we had reported to Facebook first. Everything I have written here, including granular data, we had shared at some point with Facebook, hoping against hope that it would act.

In the instances when Facebook did act, it often made the problem and the spread of disinformation worse. One example was shutting down the API, the application programming interface, that enabled third parties to gather data. The move was intended to prevent another Cambridge Analytica scandal, but it also prevented researchers like us from understanding the platform. Rappler had been among the first to focus on the astroturfing of comments, which had deceived the public into believing that certain political campaigns had grassroots support and consensus. But without the API, researchers couldn't do that kind of analysis anymore. Instead of making the platform more transparent, as Mark claimed to be doing, the company made sure that no one but Facebook had the data to see the whole picture.[15]

Even when the company produced its own disturbing internal research findings, its executives refused to act. A 2016 internal presentation about Germany detailed that "64% of all extremist group joins are due to our recommendation tools," such as algorithms driving "Groups You Should Join" and "Discover." The report made a very clear statement: "Our recommendation systems grow the problem."[16]

Facebook has a staggering ability to determine the fates of news organizations—of journalism itself, even. Today it has an internal ranking for news that is supposedly determined by algorithms; however, not only did a human code those algorithms, but Facebook decides whether a given user is fed more hate or more facts. After the January 6, 2021, violence on Capitol Hill, Facebook released its mode of response to worst-case scenarios (called "break glass" measures).[17] One of them was to dial up facts. That meant that in the algorithmic mix for distribution it would increase what it calls "news ecosystem quality" scores,[18] a secret internal ranking for news publishers based on the quality of their journalism. Recommendations of news sites like CNN, the *New York Times*, and NPR spiked while those of hyperpartisan pages such as Breitbart dropped. So we know that Facebook can do it.

Restoring a "nicer news feed" is one of the demands of the Real Facebook Oversight Board, something the Philippines would need leading up to our crucial presidential election on May 9, 2022, and something all countries would need for their own elections.

I have always been certain about Facebook's influence on our democracies because Rappler had the data and we lived through its harmful impact. Throughout the 2020 pandemic year, our staff kept working, researching, and discovering.

Our Sharktank database is now available to academic institutions and researchers who want to understand how information operations can transform a robust democracy into authoritarian rule.[19] By August 2021, the Sharktank database had captured 382,633,021 public posts and 444,788,994 comments from 68,097 public pages, 23,736 public groups, and 4,759,678 users on Facebook. It had also captured 11,400,241 unique links from 235,265 websites. Once YouTube overtook Facebook as the number one social media platform in the Philippines in 2021, we began monitoring public channels and now have insights into content from 331,471 YouTube channels.

The chart below is an example of how we can map our information ecosystem. Each circle is a Facebook page, and its size is based on eigenvector centrality, or its power to distribute. From 2016 to 2019, we were able to see how traditional news groups were pushed from the center to the periphery.

By then, Facebook had launched its international fact-checking program in the Philippines. Rappler and Vera Files, a small media nonprofit, became Facebook's local fact-checking partners.[20] I have long maintained that fact-checking is a whack-a-mole game, but doing it enabled

The network map above is from October 2018, right before midterm elections in May 2019. The center is dominated by pro-Duterte, pro-Marcos, and government accounts, what I have referred to as the propaganda machine, spewing half-truths and lies. News organizations were pushed away from the center—represented by some of the circles on the left. The two right-hand clusters are largely fast-growing Facebook meme pages, ready to be deployed for election campaigns, which did happen during the 2019 elections.

us to identify the posts that are meant to mislead. The Duterte administration immediately complained.[21]

Our first step in the fact-checking process was to find the lies. As mentioned previously, the best lies are half-truths that work to support a metanarrative, like "Duterte is the best leader" or "Journalists are criminals." Step two was to use natural language processing, using computers to process large amounts of text to pull out the consistent messages of networks of disinformation. Doing that led us to step three, which was identifying the websites and other digital assets associated with those networks, including those profiting off the enterprise.[22]

Duterte had consolidated power and polarized the society by often using asymmetrical warfare, with small groups like us trying to stand up for the facts against the disinformation that was more likely to travel over pro-Duterte and pro-Marcos disinformation networks.

One of the first times when there was a near-even split in our information ecosystem was when I was arrested on February 13, 2019. You can see below how most Filipinos shared and amplified traditional news organizations, giving news a higher eigenvector centrality. You can also

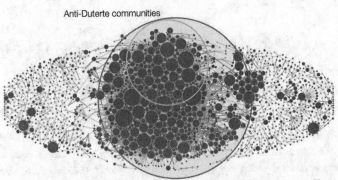

Anti-Duterte communities

Pro-Duterte/Marcos communities

The pro-Duterte communities actively share and spread each other's content within a large, coordinated network. While anti-Duterte communities have started to organize themselves online, they are still behind in terms of sheer quantity.

Visualization: https://public.flourish.studio/visualisation/2297941/

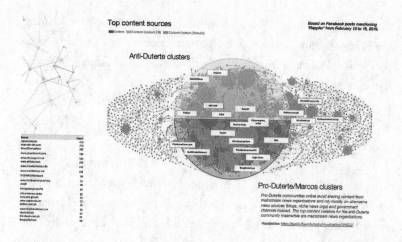

Top content sources

Based on Facebook posts mentioning 'Rappler' from February 12 to 19, 2019.

Anti-Duterte clusters

Pro-Duterte/Marcos clusters

Pro-Duterte communities online avoid sharing content from mainstream news organizations and rely mostly on alternative news sources (blogs, niche news orgs) and government channels instead. The top content creators for the anti-Duterte community meanwhile are mainstream news organizations.

Visualization: https://public.flourish.studio/visualisation/229412/

see how the Duterte-Marcos networks are directly linked to government accounts and are actively sharing Facebook groups like VOV Ph that have been repeatedly fact-checked and shown to join and fuel information operations.

These government propaganda efforts are often aided and abetted by foreign actors. In December 2018, Rappler Research found links to Russian disinformation networks[23] from the Facebook page of the Daily Sentry in the Philippines, which had quickly become the most powerful account attacking Rappler.

Facebook would take down the Daily Sentry page in January 2019. In September 2020, Facebook also took down Chinese information operations: pages that targeted me; polished the Marcos image; supported Sara Duterte, the president's daughter; and created fake accounts using AI-generated photos for the US presidential election.[24] And due in part to Rappler's reporting, Facebook took down police and military accounts that were doing what is called "red-tagging"—branding human rights activists, journalists, and politicians as "terrorists."[25]

In 2021, Rappler Research embarked on one of its most important projects.[26] We wanted to do a deep dive to look for the signals that turn online violence into real-world violence. Our subject was the human rights group Karapatan, which saw fifteen of its members killed during the Duterte administration. We discovered that the online accounts of the victims hadn't been individually targeted online; only high-profile figures and the groups themselves had been targeted. But the violent messaging still created a kind of enabling environment for the murders of Karapatan's members, including Zara Alvarez,[27] who had asked for court protection that never arrived.

One evening, she was walking down the street with a friend. She had just bought dinner when a gunman shot her from behind. Then, to make sure she was dead, the assassin stood over her fallen body and pumped more bullets into her. It was a brutal and brazen act of politically motivated killing that should have generated widespread outrage and horror. But there again, the propaganda machine sprang into action. The Philippine government had created a very well funded military-led entity called the National Task Force to End Local Communist Armed Conflict (NTF-ELCAC), which soon launched its own kind of anti-Communist, McCarthyist crusade.

The graphic below compares the Facebook presence of Karapatan with that of the NTF-ELCAC. You can see that the reach of the human rights group is severely limited because it lacks the digital funnel to public hubs. NTF-ELCAC, on the other hand, uses a red-tagging network built on state accounts as well as its disinformation network. The end result was that the stories about the activists targeted and killed tended to stay within the bubble of progressive groups and the few media organizations that carried the stories.

This speaks to the evolution of the Philippines' information ecosystem and why the NTF-ELCAC has played such a prominent role since it was formed. This graphic shows how effective the combined force of NTF-ELCAC and government agencies—using tried and tested methods in the drug war and evolving after three Facebook takedowns in 2018 and 2019—can be at amplifying disinformation and abuse. This was the second wave of the Duterte administration's use of violence and fear, the creation of an enabling environment for more real-world violence, another version of "us against them."

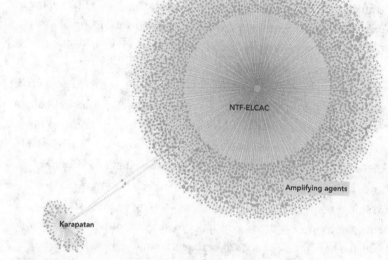

Facebook conversations about activists killed

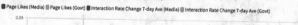

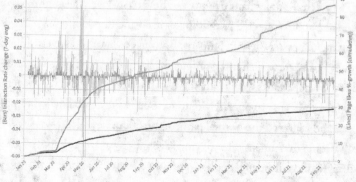

Page Likes of Government Agencies and Media Organizations

The following shows the growth of Facebook pages of selected government agencies and media organizations in the Philippines from January 1, 2020 to September 30, 2021. The bars show the daily interaction rate change (as a 7-day moving average) while the line charts show the cumulative increase of the page likes (expressed as a %-increase).

This was made worse by the pandemic, another example of how best intentions pave the way to Hell. Facebook's decision to prioritize the Department of Health meant that journalists' ability to hold power to account was further diminished, because that also enabled the government to grow its pages faster—much faster than those of news organizations. Among the government pages that grew significantly were the police- and military-operated pages that have been involved in red-tagging activists and journalists. By prioritizing "official" sources, Facebook made attacks against journalists carried out by state assets more effective and harder to counteract.

What can be done? When asked whether activists should create fake accounts or use the same tactics, I replied the same way: don't become a monster to fight a monster. Which brings us back to the platforms themselves. The platforms' impunity must stop; they must be held accountable.

For the government and political players who exploit the platforms, I've tried many different ways to fight back: ignoring them (it doesn't work—you lose without even knowing it); responding to them (massive time suck, much too atomized). Finally, I settled on my own North Star, what had also been the elevator pitch of Rappler: build communities of action.

How can we create a whole-of-society approach that uses technology, data, and civic engagement to fight back? That's what we set out to do for the May 2022 elections.

But first, Rappler had to figure out how to survive. The continued online attacks affected both Rappler itself and our community and had a financial impact on our company. Both page views and advertising revenues had decreased after the online attacks had begun in October 2016. But the legal attacks were really the last straw. The January 2018 order revoking our license to operate would have been the death knell of Rappler if we had followed the normal path. Some of our key advertisers received calls from government officials (message: stay away), and Rappler—once admired and considered cool—was pushed to near bankruptcy.

The legal cases and investigations that followed meant that within four months, we lost 49 percent of our revenues. Our future was clear: if we followed that path without doing anything differently, we wouldn't be able to make payroll. We needed to create a new, sustainable business model or die.

The government seemed certain that it would win in a war of attrition, and for a while, things looked bleak. Our legal fees ballooned to nearly a third of our monthly operating expenses. The money I had set aside to build a new tech platform went to pay for some of that, setting our technology plans back years.

But that existential moment brought out our best ideas and our best selves. I joked that all the friction of managing a newsroom had fallen aside: it was all for one, and one for all. You could feel the energy from every member of Rappler; the editorial team, which was under attack publicly, was supported by graphics, video production, technology and data, administration–human resources, finance, and most of all, sales.[28]

Our commercial team, working with our core managers, found the solution in our investigative journalism: the very same processes we had developed to track networks of disinformation online became the foundation of a data- and tech-based business model that grew by 12,000 percent from 2018 to 2019, helping power our first year of profitability.

Until 2016, we had been powered largely by advertising. Once the online attacks began and our advertising revenue dropped, we pivoted the company toward other tech services, which prepared us for the pandemic lockdown.

Then our community kicked in. We began a crowdfunding campaign that helped pay our legal bills. At the end of 2018, we began Rappler+, the first news membership program in the Philippines. Its members are our most devoted users, emotionally linked to our mission and values. They kept asking us, "How can we help?" And they did.

Three years of growth—that was what the government attack cost us, but I'm not sure it's an even trade. The business model of news—

advertising—is dead. The government's attacks in 2016 just forced us to confront that fact head-on, find a solution, learn to innovate, and build for the future. In 2019, Rappler hit its break-even year,[29] marking four years of turning crisis into opportunity. We decided to give every Rappler the same bonus when we hit that benchmark, from our messenger to the CEO. It was small but large enough to show our appreciation for the ideals, creativity, and courage of our entire team.

Friedrich Nietzsche was right: what doesn't kill you makes you stronger.

A ll stand!" someone yelled, bringing all of us to our feet. It was June 15, 2020, and we were at Manila Regional Trial Court, Branch 46. It was inside a decrepit condemned building with broken tiles, chipped and peeling paint, and holes in the walls. Most of the time, the elevator didn't work, so I had to climb four flights up a broken stairwell littered with scaffolding, signs that building maintenance was just trying to hold it all together.

We were there for my case: a 2019 charge of cyberlibel.[30] It was for a story Rappler had published in May 2012, before the law we had allegedly violated had even been enacted. It showed links between a businessman and the then chief justice of the Supreme Court, who was involved in an impeachment trial that later removed him from office. The story was a standard piece of reporting: when even the indictment is a flip-flop, even to explain the details of the accusation is to get lost in weeds of nonsense. When accusations and legal charges are that absurd, incoherent, and corrupt, to explain them is almost like legitimizing something that never should have happened in the first place.[31]

I knew the deck was stacked against us. The eight charges the government had brought against me—for cyberlibel, for tax evasion, for securities fraud—carried a cumulative maximum prison sentence of more than a hundred years.

The thirty-seven-year-old judge, Rainelda Estacio-Montesa, walked in. Unlike the rest of us, she wasn't wearing a mask, which made her bright red lipstick and fresh makeup stand out in the dreary courtroom. The small, dank, windowless space she ruled had been transformed by covid-19, so only a few of us were allowed inside. No court observers were allowed; no one from the diplomatic community could be in the room. Plastic dividers partitioned the space, making it seem smaller but cleaner.

Immediately facing the judge was my lawyer, Ted Te, a former Supreme Court spokesman, next to his counterpart from the Department of Justice, prosecutor Jeannette Dacpano (who had gone on government-funded trips with our judge).[32] Behind her sat a team of prosecution lawyers, hired to strengthen the government's case. At every hearing in the case, the prosecution always vastly outnumbered us, the defense.

There were two short benches behind the prosecution lawyers. My co-accused and former colleague, Rey Santos, and I sat on the first bench. Rey, slight of frame, quiet, and mild mannered with wire-framed glasses, had first been a researcher at Rappler, often helping in our investigative stories, before he had become a reporter. The irony was that he now worked for the government.[33]

In moments like that, I needed to stay busy, so I tweeted what was happening. When prayers were done, we sat while the court clerk did the roll call. Then the clerk told us to rise for the reading of the verdict.

I stood up, grabbed my notebook, and started taking notes.

"The right of every person to freedom of speech is a right guaranteed by our Constitution," the clerk said. "It is a right to speak freely without fear of retribution or retaliation. The right of the press to freely report news and opinion without undue restraint is guaranteed no less."

I was writing everything nearly word for word. I began to feel some hope.

"These rights are imbued with vast powers to advance the common good, to effect change and influence the minds of others in the hope of building a society where every person can be free. But when abused, this freedom can sow animosity and engender divisiveness and resentment that may lead to disorder and chaos."

That was when my hope began to die.

I shut my notebook, put it down on the bench, and looked ahead. I stared at Estacio-Montesa, her red lipstick. I tried to catch her eye while the clerk continued reading. She looked down. "There is no curtailment of the right to freedom of speech and the press. . . . What society expects is a responsible free press. It is in acting responsibly that freedom is given its meaning. The exercise of a freedom should and must be used with due regard to the freedom of others. As Nelson Mandela said, 'For to be free is not merely to cast off one's chains but to live in a way that respects and enhances the freedom of others.'"

Mandela must have been rolling in his grave. I was being convicted for a story I hadn't written, edited, or supervised, for a crime that hadn't even existed when the story had been published. In order to do that, Estacio-Montesa not only changed the period of prescription of libel from one year to twelve years; she also accepted a novel theory of "republication." I could go to jail because someone in Rappler had in 2014 fixed a misspelled word, changing one letter of one word. The court found us "guilty beyond a reasonable doubt" and sentenced each of us to up to six years in prison (which now may be eight, depending on one's interpretation of the law).

Estacio-Montesa made a point of saying that there had been no government influence on her decision. I shook my head. She allowed us to remain free on bail pending our appeal—which, of course, we would do.

I let out a long breath. I had packed a bag and put it into the car that morning. My worst-case scenario was that I would be thrown directly into jail. So in a way, this was a little better.

She then addressed me directly and said that I would now have to ask the Court of Appeals for permission to travel. Then she asked me if I had anything to say.

I stared at her. I smiled.

Estacio-Montesa banged her gavel, and a flurry of activity followed. No one would look me in the eye. We made our way to Manila City Hall to face the media. I had a funny taste in my mouth and a throbbing in my stomach. I somehow maintained control.

Thanks to covid-19, it was the first time many of us had left our homes in three months. While the journalists were setting up their microphones and live shots, I reassured Rey, whose eyes looked haunted above his mask. "Don't worry," I told him, "we'll appeal this. We'll take care of you and your legal fees." I would shield him. Ted was on my right talking to some of the journalists. The microphones were placed in front of me.

I began to speak. My voice echoed in the hall, and as I searched for familiar faces, I felt as though I were floating. I couldn't tell who I was talking to, so I concentrated on the hard lump in the pit of my stomach.

"I appeal to you—the journalists in this room, the Filipinos who are listening—to protect your rights," I told them. "We are meant to be a cautionary tale. We are meant to make you afraid, right?" My voice broke slightly. "Don't be afraid. Because if you don't use your rights, you will lose them."

Behind me, one of the members of the National Union of Journalists of the Philippines held up a sign that read HANDS OFF THE PRESS.

"Freedom of the press is the foundation of every single right you have as a Filipino citizen," I continued. "If we can't hold power to account, we can't do anything. If we can't do our jobs, then your rights will be lost."

Before the lockdown began in March 2020, I warned that we shouldn't let the virus infect our democracies,[34] but that was exactly what happened. Power consolidated more power. On May 5, the government shut down ABS-CBN.[35] It happened partly because we were in quarantine. There was no need for Duterte to declare martial law like Marcos had in the 1970s. The pandemic did it for him.

I lost my right to travel starting in August 2020. Despite my having returned home from international travel more than thirty-six times, the Court of Appeals handling the cyberlibel case ruled four times in favor of the solicitor general, Jose Calida, who called me a flight risk, unjustly (and absurdly) comparing me to Imelda Marcos in its ruling.[36]

One of the requests the Court of Appeals denied was when my mom was diagnosed with cancer and needed surgery in Florida. Mom and Dad had aged, and being isolated from their children and grandchildren didn't help. I wanted to be there to help them with logistics as well as with the psychological impact of the pandemic. Plus it was Christmas.

It was a particularly cruel turn of events: I had received approval to travel from courts handling eight of what had now become nine charges against me. The Court of Appeals released its denial near 5:00 p.m. the Friday before my flight was scheduled to leave the next morning. My parents had prepared my room and were excited about my arrival. The government dragged them into the emotional roller coaster that its harassment triggers. I can weather that fine, but to make me take my aged and ailing parents along was inhumane.

I absorbed the pain, reassured my family, and coped the best way I knew how: I worked.

Chapter 12

...

Why Fascism Is Winning

Collaborate, Collaborate, Collaborate

Inside the deliberation room of the Norwegian Nobel Committee with its members. *From left to right:* Asle Toje; Nobel laureate Dmitry Muratov (standing above me); David Beasley, representing 2020's Nobel Peace Prize winner the World Food Programme; Berit Reiss-Andersen; Anne Enger; Kristin Clemet; Jorgen Watne Frydnes. (© *Nobel Prize Outreach. Photo: Geir Anders Rybakken Ørslien*)

The week of October 8, 2021, Rappler was covering the filing of certificates of candidacy in the Philippines' crucial May 2022 elections, when Filipinos would vote for more than eighteen thousand officials, including the president.

Duterte, unlike many other autocrats, finally seemed willing to relinquish power. A Filipino president can serve only one six-year term, but for some time, he had threatened to run for vice president. That week of October, he announced his retirement. Most Filipinos suspected that he was preparing for a successor. There was talk that his daughter Sara would run for president; she announced her candidacy for the vice presidency, to make way for someone else: Ferdinand Marcos, Jr., nicknamed "Bongbong," the son of a former dictator.

Nearly thirty-six years after his family had been ousted in a People Power revolt and after his father had imprisoned and murdered thousands of people and plundered $10 billion from his country's Treasury, a Marcos was returning. The opposition leader, Leni Robredo, long a target of daily information operations by the Duterte government, also filed her certificate for president, and the groundswell of support seemed to surprise even her.

Now, less than half an hour until the Commission on Elections closed, I was in a webinar with two other heads of independent news groups in Indonesia and Malaysia titled "Press in Distress: Will Independent Journalism Survive in Southeast Asia?"

Manila was again in a pandemic lockdown, the only mitigating measure that the Duterte administration had enforced in nearly nineteen months of dealing with covid-19. The government was playing catch-up with vaccines because it had been about half a year late[1] in getting a viable supply, and when it finally had, it had prioritized the Chinese-made Sinovac, which had the lowest efficacy of the available vaccines. Contact tracing remained largely aspirational, and now the Senate was investigating corruption charges for some of the largest pandemic deals that seemed to link Duterte to the dubious companies of his Chinese friend and economic adviser, Michael Yang.[2]

By then two of my cases had been dismissed. The constant legal battles were taking a toll on me, but I was determined to not let them stop my mission of getting out in the world and sounding the alarm. Just three days earlier, despite what seemed like a de facto ban on my travel, I had put in another travel request to the courts, this time to take a one-month fellowship at Harvard's Kennedy School. I wanted open confrontation.

Then my cell phone began flashing. I looked at the number. It was from Norway.[3] "Hello, am I talking to Maria Ressa?"

"Yes, you are," I replied.

"I'm Olav Njølstad, calling from the Norwegian Nobel Institute in Oslo. I'm calling you on behalf of the Norwegian Nobel Committee, and it's a great pleasure for me, Maria, to inform you—"

My eyes widened. I leaned back. It couldn't be.

"—that at eleven o'clock local time here in Oslo, it will be announced that you are awarded the Nobel Peace Prize for 2021—"

"Oh, my gosh," I whispered. I reached for my pen but didn't know what to write.

"—for your courageous fight for freedom of expression in the Philippines, and you will be sharing the prize with another candidate, which I cannot disclose the name of right now because I will need to call that person first."

"Oh, my gosh."

"I will only congratulate you on behalf of the committee, and we will come back to you later with more information. But I would be delighted to hear your immediate spontaneous reaction to this news."

"I . . . I . . . I'm speechless. I'm actually live at another event, but oh, my God. Oh, my gosh. I'm speechless. Thank you so very much." I was stunned.

My heart was pounding. I immediately sent a Signal message to the *manang*s: "I won!" and took a deep breath, staying still, feeling my heart pound faster. We knew I had been nominated, but to actually be chosen had been beyond our collective imagination. They responded quickly, my usually articulate *manang*s reduced to "OMG!" and "OMGG!"

When the news broke publicly twenty minutes later, every device

I had on my desk—two cell phones, two computers—began ringing. I rushed to mute everything, and I heard the moderator asking me to react. I turned on my audio and started to speak. "This is for all of us," I started. Then it hit me. "Oh, my God, you know that I'm in shock. See what I mean . . ." My voice cracked, so instead of hiding it, I stopped and pulled back. "I'm sorry. I think it's a recognition of how hard it is to be a journalist and how hard it is to keep doing what we do . . . it's a recognition of the difficulties, but also, hopefully, of how we are going to win the battle for truth, the battle for facts. We hold the line."[4]

It wasn't a win for me alone; it was a win and vindication for Rapplers—a private moment when we cried, laughed, and soared together. Still, I'm suspicious of such emotional releases, and I reminded the team that this could also mean things could get worse. I hated to rain on our parade at that moment of joy, but I didn't want us to be complacent. One of the *manang*s Signaled me: Let them celebrate.

That recognition went far beyond Rappler. I was the only woman that year and the first Filipino ever to win the Nobel Peace Prize, and my award shone a light not only on my country but on the Global South.

It was also a win for Filipino journalists looking for hope and encouragement to keep going despite how difficult things had become. Ryan Macasero, our Cebu bureau chief, reminded[5] us of twenty-three-year-old Frenchie Mae Cumpio, who had been in prison now for more than a year,[6] and of the journalist Rex Cornelio, whose wife, Coleen, had been riding behind him on his motorcycle when he had been shot and killed in May 2020.[7]

"For as long as there are good people, there is hope," Coleen had said. "Those in power, they won't be in power forever. And whatever wrong they do, it will come back to them."

That search for justice is why we became journalists. That faith in the good is integral to my worldview. In recognizing me and *Novaya Gazeta*'s Dmitry Muratov, the Norwegian Nobel Committee told every journalist around the world, "We see your pain, sacrifice, and suffering."

It was a recognition that the devastation we were personally feeling from the invisible atom bomb that had exploded in our information ecosystem was being seen and felt by others.

We are with you, said the Nobel Committee, and we can do something together.

Shortly after the Nobel announcement and a de facto travel ban, Philippine courts gave me approval to travel to Boston and stay in Harvard for a month. It was glorious to be a Hauser Leader at the Harvard Kennedy School's Center for Public Leadership[8] and a fellow at its Shorenstein Center on Media, Politics and Public Policy.[9] I could focus on what had increasingly become my obsession: how technology and journalism were shaping politics and public policy as well as what it means for public leadership. When the wrong behavior is constantly rewarded, how do our leaders of tomorrow decide their values? What does leadership look like in our upside-down world?

Though I felt the constant pressure of Rappler and the court cases, living like Sisyphus and Cassandra combined, being awarded the Nobel Prize forced me to rethink and reshape what I wanted to tell a world that was listening. I went back to revisit ideas within that new context, immersing myself in exhilarating conversations and explorations at Harvard. One of the highlights was the time I spent with Shoshana Zuboff, whose work had influenced me so deeply. We had worked together virtually for more than a year at the Real Facebook Oversight Board, among other places, but now she invited me to her home overlooking a picturesque lake in Maine. We took walks together as she meticulously explained a worldview and experiences that included many firsts, like being the first tenured female professor at the then-male-dominated Harvard Business School. As professor emeritus, she studied and taught the patterns and trends that shaped—and destroyed—the vision of an inclusive internet.

For Shoshana, every other problem is a distraction and by-product of the original sin of "primary extraction"—even those words were her creation. She uses the term to describe how the social media companies took our private actions and lives by using machine learning and artificial intelligence to collect and organize our personal data and building models of each of us, then publicly declared that they now own those corporate assets, which are then used to create algorithms that insidiously manipulate us for profit. They offer no compensation, and they don't have to ask us for permission. Primary extraction is a morally reprehensible practice that Shoshana compares to slavery; she demands that it be outlawed. If that original sin is corrected, every other problem it has created, the cascading failures it has allowed, would be addressed, including safety, competition, and privacy.[10]

She reminded me of the first follower theory and the fact that those who follow often take on the risks of the leader. Though many of us had sounded the alarm as early as 2016, it had taken Shoshana to connect the technology to the business and give it a name, "surveillance capitalism": bringing in power and money and bringing us to a galvanizing point. She felt that we were now in the third phase of it and reminded me how far the public debate had come, especially after the devastating internal documents released by Facebook whistleblower Frances Haugen. Except it wasn't far enough for those of us on the front lines. Every day of inaction is a day of injustice for me and others like me.

My time with Shoshana produced a constant, invigorating back-and-forth and push and pull of ideas. We discussed the big picture versus atomized experience, the now against the next decade. Our last day together we spent in her outer room in front of a crackling fire, focused on my question of what the world should be doing now. I was looking for quick, easy steps that we could push platforms like Facebook and You-Tube to adopt. She took every suggestion and showed why what I was recommending was inadequate and why nothing less than attacking the business model directly could bring true change. She was as obstinate as I was stubborn.

"Journalism as an institution has to be reinvented for the twenty-first century," she told me. "How do you do journalism in a digital world? It's not surveillance capitalism—you're not competing with surveillance capitalists for the same surveillance dividend. Which is what they're doing now. It's the only way they know how to do it."

"And we feed into this, using their social sharing buttons so we give them our most precious resource—our relationships," I replied, thinking aloud. "It degrades the quality of our journalism as well." I had long been saying that reducing journalism to page views commoditized our work, and since our journalism was being distributed on social media, which rewarded the opposite incentives, our audience reach was limited because we could never compete on outrage. It goes against our standards and ethics manuals.

"The journalism is coerced into self-optimization for social media." Shoshana finished my thought. Social media was shaping journalism, much like Facebook told advertisers and publishers that video would get greater distribution[11] so news groups around the world had laid off editorial staff and hired video teams and advertisers had placed their ads on video on Facebook. Except that Facebook lied: it inflated the number of its video views[12] by as much as 900 percent, and, according to its internal documents, it lied about its mistake, keeping it secret for more than a year.

"Ultimately, it's surveillance capitalism that is deciding what journalism survives." Shoshana pounded it in.

The technology companies are not satisfied with destroying democracy; left unchecked, they are capable of destroying much more.

While I was literally fighting for my freedom and safety, information operations were chipping away and reshaping my country's past. In plain sight, it was death by a thousand cuts of history. The seeding of metanarratives, and outright lies, would play no more disturbing or prominent role than in the rise of a dictator's son.

On Tuesday, February 8, 2022, thirty-six years to the month since the Marcos family had been forced into exile by People Power, Ferdinand Marcos, Jr., the front-runner for president, launched his campaign[13] using words, slogans, and songs from his father's repressive rule. On a massive stage in front of giant LED screens, the Marcos martial law anthem from the 1970s, "Bagong Lipunan" (New Nation),[14] was given a new beat[15] and rolled out for a new generation: "There's a new birth / There's a new life / A new country, a new path / In the New Society!"[16] The father called it "constitutional authoritarianism" and said it was needed for reforms and to create a "new society." Until today, he held the Guinness World Record for the "greatest robbery of a government," siphoning away up to $10 billion[17] through an intricate kleptocracy best symbolized by Imelda's shoe collection. As of the end of 2020, only $3.4 billion had been recovered. On the human rights front: 70,000 detained, 34,000 tortured, 3,240 killed.

There are two photos seared into my memory of the only son of Ferdinand and Imelda Marcos right before their family fled into exile: the young Bongbong on the balcony of the palace, a gun tucked into his fatigues; and Bongbong partying on the presidential yacht with the Philippine flag painted on his cheek. Now here he was onstage, sixty-four years of age, literally dressed in his father's clothes, a 1960s-style shirt and pants, complete with the same hairstyle. The nearly three-hour campaign event bastardized history, past and present. Marcos said little of substance but used motherhood statements for "unity," a Filipino word he mentioned twenty-one times in twenty minutes, including sentences I had heard from his mother. The present moment of the past is horrifying because it showed exactly how information technology can help any digital populist rise, especially one connected to a repressive past.

What are Bongbong's qualifications? Even his father complained in his diary about his son's profligate and undisciplined ways.[18] Yet the father enabled the twenty-two-year-old Bongbong's election to governor in their home province of Ilocos Norte, about 273 miles north of Manila. His older sister, Imee, jokingly complained about her jobless brother,[19] and aside from politics, he seems to not have held a job in fourteen years.[20] He first won a congressional seat in 1992, then became governor. In 1995, he ran for and lost his first nationwide post, but in 2010, he became a senator.

In 2016, Bongbong ran for vice president, losing by about two hundred thousand votes but setting himself up perfectly to run for president. His mother, Imelda, is straightforward: she says it is Bongbong's "destiny"[21] to become president, his rise to power engineered meticulously on the ground through patronage-driven alliances that never really went away and given the final push by social media.

Until today, Marcos has denied any connection to "trolls,"[22] despite the data that we at Rappler exposed in a three-part Marcos propaganda series in 2019. Not so subtly, the messaging on his social media accounts began with changing the past. To begin with, he repeatedly lied about his education at Oxford University and Wharton. After being caught in the lie by a Rappler exclusive,[23] his Senate office quietly changed his résumé on the Senate website, but he doubled down on the lie,[24] a lesson many people, including Donald Trump and Mark Zuckerberg, have learned is easily facilitated by social media.

His disinformation network also hijacked popular pages and news groups with copied-and-pasted comments that slowly chipped away at the legacy of the Aquino family, long seen as his family's nemesis—all the while rehabilitating the image and the role of the Marcoses. The network, which crossed from websites to Facebook pages and groups, YouTube channels, and social media influencers, pumped out propaganda on a massive scale to first downplay or outright lie about the Marcos regime's excesses, kleptocracy, and human rights violations, exaggerate Marcos's achievements, and vilify critics, rivals, and mainstream media.

The creation of Marcos pages on Facebook began to ramp up in 2014, shortly after Imelda Marcos hinted about a Marcos return to the presidency.[25] In a post from 2014 on the popular Facebook page Pinoy Rap Radio, Marcos Jr. claimed that there was no proof of the Marcoses' stolen wealth and that his mother had "won every corruption case" against her. Both those statements are lies.

Still, that Facebook post was shared 331,000 times and garnered more than 38,000 comments and more than 369,000 reactions before it was discovered and fact-checked by Rappler on November 15, 2018. It had spread unchecked for four years within what had become an echo chamber whose members now believe the lie. The fact-check had a pitiful reach: 3,500 shares and 2,100 comments.

This is why propaganda networks are so effective in rewriting history: the distribution spread of a lie is so much greater than the fact-check that follows, and by the time the lie is debunked, those who believe it often refuse to change their views, matching social media's impact on behavior in other parts of the world.[26]

The Marcos networks worked hand in hand with the Duterte disinformation and propaganda networks, using common themes to achieve their common goals. By 2018, the center of the Philippines' Facebook information ecosystem was dominated by the Marcos-Duterte networks, pushing news organizations to the periphery. Many of the claims by these networks were proven false by fact-checkers, and in 2018, parts of them were taken down by Facebook for "coordinated inauthentic behavior."[27] One of the fastest-growing sites on Facebook that year was Daily Sentry; its links to Russian disinformation were exposed by Rappler[28] (it was, not coincidentally, Rappler's top attacker) before it was taken down. In 2020, Facebook would also take down information operations from China that were burnishing the Marcos image and attacking me and other journalists. Yet the Marcos network continues to grow, producing and amplifying content on a scale that far outstrips that of the mainstream media in the Philippines.[29]

By the time Marcos declared he would run for president in 2021, the Marcos networks dominated social media. Perhaps that was why he spent no money on Facebook advertising early on and why he refused debates and interviews with journalists who he expected would ask tough questions.[30] He didn't need to win anyone over, as he already had a captive audience. After all, he said, the time to talk about thirty-five-year-old issues is over. His twenty-minute speech kicking off his campaign offered no platform, no hows and whys, and certainly no mention of the thousands of people killed under his father, the millions of people who had lost their jobs, the trillions of pesos of national debt incurred, and the corruption scandals that came with all that. He did, however, repeatedly paint a glowing future and promised to make the Philippines great again.

By now the global problem in our information ecosystem was clear. I had spent much of 2020 trying to figure out how to fight the technology that was turning our world upside down. I realized that the rest of the world could once again look at the experience of Rappler in the Philippines, use it to understand its own political context and situation and how to fight back.

My hope is that others can replicate our three pillars: technology, journalism, and community to fight back and build forward.

First, we must demand accountability from technology.[31] This has to start with government action, as the social media companies regard public pressure and outcry as something that can be safely ignored. But aside from legislation, the only way to fight technology is with technology. One thing we've done at Rappler is to build and roll out Lighthouse, a technology platform built by journalists to try to preserve public discourse around facts.

The second pillar is to protect and grow investigative journalism. One global initiative I've helped lead is the International Fund for Public Interest Media, an immediate short- and medium-term solution to the drop in advertising revenues of news groups all around the world. If you are a government that believes in democracy, put your money where your values are—well, that was the idea, to increase the 0.3 percent of the Official Development Assistance (ODA) fund to find new money for journalism.[32]

After funding, journalists need protection, starting with the law. Impunity must stop. Working with Amal, Caoilfhionn, and the Covington team showed me how frail the legal protections are for journalists around the world. In many ways, lawyers are also playing a whack-a-mole game, and just as with the official development assistance funds from democratic nations, there needs to be a concerted systemic effort for international law. It makes sense that if we don't have facts, we can't have law and we have no democracy.

Beyond the law are the old-world dangers: physical harassment and violence, misogyny and hate speech. Autocrats are using technology better, spying on journalists and human rights activists with impunity. And they are learning from one another, perfecting the dictator's playbook, defending each other against outdated moves from the West's toolbox.[33] Economic sanctions lose their power when countries like Russia and China rush in to help, like in Belarus, Myanmar, Venezuela, and Turkey, among others. New paradigms are needed from countries espousing democratic values because illiberal nations are using their collective power to weaken international institutions like the United Nations and UNESCO.

For our third pillar, we continued to build larger and larger communities of action. The mantra: collaborate, collaborate, collaborate. First, collaborate globally to protect frontline journalists. That was why the Committee to Protect Journalists, the International Center for Journalists, and Reporters Without Borders pulled together more than eighty press freedom, media, and civil society groups, initially to help Rappler—it's called the #HoldTheLine Coalition[34]—but also other journalists needing support around the world. It would later expand to help call attention to injustice involving human rights activists.

We continued to create coalitions in 2021: #CourageON connected human rights groups, many of which had seen online attacks turn into real-world violence. With more than eighty-five groups coming together, we proved that there is strength in standing up together. Mid-year, we prepared for elections with our #PHVote coalition.

But by November 2021, we realized that we needed to do something more. We needed a "break glass" measure, so, based on the data and research we were seeing and what we had lived through, I began to dream of a whole-of-society approach we called #FactsFirstPH,[35] with a call to action to our communities.

We start with the facts. I had pushed since 2016 to have major news groups collaborate in a common defense of facts. Competition stopped that in the Philippines, to our collective detriment, allowing news organizations to be sidelined by the Duterte-Marcos disinformation networks that had turned information operations into information warfare. The goal is to try to pull our collective digital footprints together.

This idea started with a change in Rappler's mindset: instead of acting in our company's interest alone, we took the lessons we had learned and shared them with our competitors—a risk for our company, but in the battle for our democracy, it seemed to be the right moral choice. That includes how to reach more than 64 percent of our audience from search engines.[36] We made the switch from social to search once we realized that social media was actually degrading quality journalism.

So we created four layers working together, connected by a data pipeline that would help shorten the time it takes to correct the lies, to have civil society act, and to have the legal system prevent impunity. I set three goals: scale, impact, deterrence.

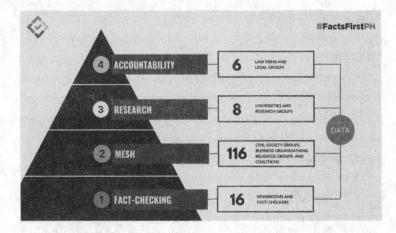

At the foundation is the core of journalism, largely present no longer: fact-checking. Four major news groups in the Philippines anchor the coalition: ABS-CBN, News5, Interaksyon, and Rappler. They're joined by rural and provincial news groups for geographic and hyperlocal distribution. Once each news group finishes a fact-check, it moves to the second layer, which I nicknamed "the mesh." Every member of the group can take each fact-check and repost or repurpose it, attributing the work to the original news group. We also promised to share that news group's social post. This accomplishes two goals: the links on each of our sites tie us all together for Google search while our sharing sends algorithmic signals for distribution.

Layer two of the #FactsFirstPH process involves civil society groups, human rights groups, NGOs, business groups, and the Church—in all, more than a hundred groups that take facts and amplify them to their communities with instructions to share them with emotions. The collaborative mesh not only would allow us to discuss and work together in real time; it would also strengthen algorithmic amplification, which would help all of us rise together, ensuring greater distribution of the fact-checks.

Layer three is composed of at least seven disinformation research groups that take the data, make sense of it, and release a weekly report that tells us how the public sphere is being manipulated. The inspiration for it came from the Election Integrity Partnership formed in the United States for the 2020 elections.[37] I hoped that by connecting it to the first two layers, we would not only shorten the time to action but would encourage more collaboration and further increase distribution. From March to May 2020, the research groups released twenty-one weekly reports telling our community how they were being manipulated, who was benefiting, and who was being attacked.

Finally, there was the last crucial layer that had been silent too long: the lawyers, groups dedicated to maintaining rule of law and demanding accountability. From the Movement Against Democracy to the Integrated Bar of the Philippines, the Philippine Bar Association, and the Free Legal Assistance Group, this legal layer provides protection for those under attack and finds systemic legal solutions for platform design choices, filing strategic and tactical litigation.

Will it work? I don't know, but I didn't know either when we started Rappler as a Facebook page in August 2011. Without any real solution from the tech platforms, we can't just throw our hands up in the air. Not when the integrity of our elections is at stake. We knew a solution wouldn't just magically appear. So we do our best with what we have: we act, and each day we iterate. This, so far, is our only collective defense. The only way to find a solution is to act.

We launched about a hundred days before the presidential vote, after it had become clear that lies were spreading faster than facts. More than 140 groups from media, civil society, the Church, academe, business, and lawyers banded together—a whole-of-society approach to fighting disinformation and ensuring the integrity of our elections.

Even though it took nearly three months to organize, it was exciting because we were no longer just victims. It was like creating a national startup, and we had help, relying on the Google News Initiative and the San Francisco startup Meedan, which provided a tech and data platform that connected the layers of the pyramid.[38] The launch was exciting, and we were all in.

The first sign of success came two weeks after what I started calling our "Avengers, assemble" moment, when Solicitor General Jose Calida, who had led the weaponization of the law, filed a petition at the Supreme Court against Rappler and the Commission on Elections, accusing Rappler of manipulating elections and calling fact-checking "prior restraint."[39] We met his challenge head-on and continued to grow our communities, successfully creating an organic mesh and distribution system for facts.

Did it work? Absolutely. That's what the data shows.

If your nation has elections coming up, organize your #FactsFirst pyramid a year earlier. The very minimum is six months.

Then the world changed drastically. On February 24, 2022, Russia invaded Ukraine. A day later, during the thirty-sixth anniversary of People Power, the holiday that marks the ousting of the Marcos dictatorship, Leni Robredo's campaign rallies began to draw massive crowds. Both Ukraine and Robredo had long been targets of disinformation, but in the following weeks, collective action by real people began to turn the tide, creating cracks of hope and light.

Vladimir Putin had invaded Crimea in 2014, annexing the territory from Ukraine by using the same two-pronged strategy that would later be used around the world: suppress and repress unfavorable facts, then replace them with the metanarrative you want. In that case the narrative was that Russia's enemies were anti-Semitic fascists preventing Crimeans and Ukrainians from doing what they wanted: to unite with Russia.

Eight years later, Putin would use the same metanarrative to invade Ukraine, tearing reality apart for both Russians and Ukrainians. What he didn't count on was a comedy actor turned president, Volodymyr Zelensky, who refused to leave Ukraine and called on his nation to fight.

That decision by one man foiled Putin's plans, inspiring not just Ukrainians but people all around the world.

In the Philippines, Leni Robredo's campaign rallies began to gather tens of thousands to hundreds of thousands of people in city after city, igniting a spirit of volunteerism that our country had never seen before.[40] To fight disinformation, they began to go door to door.

Those developments made March a month of action. Our #Facts FirstPH pyramid grew in parallel with Robredo's on-the-ground mobilization.

But it wasn't enough.

Passion fails when confronted by systematic execution backed by decades of preparation—from political machinery to allies in a feudal patronage-driven political system. The war in Ukraine ground on, with thousands of Ukrainians dying and millions displaced. And the information operations and online networks created since 2014, along with Sara Duterte as his running mate, brought Marcos back to power in the Philippines.

On May 9, 2022, in the Philippines, the inevitable came to pass.

Don't forget: Where we go, you go.

"The struggle of man against power," wrote Milan Kundera, "is the struggle of memory against forgetting."

We have been laughing at memes and forgetting our history. Even our biology, our brains and hearts, have been systematically and insidiously attacked by the technology that delivers our news and prioritizes the distribution of lies over facts—by design.

I have lived through several cycles of history, chronicling the wild swings of the pendulum that would eventually stabilize and find a new equilibrium. When journalists were the gatekeepers to our public information ecosystem, those swings took decades. Once technology took over and abdicated responsibility for our emotional safety, history could be changed in months. That's how easy it became to shift our memory through our emotions.

When that happened, it destroyed the old checks and balances on power and transformed our world. We elected incompetent populists who stoked our fears, dividing us and turning us against one another, fueling and feeding off our fear, anger, and hate. They appointed officials like themselves; their goal was not good governance but power. When termites eat away at wood, we didn't see that the floor we stood on could collapse at any minute. Concerned with power plays, those leaders ignored the existential problems that demanded a global response.

Technology didn't do all this alone; it was the accelerant to set fire to the kindling built up by decades of liberal progress. After all, for every action, there is an equal and opposite reaction, Newton's third law of motion. The more progressive we became—women's rights, gay marriage, more pluralistic societies—the greater the nostalgia for a simplicity that never really existed. The election of Barack Obama had an equal and opposite reaction, the perfect storm sparking the reemergence of fascism under a new name: white replacement theory. You only have to watch a hearing of the Select Committee to Investigate the January 6th Attack on the United States Capitol to know that.

Today, an emergent wave of right-wing populist leaders uses social media to question and break down reality, triggering rage and paranoia on a bed of exponential lies. This is how fascism is normalized and where political outrage meets terrorism, the vanguard of mass violence.

These ideas have recurred in history again and again with violent consequences, from Benito Mussolini to the Ku Klux Klan to Adolf Hitler, who wrote in *Mein Kampf*, "This pestilential adulteration of the blood, of which hundreds of thousands of our people take no account, is being systematically practiced by the Jew to-day. Systematically these negroid parasites in our national body corrupt our innocent fair-haired girls and thus destroy something which can no longer be replaced in this world."

Here's the modern-day echo in May 2022 by Hungary's prime minister, Viktor Orbán, who includes replacement theory in state ideology: "I see the great European population exchange as a suicidal attempt to replace the lack of European, Christian children with adults from other civilizations—migrants."[41]

That same week, he was the star speaker at the US Conservative Political Action Conference (CPAC), held for the first time in Hungary, uniting the far Right on both sides of the Atlantic. In a straw poll held then, 59 percent of GOP members there said they would vote for Donald Trump if the Republican primary were held then.[42]

What's the harbinger? Mass shootings. Replacement theory is embedded in the manifestos of self-declared fascists radicalized on the internet from Oslo, Norway, to Christchurch, New Zealand, to Buffalo, New York.

It's going to get worse before it gets better.

So how do you stand up to a dictator?

By embracing values, defined early—they're the subtitles of the chapters you've read: honesty, vulnerability, empathy, moving away from emotions, embracing your fear, believing in the good. You can't do it alone. You have to create a team, strengthen your area of influence. Then connect the bright spots and weave a mesh together.

Avoid thinking in terms of "us against them." Stand in someone else's shoes. And do unto others as you would have them do unto you. Technology has proven that human beings have far more in common than we have differences; the tech platforms insidiously manipulate our biology regardless of our nation or culture. Fascist ideology, whether you call it "the great replacement" or not, pits homogeneity against domestic enemies, who invariably champion democracy and its ideals. It's happening not just in the West, but in India, Myanmar, Sri Lanka, the Philippines. We all have our own Pol Pots who encourage mass violence based on us against them.

In 2018, in Washington, DC, I appealed to the future, to governments and politicians: don't manipulate the worst of human nature for power, because it cripples the next generation. They didn't listen. Why give up a sure path to power? To social media platforms, I said, "Your business model has divided societies and weakened democracies. Personalization says my reality is different from yours, and we can all have our realities. But all these realities have to coexist in the public sphere. You can't tear us apart to the point that we don't agree on facts." They didn't listen, and we're worse off today. I asked journalists and activists to stay the course, and we have—with great sacrifice.[43]

As for me, there are times I struggle. Because I refuse to stop doing my job, I've lost my freedom to travel. I can't plan my life because I still have seven criminal cases that could send me to jail for the rest of it. But I refuse to live in a world like this. I demand better. We deserve better.

In my Nobel lecture, I asked for a person-to-person defense of our democracies—of our freedom, of equality. I've tried to flesh that out in this book: how fighting back goes from the personal to the political, from individual values to a pyramid for collective action. There are solutions: in the long term, the most important thing is education, so start now; in the medium term, it's legislation and policy to restore the rule of law in the virtual world—to create a vision of the internet that binds us together instead of tearing us apart. In the short term, now, it's just us: collaborate, collaborate, collaborate. And that begins with trust.

It won't be easy. You'll feel like giving up, burying your head in the sand, but if you do that, you're helping assure the destruction of our world, the manipulation of your children, the destruction of their values, and the ravaging of our earth. It's an existential moment.

When I felt like giving up, Twink's essay woke me up. She was dying, and she chose to fight: for me, for Filipinos, for the greater good. We can't feel sorry for ourselves. Now is the time to act.

I believe in *you*.

I believe in *us*.

Epilogue

Sometimes you have to skate through life, sliding on the surface because it's just too hard to feel. So you keep going. Keep busy. Fill the days, hours, and minutes, hoping to come out on the other side. Stopping to try to understand *why* causes too much pain. Revisiting the past, I thought, accepting an invitation to return to Toms River, would help me cope. Like our elections, it was back to the future.

And it was quite a reunion! My family and friends stepped into our old selves and slowly expanded them into the people we had become. The last time we had all been together had been forty years before, when I had graduated from Toms River High School North in 1982. On Sunday, May 22, 2022, I was inducted into the Toms River Regional Schools Hall of Fame. On Monday morning, the school staff unveiled a huge blue plaque over the main entrance of the newly renovated space I had once known so well, declaring it the Maria Ressa Auditorium, seating more than a thousand.

I know the auditorium well, and it was incredible to sing first the US national anthem followed by the national anthem of the Philippines, uniting my two worlds. My parents and family were in the front row, and about thirty of my classmates were behind them. I looked out at the students—more than six hundred of them, said Principal Ed Keller, from North, as well as the other Toms River high schools, South and East. I decided to talk about meaning—and why they couldn't find it on social media.

"What gets our attention is what gives our lives meaning," I told them. "Where we spend our time determines what we accomplish and what we become good at. The battle for our minds—and this is a battle for *your* minds—is waged and won, not by helping you think. It's won by manipulating your emotions. Anger and hate are literally shaping who we will become as a people. It's pumping toxic sludge through us. So if you feel angry or you feel like you hate another group, step back and take a deep breath."

I had said nearly the same thing at our family dinner our first night in Toms River. Out of about a dozen of us around the table, three were Democrats. We were at the home of my cousin Vinnie, who used to ride his big wheel up and down our driveway. No longer a small child with curly black hair, he is now a captain in the Manchester police force. His brother, Peter, is a former marine, former fireman, and policeman now out on disability.

They talked about affirmative action in the police force, how standards had been lowered three times to hit the quota, and how that wasn't fair. They talked about immigration and how everyone has to sacrifice for those who don't want to work (never mind that we were a family of immigrants from Italy and the Philippines). My parents live in Florida, voted for Clinton, then switched to Trump after Obamacare raised the prices of their medicines. My siblings and I sensed their anger being fueled by something. When Facebook took down the Russian information operations, their accounts went down, too.

When voices started rising at the table, I told my family that we should guard against hate. Vinnie told me that Toms River, with its ninety-five thousand residents, had been mentioned by the Buffalo shooter in his 180-page manifesto a week earlier because of its growing Hasidic community.[1] The police had increased security around the area, and the Ocean County prosecutor had tamped down fears: "I can state, unequivocally, that there is no evidence that the shooter had any intention or inclination to travel to anywhere in Ocean County." He added,

"The document includes despicable anti-Semitic, white supremacist and radicalized racist memes and tropes with repeated references to 'replacement theory.'"[2]

I looked at the students in the auditorium. You could hear a pin drop. I put down my prepared statement and began to speak extemporaneously. How much more difficult life must be for them today, when the insecurity of discovering who you are must be done in the public spotlight with a mob waiting to pounce on you; when life is about performance instead of discovery and mistakes can seem fatal, showered with anger and hate. I pointed out that Toms River North and South can compete in sports and their students can stay friends, but politics has become so divisive that it's a gladiator's battle to the death.

"My generation has failed, and we are handing you a broken world, which means you have to be stronger and smarter than we are," I said, wondering whether they could even name what's wrong with their world today. It's all they know. So I asked them to think for themselves, be skeptical of social media, and walk in someone else's shoes. Put your phones away, I said, because in the end what matters is the people you love. You find meaning by choosing where to spend your precious time. "What you remember are the people whose lives you've touched and those whose lives have changed yours."

A day after the auditorium dedication, a shooter in the largely Latino town of Uvalde, Texas, killed twenty-one people: two teachers and nineteen students.[3] By that night, Ocean County announced that it would increase security and the local police presence at my old high school.[4]

2021 Nobel Peace Prize Laureates Maria Ressa and Dmitry Muratov's 10-Point Plan to Address the Information Crisis

Presented at the Freedom of Expression Conference, Nobel Peace Center, Oslo, Norway, on September 2, 2022

We call for a world in which technology is built in service of humanity and where our global public square protects human rights above profits. Those in power must do their part to build a world that puts human rights, dignity, and security first, including by safeguarding scientific and journalistic methods and tested knowledge.

To build that world, we must: Bring an end to the surveillance-for-profit business model; end tech discrimination and treat people everywhere equally; and rebuild independent journalism as the antidote to tyranny.

We call on all rights-respecting democratic governments to:

1. Require tech companies to carry out independent human rights impact assessments that must be made public as well as demand transparency on all aspects of their business—from content moderation to algorithm impacts to data processing to integrity policies.

2. Protect citizens' right to privacy with robust data protection laws.

3. Publicly condemn abuses against the free press and journalists globally and commit funding and assistance to independent media and journalists under attack.

We call on the European Union to:

4. Be ambitious in enforcing the Digital Services and Digital Markets Acts so these laws amount to more than just 'new paperwork' for the companies and instead force them to make changes to their business model, such as ending algorithmic amplification that threatens fundamental rights and spreads disinformation and hate, including in cases where the risks originate outside EU borders.

5. Urgently propose legislation to ban surveillance advertising, recognizing this practice is fundamentally incompatible with human rights.

6. Properly enforce the EU General Data Protection Regulation so that people's data rights are finally made reality.

7. Include strong safeguards for journalists' safety, media sustainability and democratic guarantees in the digital space in the forthcoming European Media Freedom Act.

8. Protect media freedom by cutting off disinformation upstream. This means there should be no special exemptions or carve-outs for any organization or individual in any new technology or media legislation. With globalized information flows, this would give a blank check to those governments and non-state actors who produce industrial scale disinformation to harm democracies and polarize societies everywhere.

9. Challenge the extraordinary lobbying machinery, the astroturfing campaigns and recruitment revolving door between big tech companies and European government institutions.

We call on the UN to:

10. Create a special Envoy of the UN Secretary-General focused on the Safety of Journalists (SESJ) who would challenge the current status quo and finally raise the cost of crimes against journalists.

Acknowledgments

The kindness of strangers. That's what these last few years reminded me. That in the middle of so much bad, it's the unexpected generous gesture that keeps you going. It's a minor miracle that little Rappler survived six years of Rodrigo Duterte, and we did that with the support of so many people in the Philippines, many asking to stay quietly behind the scenes, others running ahead and helping lead the charge. What most surprised me was how much our battles at home reverberated around the world, and the global support we received. Thank you to the hundreds of journalists and news organizations who chose to tell our story.

If I don't know you and you have supported us, thank you! My optimism gains strength from your energy because your kindness and attention kept us going: that outpouring of so much generosity dampened the hate and helped fuel our hopes for a better future.

It strengthens my faith in our collective humanity. And that has made all the difference.

When you're in the Upside Down, struggling to turn everything right-side up, time is the scarcest commodity. So let me start with the most important antidote to hate: love.

For Rapplers, past and present, every one of you has left your mark on each of us because we had a dream and embraced the spirit of creation together. What we are today has part of you in it.

For my family: my parents, Peter and Hermelina, my sisters Mary

Jane, Michelle, and Nicole, my brother Peter Ames, my nieces and nephews—Gia, Miguel, Diego, Gelli, Anthony, Michael, and Jessica. I don't say I love you enough. Thank you for always being patient because I work all the time.

For those who never left us: Benjamin Bitanga, our true angels Benjamin and Jenalyn So, Manny Ayala, our shareholders and directors, and our partners who continue to courageously stick their necks out in our #FactsFirstPH pyramid and our #CourageON and #PHVote coalitions, thank you for helping us #HoldTheLine.

For Stephen King, Nishant Lalwani, Marcus Brauchli, Stuart Karle, and Sasa Vucinic, thank you for believing in ideas we made real in Rappler. For Jim Risen of the Press Freedom Defense Fund: your wisdom, and empathy helped me rise to the challenge of the unexpected problems we faced.

For the core organizers and the more than 80 organizations in the #HoldTheLine Global Coalition—thank you to the Committee to Protect Journalists, Reporters Without Borders, the International Center for Journalists for organizing that. For Sheila Coronel, who fought the good fight and became a friend in adversity, a true boundary spanner, and for Harlan Mandel and Elena Popovic of the Media Development Investment Fund, thank you for sharing lessons learned at breaking-news speed.

For my Princeton friends, led by Olivia Hurlock and Leslie Tucker, who remains my writing partner since college. They created a gofundme for food, reaching across the oceans to let me know that we are not alone, and that even in a lockdown, we can have meals and wine together. For Kathy Kiely, who came out of nowhere and organized campaign after campaign of support for us, with Princeton's journalists leading the charge. For the great class of '86 and our class president Elisabeth Rodgers and the hundreds of Princetonians across the ages, who threw their voices and energy behind us.

For Domingo Magora, who kept my crazy hours for more than two decades, and Taffy Santiago, who has helped streamline my life since 1987. Her organizational skills have cleaned out cobwebs, set up safe houses, and chartered evacuation flights—only some of her many unorthodox tasks through our years with CNN, ABS-CBN, and Rappler.

For Ramona Diaz, Leah Marino, and the Frontline team led by Raney Aronson-Rath, who documented all we were living through. Thank you for helping us shine the light. *A Thousand Cuts* is part of more than 800 hours they spent with us.

For my friends in the technology companies, Google, Facebook (now Meta), Twitter, and Tiktok, among them Richard Gingras, Kate Beddoe, Madhav Chinnappa, Irene Jay Liu, Kathleen Reen, Nathaniel Gleicher, Brittan Heller, and the many who have tried to help.

For my friends at the UN and UNESCO, who always come through, including former special rapporteur for freedom of opinion and expression David Kaye and his successor, Irene Khan.

For the people who made this book possible: from the cold email and ideas of Hana Teraie-Wood reminding me I should be writing, to reconnecting with Rafe Sagalyn, and working with Amanda Urban. Thank you, Suzy Hansen, for the many hours we spent threshing out what and how to fix, and to Jonathan Jao, for your masterful edits. Thank you to the teams at HarperCollins and Penguin Random House for turning this into a reality.

For our lawyers, who have gone above and beyond: in the Philippines, John Molo and Mosveldtt; our formidable ACCRALaw team headed by former Philippine stock exchange president Francis Lim, Eric R. Recalde, Jacqueline Tan, Patricia Tysmans-Clemente, and Grace Salonga; Diane Desierto and Desierto & Desierto; former Supreme Court spokesman Theodore Te and the Free Legal Assistance Group; and to many more who have offered help at key moments.

For Amal and George Clooney, who focused their massive klieg lights on our battle, and who unexpectedly opened their home and hearts to me. Amal brought in her brilliant Doughty Street colleagues and her co-lead for our international legal team, Caoilfhionn Gallagher KC as well as Can Yeginsu and Claire Overman. Their care and counsel, thinking many steps ahead allowed me to focus on my work. For my Princeton classmate Peter Lichtenbaum, who offered us pro bono help from Covington and Burling, LLP, bringing along Dan Feldman, Steven Rademaker, Brad McCormick, and the late Kurt Wimmer.

For Jonas Gahr Stor, who nominated me for the Nobel Peace Prize, and after Dmitry and I were announced, became Norway's Prime Minister. Talk about the kindness of strangers! And for the Norwegian Nobel Committee and its chair, Berit Reiss-Andersen, your prescient analysis of the impact of freedom of information on democracy reminded journalists all around the world that we are not alone.

For the *manangs*, Glenda, Chay, and Beth, for sharing the pain and teaching me lessons I could never have learned without you. For always being there. For reinforcing my belief that we can trust. Even when we're frightened, we hold the line. Even when it's dark, we stumble ahead, and because we're together, I know others will follow.

I felt that love at the August 2022 wake of one of our Rappler stalwarts, photographer and activist Melvyn Calderon, Glenda's partner and the father of Leona, who started her first day at college a day after he was cremated. Melvyn was jailed under the Marcos father, defended us all like the swashbuckler he was during our worst attacks, and as the pandemic lockdown ended, he left us, reminding us that life is short.

Death is devastating, and we have dealt with so much loss. But we find a way to move on. And the more horrific things have become, the more we turn to love.

That sustains us against overwhelming odds.

Notes

Prologue: The Invisible Atom Bomb

1. Howard Johnson and Christopher Giles, "Philippines Drug War: Do We Know How Many Have Died?," BBC, November 12, 2019, https://www.bbc.com/news/world-asia-50236481.
2. Kyle Chua, "PH Remains Top in Social Media, Internet Usage Worldwide—Report," Rappler, January 28, 2021, https://www.rappler.com/technology/internet-culture/hootsuite-we-are-social-2021-philippines-top-social-media-internet-usage. The global annual report can be accessed here: https://wearesocial.com/digital-2021. The report specific to the Philippines can be accessed here: https://wearesocial.com/digital-2021.
3. Craig Silverman, "The Philippines Was a Test of Facebook's New Approach to Countering Disinformation. Things Got Worse." Buzzfeed, August 7, 2019, https://www.buzzfeednews.com/article/craigsilverman/2020-philippines-disinformation.
4. Peter Dizikes, "Study: On Twitter, False News Travels Faster Than True Stories," *MIT News*, March 8, 2018, https://news.mit.edu/2018/study-twitter-false-news-travels-faster-true-stories-0308.
5. "Maria Ressa, Nobel lecture," https://www.nobelprize.org/prizes/peace/2021/ressa/lecture/.
6. Here's a concrete example of how a top-down government official can cement a manufactured reality: on May 3, 2014, Russia's foreign minister Sergey Lavrov addressed the UN Council and told them that "we all know well who created the crisis in Ukraine and how they did it . . . west Ukrainian cities were occupied by armed national radicals, who used extremist, anti-Russian and anti-Semitic slogans. . . . We hear requests to restrict or punish the use of Russian."

    What he didn't say is that just a day earlier, a fake account, amplified by a network of accounts, seeded that same exact narrative. A Facebook account that had no followers and no friends, created on May 2, 2014, just as violent clashes broke out between pro-Russian separatists and supporters of an independent Ukraine, mimicked nearly word for word what Russia's foreign minister would present at the UN a day later. That account by Dr. Igor Rozovskiy about how Ukrainian nationalists prevented him from treating a wounded man and how they threatened that "Jews in Odessa would meet the same fate" went viral and was miraculously translated into other languages. For good measure, he wrote that "nothing like this happened in my city even under fascist occupation." People around the world believed this fake post from a manufactured account and combined with Lavrov's speech showed the power of bottom-up and top-down efforts to shape reality globally.

7. "2022 National Results," Rappler, https://ph.rappler.com/elections/2022/races/president-vice-president/results.

8. Ben Nimmo, C. Shawn Eib, Léa Ronzaud, "Operation Naval Gazing," *Graphika*, September 22, 2020, https://graphika.com/reports/operation-naval-gazing.

Chapter 1: The Golden Rule

1. The US bases in the Philippines renegotiated their terms after nationalists refused to grant an extension in 1992. By 1999, the US Library of Congress changed "the insurrection" to "the Philippine-American War."

2. Stanley Karnow, *In Our Image: America's Empire in the Philippines* (New York: Ballantine, 1990), 18.

3. Marge C. Enriquez, "Remembering Conchita Sunico: The Philippine Society's First 'It Girl' and Grand Dame," Tatler, September 22, 2020, https://www.tatlerasia.com/the-scene/people-parties/conchita-sunico-philippine-societys-first-it-girl-and-grand-dame.

4. "Raul M. Sunico: Pianist," https://raulsunico.com.

5. Soon after the winner of the Nobel Peace Prize was announced, I woke up to an email from Miss Ugland, who now lives in Norway.

6. We were a fixture at pop concerts in the auditorium, which my school system announced in 2021 it would name after me.

Chapter 2: The Honor Code

1. Alice Miller, *The Drama of the Gifted Child: The Search for the True Self*, 3rd ed. (New York: Basic Books, 1997), Kindle ed., 5.

2. Ibid., 6.

3. This is a phrase I pulled from Janwillem van de Wetering's *The Empty Mirror*, assigned in my World Religions class.

4. "Apartheid Protesters Arrested at Princeton," *New York Times*, May 24, 1985.

5. Artemio V. Panganiban, *Philippine Daily Inquirer*, August 26, 2018, https://opinion.inquirer.net/115635/masterminded-ninoys-murder.

6. "How Filipino People Power Toppled Dictator Marcos," BBC, February 16, 2016, https://www.bbc.com/news/av/magazine-35526200.

7. Mark R. Thompson, "Philippine 'People Power' Thirty Years On," *The Diplomat*, February 09, 2016, https://thediplomat.com/2016/02/philippine-people-power-thirty-years-on/. "Czech President Ends Philippine Visit," UPI Archives, April 7, 1995, https://www.upi.com/Archives/1995/04/07/Czech-president-ends-Philippine-visit/9128797227200/.

Chapter 3: The Speed of Trust

1. Some amazing folks were part of that unit in our youth; they later became industry leaders, including the animator and director Mike Alcazaren and the talent manager Jojie Dingcong.
2. "Secretary Delfin L. Lazaro," Republic of the Philippines Department of Energy, https://www.doe.gov.ph/secretary-delfin-l-lazaro?ckattempt=1.

Chapter 4: The Mission of Journalism

1. Author interview with Eason Jordan on May 13, 2021.
2. Piers Robinson, "The CNN Effect: Can the News Media Drive Foreign Policy?" *Review of International Studies* 25, no. 2 (1999): 301–9, http://www.jstor.org /stable/20097596.
3. Much of this I wrote or spoke about shortly after the 9/11 attacks. Some of the ideas that follow come from a speech I delivered to the International AVSEC Conference in Hong Kong on May 11, 2011.
4. Maria Ressa, "The Quest for SE Asia's Islamic, 'Super' State," CNN, August 29, 2002, http://edition.cnn.com/2002/WORLD/asiapcf/southeast/07/30/seasia.state/.
5. Documented in my first book, *Seeds of Terror: An Eyewitness Account of Al-Qaeda's Newest Center of Operations in Southeast Asia* (New York: Free Press, 2003), as well as a 2005 documentary I reported, wrote, and produced for ABS-CBN: *9/11: The Philippine Connection*, available here https://www.youtube.com /watch?v=BX7ySYJXel8&t=209s.
6. "Plane Terror Suspects Convicted on All Counts," CNN, September 5, 1996, http:// edition.cnn.com/US/9609/05/terror.plot/index.html.
7. Maria Ressa, "U.S. Warned in 1995 of Plot to Hijack Planes, Attack Buildings," CNN, September 18, 2001, https://edition.cnn.com/2001/US/09/18/inv.hijacking .philippines/.
8. I spent years tracking down everyone involved in 1995 and in my first book wrote about Aida Fariscal, the police officer who turned down a bribe from Murad and whose persistence foiled the pilot. We would meet several times before she died in April 2004. See Maria A. Ressa, "How a Filipino Woman Saved the Pope," Rappler, January 15, 2015, https://www.rappler.com/newsbreak/80902-filipino-woman-save-pope/.
9. The paper trail I followed, along with interviews with investigators from at least three different countries, led to numerous exclusives in my reporting for CNN. Much of that reporting was later incorporated into the *9/11 Commission Report*, released on July 22, 2004. See "The 9/11 Commission Report: Final Report of the National Commission on Terrorist Attacks upon the United States: Executive Summary," 9/11 Commission, https://www.9-11commission.gov/report/911Report_Exec.pdf.
10. In 2005, the year I returned to the Philippines to head ABS-CBN News, I put the information I had together in an ABS-CBN documentary that aired that year, describing the terrorism links to the Philippines. It was a way of telling the story highlighting what was important to Filipinos that I couldn't have done at CNN.
11. An example of the many stories Kelli Arena and I did together was "Singapore Bomb Plot Suspect Held," CNN, July 27, 2002, http://edition.cnn.com/2002/WORLD/asiapcf

/southeast/07/26/us.alqaeda.arrest/index.html. She visited the Philippines in 2014 as a speaker at Rappler's Social Good Summit; see Jee Y. Geronimo, "PH+SocialGood: Good Journalism, and the Power of the Crowd," Rappler, September 16, 2014, https://www.rappler.com/moveph/69241-good-journalism-crowdsourcing/. The path seemed so simple then.

12. Lessons learned as reporters led us to create Rappler's own database to keep track of the digital attacks on a scale I couldn't have fathomed in the age before social media.

13. Imagine that you're in a room with six other people, and a researcher shows you a card with a line on it and another card with lines of varying lengths marked *A*, *B*, and *C*. You're asked to compare the two cards and choose which line on the second card best matches the length of the one on the first card. You're certain that the right answer is *C* but are surprised when one by one, everyone asked before you answers *B*. Then the researcher gets to you, the last to respond, and asks for your answer. Now, despite your earlier certainty, you begin to doubt yourself. You're tempted to go along with the group. Do you go with your first answer or do you follow the group? Asch coached the actors hired to prompt the test subjects, and 75 percent caved in to the pressure of the group. Left alone, those same subjects answered correctly nearly 100 percent of the time. The Asch experiment, however, had a silver lining: one-fourth, or 25 percent, of people were independent; they never conformed.

14. In Milgram's study, the test subject is the person given the power to administer an electric shock in an experiment that is supposed to help others learn. When the "learner," hidden by a screen, fails to memorize word pairs fast enough, the "helper," or test subject, applies an electric shock, increasing the voltage with each wrong answer. Milgram found that most people follow instructions to give what would have been potentially lethal shocks despite the screams and pleas of the "learner."

15. In his experiment, Stanford University students were asked to become either a prisoner or a guard in an experiment that was supposed to last two weeks. It was cut short in less than a week because the guards became sadistic.

16. Nicholas Christakis and James Fowler, "Links," Connected, 2011, http://connected thebook.com/pages/links.html.

17. See Connected (home page), 2011, http://connectedthebook.com.

18. John T. Cacioppo, James H. Fowler, and Nicholas A. Christakis, "Alone in the Crowd: The Structure and Spread of Loneliness in a Large Social Network," *Journal of Personality and Social Psychology* 97, no. 6 (December 2009): 997–91, https://www.ncbi.nlm.nih.gov/pmc/articles/PMC2792572/.

19. James H. Fowler and Nicholas A. Christakis, "Dynamic Spread of Happiness in a Large Social Network: Longitudinal Analysis over 20 Years in the Framingham Heart Study," *British Medical Journal* 337 (2008): a2338, https://www.bmj.com/content/337/bmj.a2338. Smoking: Nicholas A. Christakis and James H. Fowler, "The Collective Dynamics of Smoking in a Large Social Network," *New England Journal of Medicine* 358 (2008): 2249–58, https://www.nejm.org/doi/full/10.1056/nejmsa0706154. Sexual diseases: Elizabeth Landau, "Obesity, STDs Flow in Social Networks," CNN, October 24, 2009, https://edition.cnn.com/2009/TECH/10/24/tech.networks.connected/index.html. Obesity: Nicholas A. Christakis and James H. Fowler, "The Spread of Obesity in a Large Social Network over 32 Years," *New England Journal of Medicine* 375 (2007): 370–79, https://www.nejm.org/doi/full/10.1056/nejmsa066082.

20. I discussed this in email exchanges with Nicholas Christakis, who said the thesis should work but that he didn't have a data set to prove it as definitively as the ones he and James Fowler had used to formulate the Three Degrees of Influence Rule.

21. I was the Southeast Asia Visiting Scholar at the CORE Lab at the Naval Postgraduate School in 2011. My project, along with others, was to chart terrorist networks in Southeast Asia.

22. Maria Ressa, "Spreading Terror: From bin Laden to Facebook in Southeast Asia," CNN, May 4, 2011, https://edition.cnn.com/2011/OPINION/05/03/bin.laden .southeast.asia/.

23. "Threat Report: The State of Influence Operations 2017–2020," Facebook, https:// about.fb.com/wp-content/uploads/2021/05/IO-Threat-Report-May-20-2021.pdf.

Chapter 5: The Network Effect

1. My second CNN team in Manilla: Boying Palileo for camera; Armand Sol for tech edit; Judith Torres as producer. For the systems and workflows of a news desk, I asked CNN's Atlanta-based Lynn Felton, my longtime minder, to visit Manila and run workshops, and I cut an arrangement with the brand-new Al-Jazeera English. They could have office space inside the ABS-CBN compound if their reporter, Marga Ortigas, an ex-prober, also ran training courses with me. We were also given rights to run a set amount of Al-Jazeera's programming monthly. For the news producers and the twenty-four-hour cycle of ANC, the ABS-CBN News Channel, I asked Hope Ngo, another former colleague from CNN HK, to revamp and train that team.

2. Carlos H. Conde, "Arroyo Admits to 'Lapse' During Election," *New York Times*, June 28, 2005, https://www.nytimes.com/2005/06/28/world/asia/arroyo-admits-to -lapse-during-election.html.

3. Pauline Macaraeg, "Look Back: The 'Hello, Garci' Scandal," Rappler, January 5, 2021, https://www.rappler.com/newsbreak/iq/look-back-gloria-arroyo-hello-garci -scandal/.

4. "Proclamation No. 1017 s. 2006," *Official Gazette*, February 24, 2006, https://www .officialgazette.gov.ph/2006/02/24/proclamation-no-1017-s-2006/.

5. "States of Rebellion, Emergency Under Arroyo Administration," *Philippine Daily Inquirer*, September 4, 2016, https://newsinfo.inquirer.net/812626/states-of-rebel lion-emergency-under-arroyo-administration.

6. Raissa Robles, "Coronavirus: Is Covid-19 Task Force Duterte's 'Rolex 12' in Plan for Marcos-Style Martial Law in the Philippines?," *South China Morning Post*, April 28, 2020, https://www.scmp.com/week-asia/politics/article/3081939/coronavirus-covid -19-task-force-dutertes-rolex-12-plan-marcos.

7. Korina Sanchez, Henry Omaga-Diaz, and Ces Oreña-Drilon were the founding anchors of *Bandila*.

8. We co-opted two key ideas: crowdsourcing from James Surowiecki, who wrote the book *The Wisdom of Crowds*, and the tipping point from the book *The Tipping Point*, written more than a decade earlier by Malcolm Gladwell.

9. "Ako ang Simula," YouTube, October 20, 2009, https://www.youtube.com/watch?v =Kbm1HfW9HYs.

10. Joseph Campbell was right about the power of myth, and we thought about universal truths that would resonate for the Philippines.

11. Video call to action available here: bravenewworldressa, "Boto Mo, iPatrol Mo Maria Ressa Stand Up and Say AKO ANG SIMULA!," YouTube, January 6, 2011, https://www.youtube.com/watch?v=D13Q23BXpZg.

12. News piece about this extraordinary event in Tagalog: "Boto Patrollers Rock with Famous Artists, Bands." The title, *"Himig ng Pagbabago,"* means "the sound (or melody/music) of change." "Boto Patrollers Rock with Famous Artists, Bands," ABS-CBN News, February 20, 2010, https://news.abs-cbn.com/video/entertainment/02/20/10/boto-patrollers-rock-famous-artists-bands.

13. Alia Ahmed, "CPJ's Press Freedom Awards Remember Maguindanao," Committee to Protect Journalists, November 24, 2010, https://cpj.org/2010/11/cpjs-press-freedom-awards-remember-maguindanao/; Elisabeth Witchel, "Ten Years for Justice in Maguindanao Case Is Too Long: We Can Do Better," Committee to Protect Journalists, December 19, 2019, https://cpj.org/2019/12/ten-years-justice-maguindanao-massacre-impunity-journalists/.

14. Message sent to ABS-CBN by a citizen journalist on November 23, 2009.

15. The year 2010 was early days for Facebook, and those were the only metrics based on its baseline that were then available.

16. Maria Ressa, "#MovePH: How Social Media and Technology Are Changing You," Rappler, August 10, 2014, https://www.rappler.com/moveph/65802-moveph-how-social-media-and-technology-are-changing-you/.

17. It's fitting because Ging Reyes, the North America bureau chief, was the first person to walk into my office as head of news. A former producer of the prime-time newscast, she was an ABS-CBN original, and we used to bump into each other in the hallways in 1987. She has been the head of the news group for more than a decade now.

18. Maria Ressa, "Maria Ressa's Letter to ABS-CBN News and Current Affairs," ABS-CBN News, October 11, 2010, https://news.abs-cbn.com/insights/10/11/10/maria-ressas-letter-abs-cbn-news-and-current-affairs-team.

Chapter 6: Creating Ripples of Change

1. Writer, producer, photographer, videographer, and newscast producer Beth Frondoso studied political science at UP Diliman and worked at ABS-CBN as a supervising producer for News and Current Affairs. She currently heads Multimedia Strategy and Growth in Rappler.

   Beth's style is like a general—gather information, assign, and deploy. It made sense because production is the engine of traffic on our social media platforms, which means that her team needs to strike the balance of a factory line of video that will bring viewers in, yet also be creative enough to do the quality reports and documentaries that won us awards, and experiment with 360 video executions (well, that also won an award).

   Among Rappler's senior editors and founders, Chay Hofileña is the managing editor. She was previously head of Rappler's Investigative Desk—Newsbreak—and is in charge of training. Before joining Rappler, she was a contributing writer of *Newsbreak Magazine* and was one of its founding editors, too, in 2001. Chay cowrote with Miriam

Grace Go *Ambition, Destiny, Victory: Stories from a Presidential Election* (2011) on the 2010 elections.

She has written on media issues and authored the book *News for Sale: The Corruption and Commercialization of the Philippine Media* (2004 edition, published by the Philippine Center for Investigative Journalism). She obtained her graduate degree from Columbia University's School of Journalism in New York and is a lecturer at the undergraduate level of the Ateneo de Manila University. She has been the recipient of awards from the Jaime V. Ongpin Awards for Excellence in Journalism.

The former director of the Asian Center for Journalism at the Ateneo, Chay also teaches News Writing and Investigative Journalism to undergraduate students. She is drawn to journalism because it allows her to write stories that have the potential to make a difference.

Chay is forever the teacher, part of the reason each member of our team grows so quickly. We all shared our sources and analysis, instilling a culture that didn't exist outside Rappler or at many cutthroat and secretive news organizations—a share culture. Chay is also the recruiter who identifies the best students in her classes; we wanted people who would ask questions and whose egos could take a backseat to the mission.

Glenda cofounded Rappler in July 2011 and served as its managing editor until November 16, 2020, when she was named executive editor. She finished journalism in 1985, a year before the end of the Marcos dictatorship. She has worked for the *Philippine Daily Inquirer*, the *Manila Times*, the Philippine Center for Investigative Journalism, and for international news agencies. In the dying days of the Estrada administration, she cofounded the Philippines' top investigative magazine *Newsbreak*, which started as a newsweekly.

From 2008 to January 2011, she managed ANC, the ABS-CBN News Channel, as its chief operating officer.

Glenda earned her journalism degree at the University of Santo Tomas in Manila. A British Chevening scholar, she holds a master's degree in political sociology from the London School of Economics and Political Science (1999). In May 2018, Glenda finished her Nieman Journalism Fellowship at Harvard University.

The books that she has authored include *Under the Crescent Moon: Rebellion in Mindanao*, with Marites Dañguilan Vitug, the groundbreaking, National Book Award–winning work on the conflict in Mindanao. In 2011, she wrote *The Enemy Within: An Inside Story on Military Corruption*, with the late Aries Rufo and Gemma Bagayaua-Mendoza.

Glenda is really my partner in building the organization, the evil eye, and I smile as I write that. She's the bad cop to my good cop, the disciplinarian who lays out our expectations, and woe to whoever disappoints her. She balances the medium- and long-term with the daily, nitty-gritty of the stories that build a reporter and a news site.

2. Our founding board included Manny Ayala, a former *Probe* reporter who went on to get a Harvard MBA and become an investment banker; internet entrepreneur Nix Nolledo; and former media wunderkind Raymund Miranda, who had just left his job in Singapore as head of NBC Universal in the Asia-Pacific to come home to the Philippines. I had worked with both Manny and Raymund when we were all in our twenties, and Nix rounded out our founding board. That group was our brain trust for business and the

internet. With the exception of Nix, all of us had worked with big corporate media, so we understood news and entertainment. In 2014, we added three more board members: Felicia Atienza, a former investment banker who had engineered the leveraged buyout of Merrill Lynch Philippines and later attended the Chinese International School because she wanted her kids to learn Mandarin; former IBM country director James Velasquez; and lawyer and venture capital entrepreneur James Bitanga.

3. "MovePH," Facebook, https://www.facebook.com/move.ph.

4. Our two cameras for the livestream that day were handled by multimedia reporters Patricia Evangelista and Katherine Visconti. Students in the audience asked questions about them (and of them) because by being women doing those jobs, they broke a long-held gender stereotype of men behind the tripod.

5. Simon Kemp, "Digital 2011: The Philippines," Datareportal, December 30, 2011, https://datareportal.com/reports/digital-2011-philippines.

6. Some of this text first appeared in a paper I submitted to the International Centre for Political Violence and Terrorism Research in September 2011, playing off my presentation in Baguio and in Singapore at the International Conference on Community Engagement a week earlier; see Maria A. Ressa, "The Internet and New Media: Tools for Countering Extremism and Building Community Resilience," May 1, 2013, https://doi.org/10.1142/9781908977540_0010.

7. Much has been written and said about this. See, e.g., William Saletan, "Springtime for Twitter: Is the Internet Driving the Revolutions of the Arab Spring?," Slate, July 18, 2011, http://www.slate.com/articles/technology/future_tense/2011/07/springtime_for_twitter.html; and D. Hill, "Op-Ed: The Arab Spring Is Not the Facebook Revolution," *Ottawa Citizen*, November 16, 2011.

8. Marshall McLuhan, "The Medium Is the Message," 1964, https://web.mit.edu/allanmc/www/mcluhan.mediummessage.pdf.

9. Suw Charman Anderson, "The Role of Dopamine in Social Media," ComputerWeekly.Com, November 26, 2009.

10. Jack Fuller, *What Is Happening to News: The Information Explosion and the Crisis in Journalism* (London: University of Chicago Press, 2010), 46.

11. Suzanne Choney, "Facebook Use Can Lower Grades by 20%, Study Says," NBC News, September 7, 2010, https://www.nbcnews.com/id/wbna39038581.

12. This rolled out in the United States to select users in August 2015. The global rollout was in April 2016.

13. "Rappler Is PH's 3rd Top News Site," Rappler, September 6, 2013, https://www.rappler.com/nation/rappler-third-top-news-site-alexa/.

14. Rappler rolled out the mood meter and mood navigator in alpha in 2011. Here's an example of some of the academic analysis done on the link between mood and virality: Marco Guerini and Jacopo Staiano, "Deep Feelings: A Massive Cross-Lingual Study on the Relation Between Emotions and Virality," arXiv, March 16, 2015, https://arxiv.org/pdf/1503.04723.pdf. Facebook rolled out emojis in Q4 2015; see Nathan McAlone, "There Is a Specific Sociological Reason Why Facebook Introduced Its New Emoji 'Reactions,'" Insider, October 9, 2015, https://www.businessinsider.com/the-reason-facebook-introduced-emoji-reactions-2015-10.

15. Edmund T. Rolls, "A Theory of Emotion and Consciousness, and Its Application to Understanding the Neural Basis of Emotion," in *The Cognitive Neurosciences*, edited by Michael S. Gazzaniga (Cambridge, MA: MIT Press, 1995), 1091–1106.

16. Christine Ma-Kellams and Jennifer Lerner, "Trust Your Gut or Think Carefully? Examining Whether an Intuitive, Versus a Systematic, Mode of Thought Produces Greater Empathic Accuracy," *Journal of Personality and Social Psychology* 111, no. 5 (2016): 674–85, https://www.apa.org/pubs/journals/releases/psp-pspi0000063 .pdf; Jennifer S. Lerner, Ye Li, Piercarlo Valdesolo, and Karim Kassam, "Emotions and Decision Making," *Annual Review of Psychology*, June 16, 2014, https://scholar.harvard .edu/files/jenniferlerner/files/annual_review_manuscript_june_16_final.final_.pdf.

17. We summarized the moods of the year in annual reviews: "2012 in Moods," YouTube, December 31, 2012, https://www.youtube.com/watch?v=dRXYP7zZTtE; "2013 in Moods," YouTube, December 28, 2013, https://www.youtube.com/watch?v =-PTjYFldhes; "2014 in Moods," YouTube, December 29, 2014, https://www.youtube .com/watch?v=9kDW72xbCEo&t=76s; "2015 in Moods," YouTube, December 26, 2015, https://www.youtube.com/watch?v=UJXNzwXh0_Q&t=197s.

18. In the Philippines, Rappler is trying to figure out the role of emotion in the news. Two academic studies were done by Marco Guerini and Jacopo Staiano like this one, using data from our mood meter; see Guerini and Staiano, "Deep Feelings." See also "Study Uses Rappler to See Relationship Between Emotion, Virality," Rappler, March 30, 2015, https://www.rappler.com/science/88391-rappler-corriere-guerini-staiano-study/. Here's a later study done by US researchers: Jessica Gall Myrick and Bartosz W. Wojdynski, "Moody News: The Impact of Collective Emotion Ratings on Online News Consumers' Attitudes, Memory, and Behavioral Intentions," *New Media & Society* 18, no. 11 (2016): 2576–94.

19. "Vice Ganda Gets Flak for 'Rape' Joke," Rappler, May 28, 2013, https://www.rappler .com/entertainment/30116-vice-ganda-jessica-soho-rape-joke/.

20. #BudgetWatch, Rappler, https://www.rappler.com/topic/budget-watch/.

21. "Slides and Ladders: Understand the Budget Process," Rappler, July 20, 2013, https:// r3.rappler.com/move-ph/issues/budget-watch/27897-slides-ladders-philippine -budget-process.

22. "[Budget Game] Did Congressmen Favor Your Budget Priorities?," Rappler, June 11, 2015, https://r3.rappler.com/move-ph/issues/budget-watch/33857-national-budget-game.

23. #ProjectAgos, Rappler, https://r3.rappler.com/move-ph/issues/disasters.

24. Rappler, "How to Use the Project Agos Alert Map," YouTube, October 15, 2014, https://www.youtube.com/watch?v=TfD47KXaFMc&t=79s.

25. "Checklist: What Cities and Municipalities Should Prepare for an Earthquake," Rappler, https://r3.rappler.com/move-ph/issues/disasters/knowledge-base.

26. Rappler, "Agos: Make #ZeroCasualty a Reality," YouTube, May 18, 2015, https://www .youtube.com/watch?v=Dvrubwbeypk.

27. "#HungerProject," Rappler, https://r3.rappler.com/move-ph/issues/hunger.

28. David Lozada, "#HungerProject: Collaboration Key to Ending Hunger in the PH," Rappler, March 4, 2014, https://www.rappler.com/moveph/52036-hunger-project -launch-collaboration-ph-hunger/.

29. "#WhipIt," Rappler, https://r3.rappler.com/brandrap/whipit.

30. Bea Cupin, "#WHIPIT: Can Women Have It All?," Rappler, December 12, 2013, https://www.rappler.com/brandrap/44663-whip-it-ncr-survey-women-issues/.

31. Libay Linsangan Cantor, "#WHIPIT: The (En)gendered Numbers Crunch," Rappler, January 16, 2014, https://www.rappler.com/brandrap/profiles-and-advocacies/47950 -whip-it-engendered-numbers-crunch/.

32. Libay Linsangan Cantor, "#WHIPIT: A Filipino Campaign Goes Global and Viral," Rappler, March 18, 2016, https://www.rappler.com/brandrap/profiles-and-advo cacies/46129-whipit-gets-international-mileage/.

33. Smartmatic, *Automated Elections in the Philippines, 2008–2013*, https://www.parlia ment.uk/globalassets/documents/speaker/digital-democracy/CS_The_Philippine _Elections_2008-2013_v.9_ING_A4.pdf; and Business Wire, "Philippine Votes Transmitted in Record Time in Largest Ever Electronic Vote Count," May 9, 2016, https://www.businesswire.com/news/home/20160509006516/en/Philippine-Votes -Transmitted-in-Record-Time-in-Largest-Ever-Electronic-Vote-Count.

34. Ibid.

35. For photos and videos of the leaderless protest, see Bea Cupin, "Scrap Pork Barrel! Punish the Corrupt," Rappler, August 26, 2013, https://www.rappler.com /nation/37282-pork-barrel-protests-nationwide/; Ted Regencia, "'Pork-Barrel Protests' Rock the Philippines," Al Jazeera, August 27, 2013, https://www.aljazeera.com /features/2013/8/27/pork-barrel-protests-rock-the-philippines.

36. Dominic Gabriel Go, "#MillionPeopleMarch: Online and Offline Success," Rappler, September 11, 2013, https://www.rappler.com/nation/37360-million-people-march -social-media-protest-success.

37. For photos and videos of the leaderless protest, see Cupin, "Scrap Pork Barrel! Punish the Corrupt"; Regencia, "'Pork-Barrel Protests' Rock the Philippines."

38. "#NotOnMyWatch," Rappler, https://ph.rappler.com/campaigns/fight-corruption# know-nomy.

39. Michael Bueza, "#NotOnMyWatch: Reporting Corruption Made Easier," Rappler, September 26, 2016, https://www.rappler.com/moveph/147340-notonmywatch -chat-bot-report-corruption-commend-good-public-service/.

40. I Paid a Bribe in India was ahead of us in crowdsourcing corruption reports, but it didn't have the government partnerships that could turn the reports into action. Of course, that's now dead after Prime Minister Narendra Modi weaponized social media.

41. "WATCH: Duterte: Say 'No' to Corruption," Rappler, January 2, 2017, https://www .rappler.com/moveph/157170-not-on-my-watch-fighting-corruption-rodrigo -duterte-call/.

42. "#TheLeaderIWant: Leadership, Duterte-style," Rappler, October 29, 2015, https:// www.rappler.com/nation/elections/111096-leadership-duterte-style/ and YouTube, October 29, 2015, https://www.youtube.com/watch?v=ow9FUAHCclk.

43. Maria Ressa, "Duterte, His 6 Contradictions and Planned Dictatorship," Rappler, October 26, 2015, https://www.rappler.com/nation/elections/110679-duterte-contra dictions-dictatorship/.

44. Euan McKirdy, "Philippines President Likens Himself to Hitler," CNN, September 30, 2016, https://www.cnn.com/2016/09/30/asia/duterte-hitler-comparison.

45. "Philippines Presidential Candidate Attacked over Rape Remarks," Guardian.com, April 17, 2016, https://www.theguardian.com/world/2016/apr/17/philippines -presidential-candidate-attacked-over-remarks.

46. "Philippines President Rodrigo Duterte in Quotes," BBC.com, September 30, 2016, https://www.bbc.com/news/world-asia-36251094.

Chapter 7: How Friends of Friends Brought Democracy Down

1. Terence Lee, "Philippines' Rappler Fuses Online Journalism with Counter-terrorism Tactics, Social Network Theory," Tech in Asia, May 21, 2013, https://www.techinasia.com/how-rappler-is-applying-counter-terrorism-tactics-into-an-online-news-startup.

2. "Leveraging Innovative Solutions to Create Economic Dividends: Case Studies from the Asia Pacific Region," National Center for Asia-Pacific Economic Cooperation, 2014, https://trpc.biz/old_archive/wp-content/uploads/NCAPEC2013_StoriesOfInnovationAndEnablementFromAPEC_14Mar2014.pdf.

3. "Free Basics Partner Stories: Rappler," Facebook, April 12, 2016, https://developers.facebook.com/videos/f8-2016/free-basics-partner-stories-rappler/.

4. David Cohen, "Facebook Opens Philippines Office," Adweek, April 22, 2018, https://www.adweek.com/performance-marketing/facebook-philippines/.

5. Mong Palatino, "Free Basics in Philippines," Global Voices, March–April 2017, https://advox.globalvoices.org/wp-content/uploads/2017/07/PHILIPPINES.pdf.

6. Globe Telecom, Inc., "Facebook CEO Mark Zuckerberg: Philippines a Successful Test Bed for Internet.org Initiative with Globe Telecom Partnership," Cision, February 24, 2014, https://www.prnewswire.com/news-releases/facebook-ceo-mark-zuckerberg-philippines-a-successful-test-bed-for-internetorg-initiative-with-globe-telecom-partnership-247184981.html.

7. Miguel R. Camus, "MVP Admits PLDT Losing to Globe in Market Share," Inquirer.net, January 13, 2017, https://business.inquirer.net/222861/mvp-admits-pldt-losing-globe-market-share.

8. "Value of Connectivity," Deloitte, https://www2.deloitte.com/ch/en/pages/technology-media-and-telecommunications/articles/value-of-connectivity.html.

9. Watch the video here: Free Basics Partner Stories: Rappler, https://developers.facebook.com/videos/f8-2016/free-basics-partner-stories-rappler/.

10. The population of the Philippines was 112,579,898 as of July 3, 2022, based on the latest UN data; see "Philippines Population (Live)," Worldometer, https://www.worldometers.info/world-population/philippines-population/.

11. David Dizon, "Why Philippines Has Overtaken India as World's Call Center Capital," ABS-CBN News, December 2, 2010, https://news.abs-cbn.com/nation/12/02/10/why-philippines-has-overtaken-india-worlds-call-center-capital.

12. Such businesses include Kim Dotcom and his file-sharing site Megaupload, which, according to FBI and US court documents, operated partly from the Philippines. See David Fisher, "Free but $266 Million in Debt: The Deal That Gave the FBI an Inside Man Who Could Testify Against Kim Dotcom," New Zealand Herald, November 27, 2015, https://www.nzherald.co.nz/business/news/article.cfm?c_id=3&objectid=11551882.

13. Doug Bock Clark, "The Bot Bubble: How Click Farms Have Inflated Social Media Currency," New Republic, April 21, 2015, https://newrepublic.com/article/121551/bot-bubble-click-farms-have-inflated-social-media-currency.

14. Chris Francescani, "The Men Behind QAnon," ABC News, September 22, 2020, https://abcnews.go.com/Politics/men-qanon/story?id=73046374.

15. Clark, "The Bot Bubble."

16. Ibid.

17. Jennings Brown, "There's Something Odd About Donald Trump's Facebook Page," Insider, June 18, 2015, https://www.businessinsider.com/donald-trumps-facebook -followers-2015-6.

18. Nicholas Confessore, Gabriel J. X. Dance, Richard Harris, and Mark Hansen, "The Follower Factory," *New York Times*, January 27, 2018, https://www.nytimes.com /interactive/2018/01/27/technology/social-media-bots.html.

19. Jonathan Corpus Ong and Jason Vincent A. Cabañes, "Architects of Networked Disinformation: Behind the Scenes of Troll Accounts and Fake News Production in the Philippines," Newton Tech4Dev Network, February 5, 2018, http://newtontechfordev .com/wp-content/uploads/2018/02/ARCHITECTS-OF-NETWORKED -DISINFORMATION-FULL-REPORT.pdf.

20. Glen Arrowsmith, "Arkose Labs Presents the Q3 Fraud and Abuse Report," Arkose Labs, September 18, 2019, https://www.arkoselabs.com/blog/arkose-labs-presents -the-q3-fraud-and-abuse-report/.

21. "Software Management: Security Imperative, Business Opportunity: BSA Global Software Survey," BSA, June 2018, https://gss.bsa.org/wp-content/uploads/2018/05 /2018_BSA_GSS_Report_en.pdf.

22. Heather Chen, "'AlDub': A Social Media Phenomenon About Love and Lip-Synching," BBC, October 28, 2015, https://www.bbc.com/news/world-asia-34645078.

23. Pia Ranada, "ULPB Students to Duterte: Give Us Direct Answers," Rappler, March 12, 2016, https://www.rappler.com/nation/elections/125520-up-los-banos-students-du terte-forum/.

24. "#AnimatED: Online Mob Creates Social Media Wasteland," Rappler, March 14, 2016, https://www.rappler.com/voices/editorials/125615-online-mob-social-media -wasteland/.

25. "Duterte to Supporters: Be Civil, Intelligent, Decent, Compassionate," Rappler, March 13, 2016, https://www.rappler.com/nation/elections/125701-duterte-sup porters-death-threats-uplb-student/.

26. Gemma B. Mendoza, "Networked Propaganda: How the Marcoses Are Using Social Media to Reclaim Malacañang," Rappler, November 20, 2019, https://www.rappler .com/newsbreak/investigative/245290-marcos-networked-propaganda-social -media.

27. "#SmartFREEInternet: Anatomy of a Black Ops Campaign on Twitter," Rappler, October 8, 2014, https://www.rappler.com/technology/social-media/71115-ana tomy-of-a-twitter-black-ops-campaign/.

28. A single fake account with a broadcaster's reach. Facebook user Mutya Bautista, who joined more than a hundred Facebook groups, could have spread false information to millions of people.

29. Chay F. Hofileña, "Fake Accounts, Manufactured Reality on Social Media," Rappler, October 9, 2016, https://www.rappler.com/newsbreak/investigative/148347-fake -accounts-manufactured-reality-social-media/.

30. The three main Facebook pages that created content geared to demographics were Sass Sasot, for the educated class; Thinking Pinoy, for the middle class; and Mocha Uson Blog, for the mass base.

31. "Twitter Map: No Real Party System," Rappler, February 25, 2013, https://www .rappler.com/nation/elections/22454-twitter-map-of-political-coalitions-at-start-of -national-campaigns/.

32. Rappler Research, "Volume of Groups Tracked by Sharktank," Flourish, October 3, 2019, https://public.flourish.studio/visualisation/590897/.

33. Catherine Tsalikis, "Maria Ressa: 'Facebook Broke Democracy in Many Countries Around the World, Including in Mine,'" Centre for International Governance Innovation, September 18, 2019, https://www.cigionline.org/articles/maria-ressa -facebook-broke-democracy-many-countries-around-world-including-mine/.

34. "Explosion Hits Davao Night Market," Rappler, September 2, 2016, https://www .rappler.com/nation/145033-explosion-roxas-night-market-davao-city/.

35. "Duterte Declares State of Lawlessness in PH," Rappler, September 3, 2016, https:// www.rappler.com/nation/145043-duterte-declares-state-of-lawlessness-ph/.

36. Editha Caduaya, "Man with Bomb Nabbed at Davao Checkpoint," Rappler, March 26, 2016, https://www.rappler.com/nation/127132-man-bomb-nabbed-davao-check point/.

37. These were the specific stories on the websites that had the misleadingly repurposed Rappler story: http://ww1.pinoytribune.com/2016/09/man-with-high-quality-of -bomb-nabbed-at.html; http://www.socialnewsph.com/2016/09/look-man-with -high-quality-of-bomb.html; http://www.newstrendph.com/2016/09/man-with -high-quality-of-bomb-nabbed-at.html.

38. Rappler Research, "Davao Bombing," Flourish, July 8, 2019, https://public.flourish .studio/visualisation/230850/.

39. Ralf Rivas, "Gambling-Dependent Philippines Allows POGOs to Resume Operations," Rappler, May 1, 2020, https://www.rappler.com/business/259599-gambling-depen dent-philippines-allows-pogos-resume-operations-coronavirus/.

40. This is the now-nonexistent link to the Rappler Facebook post that was taken down: https://www.facebook.com/rapplerdotcom/posts/1312782435409203.

41. John Naughton, "The Goal Is to Automate Us: Welcome to the Age of Surveillance Capitalism," *Guardian*, January 20, 2019, https://www.theguardian.com/tech nology/2019/jan/20/shoshana-zuboff-age-of-surveillance-capitalism-google -facebook.

42. There are four books about Facebook that I would recommend: David Kirkpatrick's *The Facebook Effect: The Inside Story of the Company That Is Connecting the World* (New York: Simon & Schuster, 2010) traces the beginning and the development of Mark Zuckerberg. Published in 2010, it came out at a time of wonder. On the business model, Shoshana Zuboff coined the term *surveillance capitalism* in 2019; see *The Age of Surveillance Capitalism: The Fight for a Human Future at the New Frontier of Power* (New York: Public Affairs, 2019). Steven Levy's *Facebook: The Inside Story* (New York: Blue Rider Press, 2020) chronicled the company's fall. And finally, Sinan Aral's *The Hype Machine: How Social Media Disrupts Our Elections, Our Economy, and Our Health— and How We Must Adapt* (New York: Currency, 2020) details some of the dangers but remains a favorable view of the giant, providing the possibility of redemption.

43. Naughton, "The Goal Is to Automate Us."

44. James Bridle, "*The Age of Surveillance Capitalism* by Shoshana Zuboff Review— We Are the Pawns," *Guardian*, February 2, 2019, https://www.theguardian.com /books/2019/feb/02/age-of-surveillance-capitalism-shoshana-zuboff-review.

45. Shoshana Zuboff wants the market in our behavioral data, like the slave trade, abolished. She and I, along with Roger McNamee and other Facebook critics, meet as part of the Real Facebook Oversight Board, created by the journalist Carole Cadwalladr, who broke

the Cambridge Analytica story in 2018. That was when we launched the group; see Olivia Solon, "While Facebook Works to Create an Oversight Board, Industry Experts Formed Their Own," NBC News, September 25, 2020, https://www.nbcnews.com /tech/tech-news/facebook-real-oversight-board-n1240958.

46. Ryan Mac and Craig Silverman, "'Mark Changed the Rules': How Facebook Went Easy on Alex Jones and Other Right-Wing Figures," BuzzFeed News, February 22, 2021, https://www.buzzfeednews.com/article/ryanmac/mark-zuckerberg-joel-kaplan -facebook-alex-jones; Sheera Frenkel et al., "Delay, Deny and Deflect: How Facebook's Leaders Fought Through Crisis," *New York Times*, November 14, 2018, https://www .nytimes.com/2018/11/14/technology/facebook-data-russia-election-racism.html.

47. Maria A. Ressa, "[ANALYSIS] As Democracy Dies, We Build a Global Future," Rappler, October 13, 2020, https://www.rappler.com/voices/thought-leaders /analysis-as-democracy-dies-we-build-global-future/.

48. Maya Yang, "More Than 40% in US Do Not Believe Biden Legitimately Won Election— Poll," *Guardian*, January 5, 2022, https://www.theguardian.com/us-news/2022 /jan/05/america-biden-election-2020-poll-victory. The figures 37 percent of Americans and 10 percent of Democrats came from a private poll shared with me.

49. "Is Facebook Putting Company over Country? New Book Explores Its Role in Misinformation," *PBS NewsHour*, July 22, 2021, https://www.pbs.org/newshour /show/is-facebook-putting-company-over-country-new-book-explores-its-role-in -misinformation.

50. Lora Kolodny, "Zuckerberg Claims 99% of Facebook Posts 'Authentic,' Denies Fake News There Influenced Election," TechCrunch, November 12, 2016, https:// techcrunch.com/2016/11/13/zuckerberg-claims-99-of-facebook-posts-authentic -denies-fake-news-there-influenced-election/.

51. That was Alex Stamos, who technically reported to Sheryl Sandberg, whose responsibilities included protecting users.

52. Sheera Frenkel and Cecilia Kang, *An Ugly Truth: Inside Facebook's Battle for Domination* (New York: Harper, 2021).

53. Ibid. Facebook's policy, according to the authors, *New York Times* reporters Sheera Frenkel and Cecilia Kang, is to fire employees after they're caught doing that. Stamos argued that the company was responsible for preventing it from even happening.

54. Daniela Hernandez and Parmy Olson, "Isolation and Social Media Combine to Radicalize Violent Offenders," *Wall Street Journal*, August 5, 2019, https:// www.wsj.com/articles/isolation-and-social-media-combine-to-radicalize-violent -offenders-11565041473. See also studies on terrorism, including "The Use of Social Media by United States Extremists," National Consortium for the Study of Terrorism and Responses to Terrorism, https://www.start.umd.edu/pubs/START_PIRUS _UseOfSocialMediaByUSExtremists_ResearchBrief_July2018.pdf. On politics, including Robin L. Thompson, "Radicalization and the Use of Social Media," *Journal of Strategic Security* 4, no. 4 (2011), https://digitalcommons.usf.edu/cgi/viewcontent .cgi?article=1146&context=jss. On far-right terrorism, including Farah Pandith and Jacob Ware, "Teen Terrorism Inspired by Social Media Is on the Rise. Here's What We Need to Do," NBC News, March 22, 2021, https://www.nbcnews.com/think /opinion/teen-terrorism-inspired-social-media-rise-here-s-what-we-ncna1261307.

55. Kyle Chua, "8Chan Founder Says Current Site Owner Jim Watkins Behind QAnon—

Report," Rappler, September 29, 2020, https://www.rappler.com/technology/8chan -founder-fredrick-brennan-jim-watkins-behind-qanon/.

56. Jim Holt, "Two Brains Running," *New York Times*, November 25, 2011, https://www.nytimes.com/2011/11/27/books/review/thinking-fast-and-slow-by-daniel -kahneman-book-review.html.

57. Peter Dizikes, "Study: On Twitter, False News Travels Faster Than True Stories," MIT News, March 8, 2018, https://news.mit.edu/2018/study-twitter-false-news-travels -faster-true-stories-0308.

58. "#NoPlaceForHate: Change Comes to Rappler's Comments Thread," Twitter, August 26, 2016, https://twitter.com/rapplerdotcom/status/769085047915810816.

59. "#NoPlaceForHate: Change Comes to Rappler's Comments Thread," Rappler, August 26, 2016, https://www.rappler.com/voices/143975-no-place-for-hate-change -comes-to-rappler-comments-thread/.

60. "If there be time to expose through discussion the falsehood and fallacies, to avert the evil by the processes of education, the remedy to be applied is more speech, not enforced silence." *Whitney v. People of State of California*, 274 U.S. 357 (1927).

61. Raisa Serafica, "Collateral Damage: 5-Yr-Old Girl Latest Fatality in War on Drugs," Rappler, August 25, 2016, https://www.rappler.com/nation/144138-five-year-old -killed-pangasinan-war-drugs/.

62. Maria Ressa, "Propaganda War: Weaponizing the Internet," Rappler, October 3, 2016, https://www.rappler.com/nation/148007-propaganda-war-weaponizing-internet/; Maria Ressa, "How Facebook Algorithms Impact Democracy," Rappler, October 8, 2016, https://www.rappler.com/newsbreak/148536-facebook-algorithms-impact-democracy/.

63. Chay F. Hofileña, "Fake Accounts, Manufactured Reality on Social Media," Rappler, October 9, 2016, https://www.rappler.com/newsbreak/investigative/148347-fake -accounts-manufactured-reality-social-media/.

Chapter 8: How the Rule of Law Crumbled from Within

1. Maria Ressa, "Propaganda War: Weaponizing the Internet," Rappler, October 3, 2016, https://www.rappler.com/nation/148007-propaganda-war-weaponizing-internet/.

2. "Keyboard warriors" was what the Duterte team called their "volunteers."

3. "Aquino: 'I Hope I Showed Best Face of PH to the World,'" Rappler, June 8, 2016, https://www.rappler.com/nation/135685-aquino-best-face-philippines-world/.

4. Jodesz Gavilan, "Duterte's P10M Social Media Campaign: Organic, Volunteer-Driven," Rappler, June 1, 2016, https://www.rappler.com/newsbreak/134979-rodrigo-duterte -social-media-campaign-nic-gabunada/.

5. Gelo Gonzales, "Facebook Takes Down Fake Account Network of Duterte Campaign Social Media Manager," Rappler, March 29, 2019, https://www.rappler.com /technology/226932-facebook-takes-down-fake-account-network-duterte-campaign -social-media-manager-march-2019/.

6. Maria A. Ressa, "How Facebook Algorithms Impact Democracy," Rappler, October 8, 2016, https://www.rappler.com/newsbreak/148536-facebook-algorithms-impact -democracy/.

7. Chay F. Hofileña, "Fake Accounts, Manufactured Reality on Social Media," Rappler,

October 9, 2016, https://www.rappler.com/newsbreak/investigative/148347-fake-accounts-manufactured-reality-social-media/.

8. Rambo Talabong, "At Least 33 Killed Daily in the Philippines Since Duterte Assumed Office," Rappler, June 15, 2018, https://www.rappler.com/newsbreak/in-depth/204949-pnp-number-deaths-daily-duterte-administration/.

9. "The Kill List," Inquirer.net, July 7, 2016, https://newsinfo.inquirer.net/794598/kill-list-drugs-duterte.

10. "Map, Charts: The Death Toll of the War on Drugs," ABS-CBN News, July 13, 2016, https://news.abs-cbn.com/specials/map-charts-the-death-toll-of-the-war-on-drugs.

11. Patricia Evangelista, "The Impunity Series," Rappler, July 25, 2017, https://r3.rappler.com/newsbreak/investigative/168712-impunity-series-drug-war-duterte-administration.

12. Amnesty International, "Philippines: Duterte's 'War on Drugs' Is a War on the Poor," February 4, 2017, https://www.amnesty.org/en/latest/news/2017/02/war-on-drugs-war-on-poor/.

13. "Philippines President Rodrigo Duterte in Quotes," BBC, September 30, 2016, https://www.bbc.com/news/world-asia-36251094.

14. This same phrase had been used to attack the media in the United States, India, Brazil, South Africa, and other countries around the world. See Chryselle D'Silva Dias, Vice, "Female Journalists, Called 'Presstitutes,' Face Extreme Harassment in India," May 9, 2016, https://www.vice.com/en/article/53n78d/female-journalists-called-presstitutes-face-extreme-harassment-in-india.

15. "Atty. Bruce Rivera's Open Letter to the Biased Media Went Viral," PhilNews.XYZ, April 9, 2016, https://www.philnews.xyz/2016/04/atty-rivera-open-letter-bias-media.html.

16. Mocha Uson spoke in Filipino, https://web.facebook.com/Mochablogger/videos/10154651959381522/.

17. See https://www.facebook.com/media/set/?set=a.10209891686836139&type=3.

18. "Maria Ressa Says Journalism Is Democracy's 'First Line of Defense' and Rappler Won't Back Down," The World, December 11, 2018 (updated Feb. 14, 2019), https://theworld.org/stories/2018-12-11/maria-ressa-says-journalism-democracys-first-line-defense-and-rappler-wont-back; Rappler (@rapplerdotcom), "Ressa: Here in the Philippines, when you're reporting on something, the pressure is immense to conform. It's really the three C's – corrupt, coerce, co-opt," Twitter, September 1, 2020, https://twitter.com/rapplerdotcom/status/1300769459855142912; and Rappler, "'A Thousand Cuts' Talkback Session at Asian American Journalists Association," YouTube, September 1, 2020, 56:01, https://youtu.be/zhqBBFFrVSY.

19. Pia Ranada, "Duterte Tags Roberto Ongpin as 'Oligarch' He Wants to Destroy," Rappler, August 3, 2016, https://www.rappler.com/nation/141861-duterte-roberto-ongpin-oligarch/.

20. Sofia Tomacruz, "Big Business Winners, Losers in Duterte's 1st Year," Rappler, July 24, 2017, https://www.rappler.com/business/176500-sona-2017-philippines-big-business-winners-losers-in-dutertes-1st-year/.

21. Ralf Rivas, "Dennis Uy's Growing Empire (and Debt)," Rappler, January 4, 2019, https://www.rappler.com/newsbreak/in-depth/219039-dennis-uy-growing-business-empire-debt-year-opener-2019/; Cliff Venzon, "Philippine Tycoon Dennis Uy Eyes Asset Sale to Cut Debt," Nikkei Asia, March 23, 2021, https://asia.nikkei.com/Business/Business-deals/Philippine-tycoon-Dennis-Uy-eyes-asset-sale-to-cut-debt.

22. Bea Cupin, "Duterte Attacks 'Politicking, Posturing' De Lima," Rappler, August 17, 2016, https://www.rappler.com/nation/143353-duterte-hits-leila-de-lima/.

23. "De Lima Admits Past Relationship with Driver Bodyguard—Report," Rappler, November 14, 2016, https://www.rappler.com/nation/152373-de-lima-admits -relationship-ronnie-dayan/.

24. "De Lima Denies Starring in 'Sex Video,' Says Ex-Driver Under Threat," ABS-CBN News, August 20, 2016, https://news.abs-cbn.com/news/08/20/16/de-lima-denies -starring-in-sex-video-says-ex-driver-under-threat.

25. "Senate Ends Probe: Neither Duterte nor State Sponsored Killings," Rappler, October 13, 2016, https://www.rappler.com/nation/149086-senate-ends-extra judicial-killings-investigation-gordon-duterte/.

26. Jodesz Gavilan, "The House's 'Climax' Congressmen: Who Are They?," Rappler, November 26, 2016, https://www.rappler.com/newsbreak/iq/153652-profiles-law makers-climax-ronnie-dayan-de-lima/.

27. "'Kailan kayo nag-climax?': Nonsense Questions at the Bilibid Drugs Hearing," Rappler, November 25, 2016, https://www.rappler.com/nation/153547-nonsense -questions-ronnie-dayan-house-probe-drugs/.

28. "'Sen. De Lima Teases Jaybee Sebastian in a Pole Inside His Kubol' Witness Says," Pinoy Trending News, http://pinoytrending.altervista.org/sen-de-lima-teases-jaybee -sebastian-pole-inside-kubol-witness-says/. (Accessed October 7, 2016; no longer there on August 19, 2021.)

29. Pauline Macaraeg, "Premeditated Murder: The Character Assassination of Leila de Lima," Rappler, December 6, 2019, https://www.rappler.com/newsbreak/in vestigative/246329-premeditated-murder-character-assassination-leila-de-lima/.

30. North Base Media's founders are Marcus Brauchli, Stuart Karle, and Sasa Vucinic. Karle was the former general counsel of the *Wall Street Journal* and COO of Reuters. Vucinic cofounded and ran the Media Development Investment Fund for sixteen years. See Natashya Gutierrez, "Top Journalists' Independent Media Fund Invests in Rappler," Rappler, May 31, 2015, https://www.rappler.com/nation/94379-top-journalists -independent-media-fund-invests-rappler/; and Jum Balea, "Rappler Gets Funding from Top Media Veterans Led by Marcus Brauchli," Tech in Asia, May 14, 2015, https://www.techinasia.com/rappler-funding-marcus-brauchli-sasa-vucinic.

31. "Omidyar Network Invests in Rappler," Rappler, November 5, 2015, https://www .rappler.com/nation/109992-omidyar-network-invests-rappler/.

32. Kara Swisher, "A Journalist Trolled by Her Own Government," *New York Times*, February 22, 2019, https://www.nytimes.com/2019/02/22/opinion/maria-ressa -facebook-philippines-.html.

33. Natashya Gutierrez, "State-Sponsored Hate: The Rise of the Pro-Duterte Bloggers," Rappler, August 18, 2017, https://www.rappler.com/newsbreak/in-depth/178709 -duterte-die-hard-supporters-bloggers-propaganda-pcoo/; Maria Ressa, "Americans, Look to the Philippines to See a Dystopian Future Created by Social Media," *Los Angeles Times*, September 25, 2019, https://www.latimes.com/opinion/story/2019-09-24 /philippines-facebook-cambridge-analytica-duterte-elections.

34. Rachel Hatzipanagos, "How Online Hate Turns into Real-Life Violence," *Washington Post*, November 30, 2018, https://www.washingtonpost.com/nation/2018/11/30 /how-online-hate-speech-is-fueling-real-life-violence/. See also "From Digital Hate to Real World Violence" (video), The Aspen Institute, June 16, 2021, https://www

.aspeninstitute.org/events/from-digital-hate-to-real-world-violence/; and Morgan Meaker, "When Social Media Inspires Real Life Violence," DW, November 11, 2018, https://www.dw.com/en/when-social-media-inspires-real-life-violence/a-46225672.

35. Hatzipanagos, "How Online Hate Turns into Real-Life Violence."

36. See Natashya Gutierrez, "State-Sponsored Hate: the Rise of the Pro-Duterte Bloggers," Rappler, August 18, 2016, https://www.rappler.com/newsbreak/in-depth/178709 -duterte-die-hard-supporters-bloggers-propaganda-pcoo/.

37. Watch the video here: "Free Basics Partner Stories: Rappler," April 12, 2016, https:// developers.facebook.com/videos/f8-2016/free-basics-partner-stories-rappler/.

38. Michael Scharff, "Building Trust and Promoting Accountability: Jesse Robredo and Naga City, Philippines, 1988–1998," Innovations for Successful Societies, Woodrow Wilson School of Public and International Affairs, Princeton University (successfulsocieties.princeton.edu), July 2011, https://successfulsocieties.princeton .edu/publications/building-trust-and-promoting-accountability-jesse-robredo-and -naga-city-philippines; and transcript and audio of interview with Jesse Robredo, March 8, 2011, https://successfulsocieties.princeton.edu/interviews/jesse-robredo.

39. "#LeniLeaks: Speculations Based on Fragmented Emails," Rappler, January 9, 2017, https://www.rappler.com/newsbreak/inside-track/157697-leni-leaks-speculations -robredo-duterte-ouster/.

40. Natashya Gutierrez, "Blogger-Propagandists, the New Crisis Managers," Rappler, August 20, 2017, https://www.rappler.com/newsbreak/in-depth/178972-blogger -diehard-duterte-supporters-crisis-manager/.

41. Pia Ranada, "COA Hits PCOO for 'Massive, Unrestricted' Hiring of Contractual Workers," Rappler, July 7, 2021, https://www.rappler.com/nation/pcoo-massive -unrestricted-hiring-contractual-workers-coa-report-2020/.

42. "Gender in Focus: Tackling Sexism in the News Business—On and Offline," WAN-IFRA, November 12, 2014, https://wan-ifra.org/2014/11/gender-in-focus -tackling-sexism-in-the-news-business-on-and-offline/.

43. "Demos: Male Celebrities Receive More Abuse on Twitter Than Women," Demos, August 26, 2014, https://demos.co.uk/press-release/demos-male-celebrities-receive -more-abuse-on-twitter-than-women-2/.

44. Julie Posetti, "Fighting Back Against Prolific Online Harassment: Maria Ressa," in *An Attack on One Is an Attack on All*, edited by Larry Kilman (Paris: UNESCO, 2017), 37–40, https://unesdoc.unesco.org/ark:/48223/pf0000250430.

45. David Maas, "New Research Details Ferocity of Online Violence Against Maria Ressa," International Center for Journalists, March 8, 2021, https://ijnet.org/en/story/new -research-details-ferocity-online-violence-against-maria-ressa.

46. I finally met Nabeelah Shabbir and Felix Simon at the Frontline Club in London in November 2019. See "Democracy's Dystopian Future—with Rappler's Maria Ressa," Frontline Club, November 12, 2019, https://www.frontlineclub.com/democracys -dystopian-future-with-rapplers-maria-ressa/.

47. Julie Posetti, Felix Simon, and Nabeelah Shabbir, "What If Scale Breaks Community? Rebooting Audience Engagement When Journalism Is Under Fire," Reuters Institute for the Study of Journalism, October 2019, https://reutersinstitute.politics.ox.ac.uk /sites/default/files/2019-10/Posetti%20What%20if%20FINAL.pdf.

48. Pia Ranada, "Duterte Claims Rappler 'Fully Owned by Americans,'" Rappler, July 24, 2017, https://www.rappler.com/nation/176565-sona-2017-duterte-rappler-ownership/.

49. Bea Cupin, "Duterte Threatens 'Exposé' vs Inquirer," Rappler, July 1, 2017, https://www.rappler.com/nation/174445-duterte-prieto-inquirer-mile-long/.

50. Pia Ranada, "Duterte to Block Renewal of ABS-CBN Franchise," Rappler, April 27, 2017, https://www.rappler.com/nation/168137-duterte-block-abs-cbn-franchise-renewal/.

51. See Leloy Claudio, Facebook, October 8, 2021, https://www.facebook.com/leloy/posts/10160062758639258.

52. Maria Ressa, Twitter, July 24, 2017, https://twitter.com/mariaressa/status/889408648799076352?s=20.

53. Carly Nyst, "Patriotic Trolling: How Governments Endorse Hate Campaigns Against Critics," *Guardian*, July 12, 2017, https://www.theguardian.com/commentisfree/2017/jul/13/patriotic-trolling-how-governments-endorse-hate-campaigns-against-critics.

54. "Lauren Etter, Projects and Investigations," Bloomberg, https://www.bloomberg.com/authors/ASFjLS119J4/lauren-etter.

55. Lauren Etter, "What Happens When the Government Uses Facebook as a Weapon?," Bloomberg, December 7, 2017, https://www.bloomberg.com/news/features/2017-12-07/how-rodrigo-duterte-turned-facebook-into-a-weapon-with-a-little-help-from-facebook.

Chapter 9: Surviving a Thousand Cuts

1. Under Duterte, the Department of Justice was first headed by a political appointee, Vitaliano Aguirre II, who was replaced early on by a career official, Menardo Guevarra, who became one of the most powerful men in Duterte's government after the anti-terror law was passed in 2020.

2. Carmela Fonbuena, "SEC Revokes Rappler's Registration," Rappler, January 15, 2018, https://www.rappler.com/nation/193687-rappler-registration-revoked/.

3. "SEC Order Meant to Silence Us, Muzzle Free Expression—Rappler," Rappler, January 29, 2018, https://www.rappler.com/nation/194752-sec-case-press-freedom-free-expression/.

4. I've stared at that photo and the smiles of our team captivated me. It didn't make it to the book, but you can find it here: https://www.bqprime.com/opinion/nobel-winner-maria-ressa-on-embracing-fear-and-standing-up-to-strongmen.

5. "Stand with Rappler, Defend Press Freedom," Rappler, December 3, 2018, https://r3.rappler.com/about-rappler/about-us/193650-defend-press-freedom.

6. Fonbuena, "SEC Revokes Rappler's Registration."

7. The summary and video of our impromptu press conference is here: https://www.rappler.com/nation/193687-rappler-registration-revoked/.

8. "Fear for Democracy After Top Philippine Judge and Government Critic Removed," *Guardian*, May 11, 2018, https://www.theguardian.com/world/2018/may/12/fear-for-democracy-after-top-philippine-judge-and-government-critic-removed.

9. "Rappler's Pia Ranada Barred from Entering Malacañang Palace," Rappler, February 20, 2018, https://www.rappler.com/nation/pia-ranada-barred-malacanang-palace/; "Everything You Need to Know About Rappler's Malacañang Coverage Ban," Rappler, February 22, 2018, https://www.rappler.com/nation/196569-rappler-malacanang-ban-pia-ranada-faq/.

10. "Duterte Himself Banned Rappler Reporter from Malacañang Coverage," Rappler, February 20, 2018, https://www.rappler.com/nation/196474-duterte-orders-psg-stop-rappler-reporter-malacanang/.

11. Pia Ranada, "Duterte Admits Role in Navy–Bong Go Frigates Issue," Rappler,

October 19, 2018, https://www.rappler.com/nation/214676-duterte-admits-role-philippine-navy-bong-go-frigates-issue/.

12. Miriam Grace A Go, "'We're Not Scared of These Things': Rappler News Editor on How the Newsroom Continues Despite the Increasing Threats, Alongside Words from Their CEO Maria Ressa," *Index on Censorship* 47, no. 2 (July 2018): 48–51, https://journals.sagepub.com/doi/10.1177/0306422018784531.

13. Lian Buan, "SC Allows Other Journalists to Join Rappler Petition vs Duterte Coverage Ban," Rappler, August 15, 2019, https://www.rappler.com/nation/237722-supreme-court-allows-other-journalists-join-rappler-petition-vs-duterte-coverage-ban.

14. Mark Zuckerberg, Facebook, January 11, 2018, https://www.facebook.com/zuck/posts/one-of-our-big-focus-areas-for-2018-is-making-sure-the-time-we-all-spend-on-face/10104413015393571/.

15. Mike Isaac, "Facebook Overhauls News Feed to Focus on What Friends and Family Share," *New York Times*, January 11, 2018, https://www.nytimes.com/2018/01/11/technology/facebook-news-feed.html.

16. Alex Hern, "Facebook Moving Non-promoted Posts Out of News Feed in Trial," *Guardian*, October 23, 2017, https://www.theguardian.com/technology/2017/oct/23/facebook-non-promoted-posts-news-feed-new-trial-publishers.

17. Filip Struhárik, "Biggest Drop in Facebook Organic Reach We Have Ever Seen," Medium, October 21, 2017, https://medium.com/@filip_struharik/biggest-drop-in-organic-reach-weve-ever-seen-b2239323413.

18. Steve Kovach, "Facebook Is Trying to Prove It's Not a Media Company by Dropping the Guillotine on a Bunch of Media Companies," Insider, January 13, 2018, https://www.businessinsider.com/facebooks-updated-news-feed-algorithm-nightmare-for-publishers-2018-1.

19. Adam Mosseri, "Facebook Recently Announced a Major Update to News Feed; Here's What's Changing," Meta, April 18, 2018, https://about.fb.com/news/2018/04/inside-feed-meaningful-interactions/.

20. Sheera Frenkel, Nicholas Casey, and Paul Mozur, "In Some Countries, Facebook's Fiddling Has Magnified Fake News," *New York Times*, January 4, 2018, https://www.nytimes.com/2018/01/14/technology/facebook-news-feed-changes.html.

21. Mariella Mostof, "'The Great Hack' Features the Journalist Who Broke the Cambridge Analytica Story," Romper, July 24, 2019, https://www.romper.com/p/who-is-carole-cadwalladr-the-great-hack-tells-the-investigative-journalists-explosive-story-18227928.

22. "Philippines' Watchdog Probes Facebook over Cambridge Analytica Data Breach," Reuters, April 13, 2018, https://www.reuters.com/article/us-facebook-privacy-philippines-idUSKBN1HK0QC.

23. Cambridge Analytica and its parent company, SCL, worked in the Philippines as early as 2013. These stories provide background: Natashya Gutierrez, "Did Cambridge Analytica Use Filipinos' Facebook Data to Help Duterte Win?" Rappler, April 5, 2018, https://www.rappler.com/nation/199599-facebook-data-scandal-cambridge-analytica-help-duterte-win-philippine-elections/; and Natashya Gutierrez, "Cambridge Analytica's Parent Company Claims Ties with Duterte Friend," Rappler, April 9, 2018, https://www.rappler.com/newsbreak/investigative/199847-cambridge-analytica-uk-istratehiya-philippines/.

24. Gelo Gonzales, "The Information and Democracy Commission: Defending Free Flow of Truthful Info," Rappler, September 18, 2018, https://www.rappler.com

/technology/features/212240-information-democracy-commission-rsf-infor
mation-operations/.

25. "Forum Names 'Infodemics' Working Group's 17-Member Steering Committee," Forum on Information & Democracy, July 6, 2020, https://informationdemocracy .org/2020/07/06/forum-names-infodemics-working-groups-17-member-steering -committee/; Camille Elemia, "How to Solve Information Chaos Online? Experts Cite These Structural Solutions," Rappler, November 14, 2020, https://www.rappler.com /technology/features/experts-cite-structural-solutions-online-information-chaos/.

26. "Maria Ressa Receives Journalism Award, Appeals to Tech Giants, Government Officials," Rappler, November 9, 2018, https://www.rappler.com/nation/216300 -maria-ressa-acceptance-speech-knight-international-journalism-awards-2018/.

27. Paige Occeñola, "Exclusive: PH Was Cambridge Analytica's 'Petri Dish'—Whistle-Blower Christopher Wylie," Rappler, September 10, 2019, https://www.rappler .com/technology/social-media/239606-cambridge-analytica-philippines-online -propaganda-christopher-wylie/.

28. "Maria Ressa Receives Journalism Award, Appeals to Tech Giants, Government Officials."

29. Alexandra Stevenson, "Philippines Says It Will Charge Veteran Journalist Critical of Duterte," *New York Times*, November 9, 2018, https://www.nytimes.com/2018/11/09 /business/duterte-critic-rappler-charges-in-philippines.html?smid=url-share.

30. Lian Buan, "DOJ Indicts Rappler Holdings, Maria Ressa for Tax Evasion," Rappler, November 9, 2018, https://www.rappler.com/nation/216337-doj-indicts-rappler -holdings-tax-evasion-november-9-2018/.

31. Rappler, "Maria Ressa at Champs-Élysées During 'Yellow Vest' Protest," YouTube, December 18, 2018, https://www.youtube.com/watch?v=393JVj-oL-E.

32. "Maria Ressa Arrives in Manila amid Arrest Fears," Facebook, , Rappler, December 2, 2018, https://www.facebook.com/watch/?v=1786538544788973.

33. Rambo Talabong, "Maria Ressa Back in PH: Don't Let the Gov't Cross the Line," Rappler, December 3, 2006, https://www.rappler.com/nation/218066-maria-ressa -back-philippines-arrest-fears/.

34. Carlos Conde, "A New Weapon Against Press Freedom in the Philippines," *Globe and Mail*, December 5, 2018, https://www.theglobeandmail.com/opinion/article-a-new -weapon-against-press-freedom-in-the-philippines/.

35. Lian Buan, "Rappler to Pasig Court: Tax Charges 'Clear Case of Persecution,'" Rappler, December 6, 2018, https://www.rappler.com/nation/218340-rhc-maria-ressa-motion -quash-tax-evasion-case-pasig-rtc-branch-265/.

36. Rappler, "Pasig Court Postpones Rappler, Maria Ressa Arraignment," YouTube, December 6, 2018, https://www.youtube.com/watch?v=4_hPBu0FXXw.

37. Karl Vick, "Person of the Year 2018," *Time*, December 11, 2018, https://time.com /person-of-the-year-2018-the-guardians/.

38. "TIME Names 'the Guardians' as Person of the Year 2018," CNN, https://edition.cnn .com/videos/tv/2018/12/11/news-stream-stout-ressa-time-person-of-the-year-2018 -guardians.cnn.

39. See Paul Mozur, "A Genocide Incited on Facebook, with Posts from Myanmar's Military," *New York Times*, October 15, 2018, https://www.nytimes.com/2018/10/15 /technology/myanmar-facebook-genocide.html; Alexandra Stevenson, "Facebook

Admits It Was Used to Incite Violence in Myanmar," *New York Times*, November 6, 2018, https://www.nytimes.com/2018/11/06/technology/myanmar-facebook.html.

Chapter 10: Don't Become a Monster to Fight a Monster

1. Lian Buan, "'We'll Go After You': DOJ Probes Threat of NBI Agent vs Rappler Reporter," Rappler, February 14, 2019, https://www.rappler.com/nation/223489-doj -probes-nbi-agent-verbal-threat-vs-reporter-during-ressa-arrest/. See also Aika Rey on Twitter: "The arrest warrant vs Maria Ressa is being served at the Rappler HQ now, an officer part of the serving party who introduced himself to be part of the NBI tried to prohibit me from taking videos—WHICH IS PART OF MY JOB," Twitter, February 13, 2019, https://twitter.com/reyaika/status/1095615339721834496.

2. Dr. Pagaduan-Lopez, a professor in the Department of Psychiatry & Behavioral Medicine, College of Medicine, University of the Philippines—Manila, was a member of the United Nations Subcommittee on Prevention of Torture and Other Cruel, Inhuman or Degrading Treatment or Punishment (SPT) from 2012 to 2016. She passed away on November 20, 2021.

3. "UP Fair: More Than Just a Concert," Rappler, February 11, 2019, https://www.rappler .com/moveph/221524-up-fair-2019-more-than-just-concert/.

4. Patricia Evangelista, "The Impunity Series," Rappler, July 25, 2017, https:// r3.rappler.com/newsbreak/investigative/168712-impunity-series-drug-war-duterte -administration.

5. Rappler, "WATCH: Patricia Evangelista Reads the Statement of Rappler in UP Fair," Facebook, February 13, 2019, https://www.facebook.com/watch/?v=740 171123044662; "Rappler's Statement on Maria Ressa's Arrest: 'We Will Continue to Tell the Truth,'" Rappler, February 13, 2019, https://www.rappler.com/nation/223423 -rappler-statement-maria-ressa-arrest-cyber-libel-february-2019/.

6. Rappler, "Students, Journalists, Civil Society Groups Protest Ressa Arrest," Facebook, February 13, 2019, https://www.facebook.com/watch/?v=2085260034888511.

7. CNN Philippines Staff, "Rappler CEO Calls Arrest 'Abuse of Power,'" CNN, February 14, 2019, https://www.cnnphilippines.com/news/2019/02/14/Rappler -CEO-Maria-Ressa-abuse-of-power.html.

8. TrialWatch: Freedom for the Persecuted, the Clooney Foundation for Justice, https:// cfj.org/project/trialwatch/.

9. Agence France-Presse, "Al Jazeera Reporter Renounces Egypt Citizenship in Bid for Release," Rappler, February 3, 2015, https://www.rappler.com/world/82809 -mohamed-fahmy-renounces-egypt-citizenship/; "Rappler, The Investigative Journal to Partner on Investigative Reporting," Rappler, July 9, 2019, https://www.rappler.com /nation/234921-partnership-with-the-investigative-journal-reporting/.

10. Jason Rezaian, "Reporter Jason Rezaian on 544 Days in Iranian Jail: 'They Never Touched Me, but I Was Tortured,'" *Guardian*, February 18, 2019, https://www .theguardian.com/media/2019/feb/18/reporter-jason-rezaian-on-544-days-in -iranian-jail-they-never-touched-me-but-i-was-tortured.

11. "Amal Clooney," Committee to Protect Journalists, 2020, https://cpj.org/awards /amal-clooney/.

12. Queen's Counsel Caoilfhionn Gallagher, Can Yeginsu, and Claire Overman. I introduced

them to Peter Lichtenbaum, a Princeton classmate now working with the prestigious law firm Covington & Burling LLP, which provided me with pro bono services; "Caoilfhionn Gallagher QC," Doughty Street Chambers, https://www.doughtystreet .co.uk/barristers/caoilfhionn-gallagher-qc; "Advisors," Daphne Caruana Galizia Foundation, https://www.daphne.foundation/en/about/the-foundation/advisors.

13. "'Anger Drives a Lot of What I Do': Amal Clooney on Why She Fights for Press Freedom," *Rappler*, November 20, 2020, https://www.rappler.com/world/global -affairs/reason-amal-clooney-fights-for-press-freedom/.

14. "Rodrigo Duterte's Persecution of Maria Ressa Is Dangerous," Daphne Caruana Galizia Foundation, June 16, 2020, https://www.daphne.foundation/en/2020/06/16/maria -ressa.

15. Malou Mangahas, "The Duterte Wealth: Unregistered Law Firm, Undisclosed Biz Interests, Rice Import Deal for Creditor," *Rappler*, April 3, 2019, https://www.rappler .com/newsbreak/investigative/pcij-report-rodrigo-sara-paolo-duterte-wealth/.

16. Terry Gross, "Philippine Journalist Says Rodrigo Duterte's Presidency Is Based on 'Fear, Violence,'" NPR, January 6, 2021, https://www.npr.org/2021/01/06/953902894 /philippine-journalist-says-rodrigo-dutertes-presidency-is-based-on-fear-violence.

17. Twink Macaraig, "When the Big C Sneaks Back," *Philippine Star*, June 28, 2016, https://www.philstar.com/lifestyle/health-and-family/2016/06/28/1597196/when -big-c-sneaks-back.

18. Twink Macaraig, "Why I Fight," *Philippine Star*, March 24, 2019, https://www.philstar .com/lifestyle/sunday-life/2019/03/24/1903779/why-i-fight.

Chapter 11: Hold the Line

1. David Pegg, "Judge Makes Preliminary Ruling in Carole Cadwalladr Libel Case," *Guardian*, December 12, 2019, https://www.theguardian.com/law/2019/dec/12 /judge-makes-preliminary-ruling-in-carole-cadwalladr-libel-case.

2. Nico Hines, "Award-Winning Reporter to Counter-sue Man Who Bankrolled Brexit for 'Harassment,'" Daily Beast, July 15, 2019, https://www.thedailybeast.com/carole -cadwalladr-award-winning-reporter-to-counter-sue-man-who-bankrolled-brexit-for -harassment.

3. Ben Judah, "Britain's Most Polarizing Journalist," *Atlantic*, September 19, 2019, https:// www.theatlantic.com/international/archive/2019/09/carole-cadwalladr-guardian -facebook-cambridge-analytica/597664/.

4. Author interview with Carole Cadwalladr, "#HoldTheLine: Maria Ressa Talks to Journalist Carole Cadwalladr," *Rappler*, May 10, 2021, https://www.rappler.com/video /hold-the-line-maria-ressa-interview/carole-cadwalladr-may-2021.

5. "Maria Ressa Future-Proofs Rappler for Digital Changes, Names Glenda Gloria Executive Editor," *Rappler*, November 11, 2020, https://www.rappler.com/about /maria-ressa-future-proofs-rappler-for-digital-challenges-names-glenda-gloria -executive-editor/.

6. Olivia Solon, "While Facebook Works to Create an Oversight Board, Industry Experts Formed Their Own," NBC News, September 25, 2020, https://www.nbcnews.com /tech/tech-news/facebook-real-oversight-board-n1240958.

7. Roger McNamee and Maria Ressa, "Facebook's 'Oversight Board' Is a Sham. The

Answer to the Capitol Riot Is Regulating Social Media," *Time*, January 28, 2021, https://time.com/5933989/facebook-oversight-regulating-social-media/.

8. Rob Pegoraro, "Facebook's 'Real Oversight Board': Just Fix These Three Things Before the Election," *Forbes*, September 30, 2020, https://www.forbes.com/sites/robpegoraro/2020/09/30/facebooks-real-oversight-board-just-fix-these-three-things-before-the-election/?sh=2cb2cb3c1e6c.

9. "Is Big Tech the New Empire?," *Studio B: Unscripted*, Al Jazeera, March 27, 2020, https://www.youtube.com/watch?v=7OLUfA6QJlE.

10. Christopher Wylie, *Mindf*ck: Cambridge Analytica and the Plot to Break America* (New York: Random House, 2019).

11. "EXCLUSIVE: Interview with Cambridge Analytica Whistle-Blower Christopher Wylie," Rappler, September 12, 2019, https://www.rappler.com/technology/social-media/239972-cambridge-analytica-interview-christopher-wylie/.

12. Ibid.

13. Raissa Robles, "Cambridge Analytica Boss Alexander Nix Dined with Two of Rodrigo Duterte's Campaign Advisers in 2015," *South China Morning Post*, April 8, 2018, https://www.scmp.com/news/asia/southeast-asia/article/2140782/cambridge-analytica-boss-alexander-nix-dined-two-rodrigo.

14. "EXCLUSIVE: Interview with Cambridge Analytica Whistle-Blower Christopher Wylie."

15. Meghan Bobrowsky, "Facebook Disables Access for NYU Research into Political-Ad Targeting," *Wall Street Journal*, August 4, 2021, https://www.wsj.com/articles/facebook-cuts-off-access-for-nyu-research-into-political-ad-targeting-11628052204.

16. Jeff Horwitz and Deepa Seetharaman, "Facebook Executive Shut Down Efforts to Make the Site Less Divisive," *Wall Street Journal*, May 26, 2020, https://www.wsj.com/articles/facebook-knows-it-encourages-division-top-executives-nixed-solutions-11590507499.

17. Mike Isaac and Sheera Frenkel, "Facebook Braces Itself for Trump to Cast Doubt on Election Results," *New York Times*, August 21, 2020, https://www.nytimes.com/2020/08/21/technology/facebook-trump-election.html.

18. Kevin Roose, Mike Isaac, and Sheera Frenkel, "Facebook Struggles to Balance Civility and Growth," *New York Times*, November 24, 2020, https://www.nytimes.com/2020/11/24/technology/facebook-election-misinformation.html.

19. In 2020, Rappler began working with Sinan Aral and his team at MIT, as well as researchers at several other universities at home and abroad.

20. Bonz Magsambol, "Facebook Partners with Rappler, Vera Files for Fact-Checking Program," Rappler, April 12, 2018, https://www.rappler.com/technology/social-media/200060-facebook-partnership-fact-checking-program/.

21. Manuel Mogato, "Philippines Complains Facebook Fact-Checkers Are Biased," Reuters, April 16, 2018, https://www.reuters.com/article/us-philippines-facebook-idUSKBN1HN1EN.

22. Jordan Robertson, "Fake News Hub from 2016 Election Thriving Again, Report Finds," Bloomberg, October 13, 2010, https://www.bloomberg.com/news/articles/2020-10-13/fake-news-hub-from-2016-election-thriving-again-report-finds#xj4y7vzkg.

23. "EXCLUSIVE: Russian Disinformation System Influences PH Social Media," Rappler, January 22, 2019, https://www.rappler.com/newsbreak/investigative/221470-russian-disinformation-system-influences-philippine-social-media/.

24. Craig Timberg, "Facebook Deletes Several Fake Chinese Accounts Targeting Trump and Biden, in First Takedown of Its Kind," *Washington Post*, September 22, 2020, https://www.washingtonpost.com/technology/2020/09/22/facebook-deletes-several-fake-chinese-accounts-targeting-trump-biden-first-takedown-its-kind/; Ben Nimmo, C. Shawn Elb, and Léa Ronzaud, "Facebook Takes Down Inauthentic Chinese Network," Graphika, September 22, 2020, https://graphika.com/reports/operation-naval-gazing/.

25. "With Anti-terror Law, Police-Sponsored Hate and Disinformation Even More Dangerous," Rappler, August 13, 2020, https://www.rappler.com/newsbreak/investigative/anti-terror-law-state-sponsored-hate-disinformation-more-dangerous/.

26. Ibid.

27. Nicole-Anne C. Lagrimas, "Tagged, You're Dead," GMA News Online, October 13, 2020, https://www.gmanetwork.com/news/specials/content/170/zara-alvarez-tagged-you-re-dead/.

28. That was when I saw the resilience and courage of every Rappler and I found out that our CFO, Fel Dalafu, had always wanted to be a journalist but her parents had told her to major in something that was more predictable and stable. So she had become an accountant and went to work for ABS-CBN News, where we had worked together. When the attacks against Rappler began, she proudly declared that she was working to make sure that "the best journalists could do their jobs." We couldn't have done our job without Fel's courage; she was the perfect finance lead to help us navigate the government land mines, making sure that our company was always prepared for the worst.

29. "Rappler Ends 2019 with Income: A Comeback Year," Rappler, June 30, 2020, https://www.rappler.com/about/rappler-income-2019-comeback-year/.

30. The indictment was filed on January 10, 2019. I was arrested a month later (and the indictment was sleazy because it reversed an earlier decision junking it). See "Despite NBI Flip-Flop, DOJ to Indict Rappler for Cyber Libel," Rappler, February 4, 2019, https://www.rappler.com/nation/222691-doj-to-indict-rappler-cyber-libel-despite-nbi-flip-flop/.

31. Sheila Coronel, "This Is How Democracy Dies," *Atlantic*, June 16, 2020, https://www.theatlantic.com/international/archive/2020/06/maria-ressa-rappler-philippines-democracy/613102/.

32. Marc Jayson Cayabyab, "Cybercrime Expert? Who Is Manila RTC Judge Rainelda Estacio-Montesa?" OneNews, June 17, 2020, https://www.onenews.ph/articles/cybercrime-expert-who-is-manila-rtc-judge-rainelda-estacio-montesa.

33. Rey Santos left the government several months before the publication of this book.

34. Maria Ressa, "We Can't Let the Coronavirus Infect Democracy," *Time*, April 14, 2020, https://time.com/5820620/maria-ressa-coronavirus-democracy/.

35. Ralf Rivas, "ABS-CBN Goes Off-Air After NTC Order," Rappler, May 5, 2020, https://www.rappler.com/nation/abs-cbn-goes-off-air-ntc-order-may-5-2020/.

36. Ruben Carranza, Facebook, August 19, 2020, https://www.facebook.com/ruben.carranza.14/posts/10157883975069671.

Chapter 12: Why Fascism Is Winning

1. Sofia Tomacruz, "What Prevents Swift COVID-19 Vaccine Deliveries to Philippines' Provinces?," Rappler, February 1, 2022, https://www.rappler.com/newsbreak /investigative/what-prevents-swift-deliveries-provinces-analysis-philippines-covid-19 -vaccination-drive-2022-part-2/.

2. "Senate Halts Search for Yang, Lao, Pharmally-Linked Officials Due to COVID-19 Surge," Rappler, January 18, 2022, https://www.rappler.com/nation/senate-halts -search-michael-yang-christopher-lao-pharmally-officials-due-covid-19-surge/.

3. The exact moment when I found out, including my reactions, was captured in this video by FreedomFilmFest: "Live Reaction: Maria Ressa Wins Nobel Peace Prize," Facebook, December 9, 2021, https://www.facebook.com/freedomfilmfest /posts/10160060586766908.

4. Guardian News, "Moment Maria Ressa Learns of Nobel Peace Prize Win During Zoom Call," YouTube, October 8, 2021, https://www.youtube.com/watch?v=UtjFwNiHUbY.

5. Ryan Macasero, "[OPINION] Maria Ressa's Nobel Peace Prize Is About All of Us," Rappler, October 12, 2021, https://www.rappler.com/voices/rappler-blogs/maria -ressa-nobel-peace-prize-about-all-filipinos-media/.

6. Lorraine Ecarma, "Tacloban Journalist Frenchie Mae Cumpio Still Hopeful a Year After Arrest," Rappler, February 9, 2021, https://www.rappler.com/newsbreak /in-depth/tacloban-journalist-frenchie-mae-cumpio-still-hopeful-year-after -arrest-2021/.

7. Ryan Macasero, "Remembering Dumaguete Radio Reporter Rex Cornelio," Rappler, February 13, 2021, https://www.rappler.com/newsbreak/in-depth/remembering -dumaguete-city-radio-reporter-rex-cornelio/.

8. "Announcing Harvard Kennedy School's Center for Public Leadership Fall 2021 Hauser Leaders," Harvard Kennedy School Center for Public Leadership, August 30, 2021, https://cpl.hks.harvard.edu/news/announcing-harvard-kennedy-school's-cen ter-public-leadership-fall-2021-hauser-leaders.

9. "Maria Ressa and Sadhana Udapa Named Fall 2021 Joan Shorenstein Fellows," Harvard Kennedy School Shorenstein Center on Media, Politics and Public Policy, September 3, 2021 https://shorensteincenter.org/maria-ressa-sahana-udupa-named -fall-2021-joan-shorenstein-fellows/.

10. I first heard this from Silicon Valley investor Roger McNamee, one of Facebook's early investors, who published a book demanding better from Facebook on safety, competition, and privacy; see McNamee, "Facebook Will Not Fix Itself," *Time*, October 7, 2021, https://time.com/6104863/facebook-regulation-roger-mcnamee/.

11. Chris Welch, "Facebook May Have Knowingly Inflated Its Video Metrics for Over a Year," The Verge, October 17, 2018, https://www.theverge.com/2018/10/17/1798 9712/facebook-inaccurate-video-metrics-inflation-lawsuit.

12. "Facebook Lied About Video Metrics and It Killed Profitable Businesses," CCN, September 23, 2020, https://www.ccn.com/facebook-lied-about-video-metrics/.

13. Lian Guan, "In Chilling Nostalgia, Marcos Loyalists Show Up Big for the Son of Dictator," Rappler, February 8, 2022, https://www.rappler.com/nation/elections /loyalists-show-up-big-dictator-son-ferdinand-bongbong-marcos-jr-campaign-launch/.

14. Lenarson Music & Vlogs, "The Original Version of Bảğöňǧ Ĺîpǔňǎň 1973—Lyrics

(President Ferdinand Marcos Era 1965–1986)," YouTube, November 25, 2021, https://www.youtube.com/watch?v=KssVXnAgW0Q.

15. Plethora, "BBM—Bagong Lipunan (New Version)," YouTube, November 7, 2021, https://www.youtube.com/watch?v=2-8lbAbGGww.

16. "Martsa ng Bagong Lipunan (English Translation)," Lyrics Translate, https://lyricstranslate.com/en/bagong-lipunan-new-society.html.

17. Christa Escudero, "Marcos' 'Greatest Robbery of a Government' Guinness Record Suddenly Inaccessible," Rappler, March 11, 2022, https://www.rappler.com/nation/guinness-record-ferdinand-marcos-greatest-robbery-of-government-suddenly-inaccessible-march-2022/.

18. Antonio J. Montalván II, "The Marcos Diary: A Dictator's Honest, Candid Description of His Only Son," Vera Files, January 27, 2022, https://verafiles.org/articles/marcos-diary-dictators-honest-candid-description-his-only-so.

19. ANC 24/7, "Sen. Imee Marcos: Bongbong Marcos to Run in 2022, but Position Undecided Yet," YouTube, August 25, 2021, https://www.youtube.com/watch?v=w4hO4RzNBxA.

20. Marites Dañguilan Vitug, "Holes in Marcos Jr's Work Experience," Rappler, February 7, 2022, https://www.rappler.com/plus-membership-program/holes-ferdinand-bongbong-marcos-jr-work-experience/.

21. Patricio Abinales, "The Curse That Is Imelda Marcos: A Review of Lauren Greenfield's 'Kingmaker' Film," Rappler, November 14, 2019, https://www.rappler.com/entertainment/movies/kingmaker-movie-review/.

22. Lian Buan, "Marcos Insists He Has No Trolls, Says Fake News 'Dangerous,'" Rappler, February 7, 2022, https://www.rappler.com/nation/elections/ferdinand-bongbong-marcos-jr-claims-has-no-trolls-fake-news-dangerous/.

23. Marites Dañguilan Vitug, "EXCLUSIVE: Did Bongbong Marcos Lie About Oxford, Wharton?," Rappler, February 24, 2015, https://www.rappler.com/newsbreak/investigative/84397-bongbong-marcos-degrees-oxford-wharton/.

24. "Bongbong Marcos: Oxford, Wharton Educational Record 'Accurate,'" Rappler, February 24, 2015, https://www.rappler.com/nation/84959-bongbong-marcos-statement-oxford-wharton/; Cathrine Gonzales, "Bongbong Marcos Maintains He's a Graduate of Oxford," Inquirer.net, February 5, 2022, https://newsinfo.inquirer.net/1550308/bongbong-marcos-maintains-he-graduated-from-oxford.

25. "Imelda Marcos, Son Plot to Reclaim PH Presidency," Rappler, July 2, 2014, https://www.rappler.com/nation/62215-imelda-marcos-son-philippines-presidency.

26. Jianing Li and Michael W. Wagner, "When Are Readers Likely to Believe a Fact-Check?," Brookings, May 27, 2020, https://www.brookings.edu/techstream/when-are-readers-likely-to-believe-a-fact-check/.

27. "Tip of the Iceberg: Tracing the Network of Spammy Pages in Facebook Takedown," Rappler, October 27, 2018, https://www.rappler.com/newsbreak/investigative/215256-tracing-spammy-pages-network-facebook-takedown.

28. "EXCLUSIVE: Russian Disinformation System Influences PH Social Media," Rappler, January 22, 2019, https://www.rappler.com/newsbreak/investigative/221470-russian-disinformation-system-influences-philippine-social-media/.

29. Gemma B. Mendoza, "Networked Propaganda: How the Marcoses Are Using Social Media to Reclaim Malacañang," Rappler, November 20, 2019, https://www.rappler

.com/newsbreak/investigative/245290-marcos-networked-propaganda-social
-media.

30. Cherry Salazar, "Robredo Leads, Marcos Snubs Advertising on Facebook," Rappler, January 16, 2022, https://www.rappler.com/nation/elections/robredo-leads-marcos -snubs-facebook-advertising-as-of-december-31-2021/; "After Skipping Jessica Soho Interview, Marcos Accuses Award-Winning Journo of Bias," *Philippine Star*, January 22, 2022, https://www.philstar.com/headlines/2022/01/22/2155660/after-skipping -jessica-soho-interview-marcos-accuses-award-winning-journo-bias.

31. *Working Group on Infodemics Policy Framework*, Forum on Information & Democracy, November 2020, https://informationdemocracy.org/wp-content/uploads/2020/11 /ForumID_Report-on-infodemics_101120.pdf.

32. International Fund for Public Interest Media, "Maria Ressa and Mark Thompson to Spearhead Global Effort to Save Public Interest Media," September 30, 2021, https:// ifpim.org/resources/maria-ressa-and-mark-thompson-to-spearhead-global-effort-to -save-public-interest-media/; and Maria Ressa, "As Democracy Dies, We Build a Global Future," Rappler, October 13, 2020, https://www.rappler.com/voices/thought-leaders /analysis-as-democracy-dies-we-build-global-future/.

33. Anne Applebaum, "The Bad Guys Are Winning," *Atlantic*, November 15, 2021, https://www.theatlantic.com/magazine/archive/2021/12/the-autocrats-are -winning/620526/.

34. "Defend Maria Ressa and Independent Media in the Philippines," Committee to Protect Journalists, https://cpj.org/campaigns/holdtheline/.

35. Bea Cupin, "#FactsFirstPH: 'Groundbreaking Effort Against Discrimination,'" Rappler, January 26, 2022, https://www.rappler.com/nation/philippine-media-civic -society-groups-launch-facts-first-philippines-initiative/.

36. Isabel Martinez, "Maria Ressa Brings the Readers. But Here's How Rappler Makes Them Stay," The Ken, January 27, 2022, https://the-ken.com/sea/story/maria-ressa -brings-the-readers-but-heres-how-rappler-makes-them-stay/.

37. Please see: "Election Integrity Partnership," https://www.eipartnership.net.

38. Disclosure: I sit on the board of Meedan.

39. Dwight De Leon. "Rappler Asks SC to Junk Calida Petition vs Fact-Checking Deal with Comelec," Rappler, April 12, 2022, https://www.rappler.com/nation/elections /comment-supreme-court-junk-calida-petition-vs-fact-checking-deal-comelec/.

40. Michelle Abad, "The Pink Wave: Robredo's Volunteer Movement Defies Traditional Campaigns," Rappler, May 4, 2022, https://www.rappler.com/nation/elections /leni-robredo-volunteer-movement-defies-traditional-campaigns/; and Sui-Lee Wee, "'We Want a Change': In the Philippines, Young People Aim to Upend an Election," *New York Times*, May 1, 2022,https://www.nytimes.com/2022/05/01/world/asia /philippines-election-marcos-robredo.html.

41. Robert Tait and Flora Garamvolgyi, "Viktor Orbán Wins Fourth Consecutive Term as Hungary's Prime Minister," *Guardian*, April 3, 2022, https://www.theguardian .com/world/2022/apr/03/viktor-orban-expected-to-win-big-majority-in-hungarian -general-election; and Flora Garamvolgyi and Julian Borger, "Orbán and US Right to Bond at CPAC in Hungary over 'Great Replacement' Ideology," Guardian, May 18, 2022, https://www.theguardian.com/world/2022/may/18/cpac-conference -budapest-hungary-viktor-orban-speaker.

42. Zeeshan Aleem, "Trump's CPAC Straw Poll Shows He's Clinging On to Dominance

of the GOP," MSNBC, February 28, 2022, https://www.msnbc.com/opinion/msnbc -opinion/trumps-s-cpac-straw-poll-shows-he-s-clinging-dominance-n1290274.

43. "Maria Ressa Receives Journalism Award, Appeals to Tech Giants, Government Officials," Rappler, November 9, 2018, https://www.rappler.com/nation/216300 -maria-ressa-acceptance-speech-knight-international-journalism-awards-2018/.

Epilogue

1. Anthony Johnson, "Buffalo Mass Shooting Suspect Mentioned 3 New Jersey Towns in 180-Page Document," ABC7 New York, May 17, 2022, https://abc7ny.com/buffalo -mass-shooting-shooter-new-jersey/11861690/.

2. Vin Ebenau, "Ocean County Prosecutor: 'No Implied or Explicit Threat' Following Buffalo, NY Shooter's Mention of Lakewood, NJ and Toms River, NJ," Beach Radio, May 17, 2022, https://mybeachradio.com/ocean-county-prosecutor-no-implied-or -explicit-threat-following-buffalo-ny-shooters-mention-of-lakewood-nj-and-toms -river-nj/.

3. "'She Was My Sweet Girl': Remembering the Victims of the Uvalde Shooting," *New York Times*, June 16, 2022, https://www.nytimes.com/2022/06/05/us/uvalde -shooting-victims.html.

4. Karen Wall, "Ocean County Schools' Police Presence Increasing After Texas Shooting," Patch, May 24, 2020, https://patch.com/new-jersey/tomsriver/ocean-county-schools -police-presence-incresasing-after-texas-shooting.

About the Author

MARIA RESSA is the corecipient of the 2021 Nobel Peace Prize for her work defending freedom of expression and democracy. The CEO, cofounder, and president of Rappler, the Philippines' top digital news site, Ressa has been a journalist in Asia for over thirty-six years. She was TIME Magazine's Person of the Year in 2018 and won the UNESCO World Press Freedom Prize in 2021. Among the many other awards she has received are the prestigious Golden Pen of Freedom Award from the World Association of News Publishers, the Knight International Journalism Award from the International Center for Journalists, the Shorenstein Journalism Award from Stanford University, and the Sergei Magnitsky Award for Outstanding Investigative Journalism. She grew up in the Philippines and the United States and currently lives in Manila.